Vocabulary Power Plus for College and Career Readiness

Table of Contents

Vocabulary Power Plus for College and Career Readiness

Introduction

VOCABULARY POWER PLUS FOR COLLEGE AND CAREER READINESS combines classroom-tested vocabulary drills with reading and writing exercises designed to foster the English and language arts skills essential for college and career success, with the added advantage of successfully preparing students for both the Scholastic Assessment Test and the American College Testing assessment.

Although *Vocabulary Power Plus* is a proven resource for college-bound students, it is guaranteed to increase vocabulary, improve grammar, enhance writing, and boost critical reading skills for students at all levels of learning.

Critical Reading exercises include lengthy passages and detailed, evidence-based, two-part questions designed to promote understanding and eliminate multiple-choice guessing. We include SAT- and ACT-style grammar and writing-exercises and have placed the vocabulary words in non-alphabetical sequence, distributed by part-of-speech.

Coupled with words-in-context exercises, inferences cultivate comprehensive word discernment by prompting students to create contexts for words, instead of simply memorizing definitions. Related words context exercises forge connections among words, ensuring retention for both knowledge and fluency, and nuance exercises instill active inference habits to discern not just adequate words for contexts, but the best words in a specific context.

The writing exercises in *Vocabulary Power Plus* are process-oriented and adaptable to individual classroom lesson plans. Our rubrics combine the fundamentals of the essay-scoring criteria for both the SAT and ACT optional writing portions, with emphasis on organization, development, sentence formation, and word choice. This objective scoring opportunity helps students develop concrete understanding of the writing process and develop a personal approach to punctual, reactive writing.

We hope that you find the *Vocabulary Power Plus for College and Career Readiness* series to be an effective tool for teaching new words, and an exceptional tool for preparing for assessments.

Strategies for Completing Activities

Roots, Prefixes, and Suffixes

A knowledge of roots, prefixes, and suffixes can give readers the ability to view unfamiliar words as mere puzzles that require only a few simple steps to solve. For the person interested in the history of words, this knowledge provides the ability to track word origin and evolution. For those who seek to improve vocabulary, the knowledge creates a sure and lifelong method; however, there are two points to remember:

1. Some words have evolved through usage, so present definitions might differ from what you infer through an examination of the roots and prefixes. The word *abstruse*, for example, contains the prefix *ab–* (away) and the root *trudere* (to thrust), and literally means *to thrust away*. Today, *abstruse* is used to describe something that is hard to understand.

2. Certain roots do not apply to all words that use the same form. If you know that the root *vin* means "to conquer," then you would be correct in concluding that the word *invincible* means "incapable of being conquered"; however, if you tried to apply the same root meaning to *vindicate* or *vindictive*, you would be incorrect. When analyzing unfamiliar words, check for other possible roots if your inferred meaning does not fit the context.

Despite these considerations, a knowledge of roots and prefixes is one of the best ways to build a powerful vocabulary.

Critical Reading

Reading questions generally fall into several categories.

1. Identifying the main idea or the author's purpose. *What is this selection about?*

In some passages, the author's purpose will be easy to identify because the one or two ideas leap from the text; however, other passages might not be so easily analyzed, especially if they include convoluted sentences. Inverted sentences (subject at the end of the sentence) and elliptical sentences (words missing) will also increase the difficulty of the passages, but all these obstacles can be overcome if readers take one sentence at a time and recast it in their own words. Consider the following sentence:

> These writers either jot down their thoughts bit by bit, in short, ambiguous, and paradoxical sentences, which apparently mean much more than they say—of this kind of writing Schelling's treatises on natural philosophy are a splendid instance; or else they hold forth with a deluge of words and the most intolerable diffusiveness, as though no end of fuss were necessary to make the reader understand the deep meaning of their sentences, whereas it is some quite simple if not actually trivial idea, examples of which may be found in plenty in the popular works of Fichte, and the philosophical manuals of a hundred other miserable dunces.

If we edit out some of the words, the main point of this sentence is obvious.

> These writers either jot down their thoughts bit by bit, in short, ambiguous, and paradoxical sentences, which apparently mean much more than they say—of this kind of writing Schelling's treatises on natural philosophy are a splendid instance; or else they hold forth with a deluge of words and the most intolerable diffusiveness, as though no end of fuss were necessary to make the reader understand the deep meaning of their sentences, whereas it is some quite simple if not actually trivial idea, examples of which may be found in plenty in the popular works of Fichte, and the philosophical manuals of a hundred other miserable dunces.

Some sentences need only a few deletions for clarification, but others require major recasting and additions; they must be read carefully and put into the reader's own words.

> Some in their discourse desire rather commendation of wit, in being able to hold all arguments, than of judgment, in discerning what is true; as if it were a praise to know what might be said, and not what should be thought.

After studying it, a reader might recast the sentence as follows:

> In conversation, some people desire praise for their abilities to maintain the conversation rather than their abilities to identify what is true or false, as though it were better to sound good than to know what is truth or fiction.

2. Identifying the stated or implied meaning. *What is the author stating or suggesting?*

The literal meaning of a text does not always correspond with the intended meaning. To understand a passage fully, readers must determine which meaning—if there is more than one—is the intended meaning of the passage. Consider the following sentence:

> If his notice was sought, an expression of courtesy and interest gleamed out upon his features; proving that there was light within him and that it was only the outward medium of the intellectual lamp that obstructed the rays in their passage.

Interpreted literally, this Nathaniel Hawthorne metaphor suggests that a light-generating lamp exists inside the human body. Since this is impossible, the reader must look to the metaphoric meaning of the passage to understand it properly. In the metaphor, Hawthorne refers to the human mind—consciousness—as a lamp that emits light, and other people cannot always see the lamp because the outside "medium"—the human body—sometimes blocks it.

3. Identifying the tone or mood of the selection. *What feeling does the text evoke?*

To answer these types of questions, readers must look closely at individual words and their connotations; for example, the words *stubborn* and *firm* have almost the same definition, but a writer who describes a character as *stubborn* rather than *firm* is probably suggesting something negative about the character.

Vocabulary Power Plus for College and Career Readiness includes evidence-based follow-up questions in every critical reading lesson, as prescribed by the Partnership for Assessment of Readiness for College and Careers (PARCC) consortium, and will be used in the 2016 revision of the SAT. These questions prompt for the contextual evidence that students use to answer the primary questions.

Writing

The optional writing portions on the two major assessment tests allow approximately 30 minutes for the composition of a well-organized, fully developed essay. Writing a satisfactory essay in this limited time requires facility in determining a thesis, organizing ideas, and producing adequate examples to support the ideas.

These fundamentals are equally important for success on the Smarter Balanced Assessment Consortium ELA Performance Task, which includes a substantial essay writing assignment based on provided source texts.

Such a time-limited essay might lack the perfection and depth that weeks of proofreading and editing provide research papers. Process is undoubtedly of primary importance, but students must consider the time constraints of both reality and those of the assessments they elect to complete. Completion of the essay is just as important as organization, development, and language use.

The thesis, the organization of ideas, and the support make the framework of a good essay. Before the actual writing begins, writers must create a mental outline by establishing a thesis, or main idea, and one or more specific supporting ideas (the number of ideas will depend on the length and content of the essay). Supporting ideas should not be overcomplicated; they are simply ideas that justify or explain the thesis. The writer must introduce and explain each supporting idea, and the resultant supporting paragraph should answer the *Why?* or *Who cares?* questions that the thesis may evoke.

Once the thesis and supporting ideas are identified, writers must determine the order in which the ideas will appear in the essay. A good introduction usually explains the thesis and briefly introduces the supporting ideas. Explanation of the supporting ideas should follow, with each idea in its own paragraph. The final paragraph, the conclusion, usually restates the thesis or summarizes the main ideas of the essay.

Adhering to the mental outline when the writing begins will help the writer organize and develop the essay. Using the Organization and Development scoring guides to evaluate practice essays will help to reinforce the process skills. The Word Choice and Sentence Formation scoring guides will help to strengthen language skills—the vital counterpart to essay organization and development.

Vocabulary Power Plus for College and Career Readiness includes two styles of writing prompts. SAT-style writing prompts feature general subjects such as art, history, literature, or politics. ACT-style writing prompts involve subjects specifically relevant to high school students. Both styles of writing prompts require students to assume a point of view and support it with examples and reasoning.

Pronunciation Guide

a — tr**a**ck
ā — m**a**te
ä — f**a**ther
â — c**a**re
e — p**e**t
ē — b**e**
i — b**i**t
ī — b**i**te
o — j**o**b
ō — wr**o**te
ô — p**o**rt, f**ou**ght
ōō — pr**oo**f
u — p**u**n
ū — **y**ou
û — p**u**rr
ə — **a**bout, syst**e**m, s**u**pper, circ**u**s
oi — t**oy**
îr — st**eer**

Word List

Lesson 1
aegis
amorphous
besiege
boor
carrion
enervate
ephemeral
erotic
factious
fervent
ignoble
opulent
perspicacity
philanthropy
rectify

Lesson 2
bauble
bestial
bland
diaphanous
effete
emendation
extenuate
gloat
impale
impediment
impotent
labyrinth
maelstrom
nihilism
shard

Lesson 3
adventitious
ambiguous
antithesis
bona fide
cataclysm
chagrin
deviate
edify
fecund
glower
importune
obfuscate
optimum
parochial
pedestrian

Lesson 4
baroque
besmirch
celibate
debacle
demeanor
facetious
fortuitous
hedonism
imperative
obloquy
perfunctory
quasi-
recapitulate
sacrosanct
sadistic

Lesson 5
bowdlerize
carnal
deference
ebullient
elegy
fop
impair
imprecation
nebulous
non sequitur
panegyric
pedantic
quandary
rakish
sanguine

Lesson 6
affluence
amoral
antipathy
banal
bedlam
denouement
elucidate
eschew
imminent
obdurate
onerous
parody
peruse
scurrilous
sedulous

Word List

Lesson 7
adroit
affectation
bovine
callow
dichotomy
fatuous
ferret
knell
laconic
macroscopic
patent
peccadillo
quiddity
rationalize
sagacious

Lesson 8
agape
carcinogen
censure
gambol
gibe
grotesque
hackneyed
harbinger
immolate
imperious
martinet
neologism
olfactory
quagmire
recondite

Lesson 9
blanch
chimerical
deride
eclectic
finesse
grandiose
heterogeneous
hybrid
idiosyncrasy
machination
masochist
nubile
pejorative
raiment
sapient

Lesson 10
adulterate
bucolic
caveat
delineate
diadem
emanate
garish
gratuitous
idolatry
immutable
impecunious
impious
onus
redolent
sedition

Lesson 11
cessation
defile
desiccated
elixir
epitome
fetish
fissure
garrulous
juxtapose
kinetic
lachrymose
languid
legerdemain
libertine
scintillate

Lesson 12
ambiance
badinage
bilious
blandishment
debauchery
fastidious
garner
gumption
halcyon
hegira
kismet
malapropism
necromancy
paradigm
regress

Word List

Lesson 13
animosity
brevity
cataract
despicable
empathy
harlequin
hoi polloi
impinge
lascivious
nirvana
obsequious
offal
redundant
salutary
savant

Lesson 14
aggrandize
bombast
deign
elicit
endemic
flaunt
mendacious
obviate
orthography
paleontology
panache
paroxysm
recoil
saturnine
shibboleth

Lesson 15
aesthetic
chaff
egregious
empirical
flaccid
foment
germane
hallow
hermetic
hospice
meretricious
orifice
perdition
querulous
ratiocinate

Lesson 16
affinity
fiscal
flout
impalpable
jocular
malleable
miscreant
palliate
recant
recreant
regale
salacious
salient
sentient
specious

Lesson 17
avuncular
beguile
coalesce
desultory
ennui
ergo
hector
hiatus
insolence
lambent
nonentity
pandemic
pecuniary
rebuke
sibilant

Lesson 18
apotheosis
auspicious
contiguous
flagellate
incendiary
inimitable
malfeasance
platonic
pontificate
proletariat
prurient
refractory
sang-froid
tenacious
vociferous

Word List

Lesson 19
abnegation
acrid
apex
credulity
dross
fulminate
gravitas
hegemony
insuperable
jejune
polyglot
psychosomatic
truculent
verisimilitude
viscous

Lesson 20
acerbic
androgynous
augur
beatitude
diaspora
discursive
disseminate
extemporaneous
intractable
maladroit
politic
requiem
sinecure
tendentious
traduce

Lesson 21
bon mot
clandestine
digress
furlough
misogyny
peon
plenary
plutocrat
potboiler
redoubtable
stolid
succor
travesty
vignette
xeric

Lesson One

1. **aegis** (ē´ jis) *n.* a shield; protection
The life of the witness is under the *aegis* of the witness protection program.
syn: backing

2. **rectify** (rek´ tə fī) *v.* to correct; to make right
JoAnne tried to *rectify* her poor relationship with her son by spending more time with him.
syn: remedy; resolve

3. **enervate** (en´ ər vāt) *v.* to weaken
The record temperatures *enervated* the farmhands before noon.
syn: devitalize; exhaust *ant: energize; strengthen*

4. **philanthropy** (fə lan thrə pē) *n.* the act of donating money or work to those in need
Half of the city was built by the *philanthropy* of wealthy steel barons.
syn: altruism; charity *ant: selfishness; egoism*

5. **boor** (bôr) *n.* a rude or impolite person
The *boor* grabbed handfuls of hors d'oeuvres and walked around while he ate them.
syn: buffoon; clown *ant: sophisticate*

6. **fervent** (fûr´ vənt) *adj.* eager; earnest
We made a *fervent* attempt to capture the stallion, but he was too quick for us.
syn: burning; passionate *ant: apathetic*

7. **besiege** (bi sēj´) *v.* to overwhelm; to surround and attack
People jumped from the ground and brushed themselves off as ants *besieged* the picnic.

8. **carrion** (kar´ ē ən) *n.* decaying flesh
The *carrion* along the desert highway was a feast for the vultures.

9. **ignoble** (ig nō´ bəl) *adj.* dishonorable; shameful
Cheating on an exam is an *ignoble* way to get good grades.
syn: despicable; base *ant: noble; glorious*

10. **amorphous** (ə môr´ fəs) *adj.* shapeless, formless; vague
What began as an *amorphous* idea in Steven's dream turned into a revolutionary way to power automobiles.

11. **factious** (fak´ shəs) *adj.* causing disagreement
The *factious* sailors refused to sail any farther into the storm.
syn: belligerent; contentious *ant: cooperative; united*

12. **ephemeral** (i fem´ ər əl) *adj.* lasting only a brief time; short-lived
The gardener experienced *ephemeral* fame the year she grew a half-ton pumpkin.
syn: transient; fleeting *ant: permanent*

13. **perspicacity** (pûr spi kas´ i tē) *n.* keenness of judgment
The old hermit still had the *perspicacity* to haggle with the automotive dealer.
syn: perceptiveness *ant: stupidity; ignorance*

14. **erotic** (i rot´ ik) *adj.* pertaining to sexual love
The museum staff cancelled the exhibition when it saw the *erotic* sculptures.

15. **opulent** (op´ ū lənt) *adj.* rich, luxurious; wealthy
Despite the stock market crash, the wealthy family continued its *opulent* lifestyle.

Exercise I

Words in Context

From the list below, supply the words needed to complete the paragraph. Some words will not be used.

amorphous	**enervate**	**besiege**	**ignoble**	**factious**
ephemeral	**perspicacity**	**philanthropy**	**carrion**	

1. Carter had been walking for more than four hours since his truck ran out of fuel. The morning desert sun __________ him, bringing him closer to exhaustion. In his weary state, he chastised himself for not having the __________ to have brought an extra can of fuel on the trip. In such a barren, isolated place, Carter knew that he couldn't rely on the __________ of others for help if his truck broke down. The only living things on the road were biting flies that __________ Carter and forced him to swat his face and neck every few seconds. They continued to attack until they detected the foul smell of __________ when Carter passed a dead hare on the shoulder of the road. The departure of the flies gave him __________ relief as he continued his trudge; the bugs went away, but in the distance, Carter could see, through eyes stinging with sweat, the __________ distortions of light along the hot, desert floor.

From the list below, supply the words needed to complete the paragraph. Some words will not be used.

rectify	**factious**	**ignoble**	**erotic**
amorphous	**besiege**	**perspicacity**	

2. Some of the council approved the new zoning restriction, but a few __________ members refused to cast votes. None of them actually approved of the __________ bookstore next to the little league field, but they wanted to find a better way to legally __________ the __________ situation.

From the list below, supply the words needed to complete the paragraph. Some words will not be used.

aegis	**philanthropy**	**boor**	**fervent**
carrion	**opulent**	**ephemeral**	

3. Councilman Parker, a wealthy native of the small town, knew that a few council members had a[n] __________ desire to remove him from office. Some of them resented his __________ lifestyle, and others claimed that Parker was careless because he lived under the __________ of his wealth and thus had no fear of being fired. They also called Parker a[n] __________ because he had the habit of interrupting conversations and barging into offices without knocking.

Exercise II

Sentence Completion

Complete the sentence in a way that shows you understand the meaning of the italicized vocabulary word.

1. Bob decided to *rectify* his crime by…
2. While some critics admired Johnson's *erotic* photography, others felt…
3. Working on the roof *enervated* the contractors, especially when…
4. The *ephemeral* argument was over in…
5. The highway crew removed the *carrion* from the road because…
6. In an act of *philanthropy*, Jennifer went to the nursing home to…
7. During the summit, the *factious* ambassador caused…
8. The wounded fish was soon *besieged* by…
9. His *fervent* speech convinced…
10. A person can lose his or her job by committing an *ignoble* act, such as…
11. Features in the *opulent* mansion include…
12. Under the *aegis* of the police department, the witness could safely…
13. People called Cory a *boor* because he always…
14. The *amorphous* body of the amoeba had no discernable…
15. If it were not for dad's *perspicacity*, I would have purchased a car that…

Exercise III

Roots, Prefixes, and Suffixes

Study the entries and answer the questions that follow.

The roots *fus* and *fun* mean "melt" or "pour out."
The suffix *–ion* means "the act of."
The roots *grad* and *gress* mean "step" or "go."
The suffix *–el* means "little."
The prefix *con–* means "together."
The prefixes *di–*, *dif–*, and *dis–* mean "apart."
The prefix *e–* means "out" or "from."

1. Using *literal* translations as guidance, define the following words without using a dictionary.

   A. fusion
   B. funnel
   C. infuse
   D. regress
   E. progress
   F. congress

2. If you have an *effusive* personality, then it __________ of you.

   Motor oil will __________ across the gravel if it spills out of the can.

3. A step-by-step process is often called a[n] __________ process, and a highway crew might use a[n] __________ to smooth out a road.

4. *Egress* literally translates to __________, and if someone loses a high-paying job and takes a lower-paying job, his or her career is said to have __________.

5. List all the words that you can think of that contain the roots *grad* and *gress*.

Exercise IV

Inference

Complete the sentence by inferring information about the italicized word from its context.

1. Some slang words are *ephemeral* and will probably…

2. Brenda felt guilty for stealing the money from the register, so she *rectified* the situation by…

3. After winning a lottery jackpot, Ed took his first steps into a life of *philanthropy* by…

Exercise V

Writing

Here is a writing prompt similar to the one you will find on the writing portion of an assessment test.

Plan and write an essay based on the following statement:

> Mark Twain once said, "Show me a man who knows what's funny, and I'll show you a man who knows what's not."

Assignment: What does this paradoxical quotation mean? In an essay, explain what Mark Twain is suggesting about humor. Support your thesis with evidence from your own reading, classroom studies, and personal observation and experience.

Thesis: Write a *one-sentence* response to the above assignment. Make certain this single sentence offers a clear stat ement of your position.

Example: People react to emotional extremes, and to appreciate humor, one must appreciate misery.

____

____

Organizational Plan: List at least three subtopics you will use to support your main idea. This list is your outline.

1. ____

2. ____

3. ____

Draft: Following your outline, write a good first draft of your essay. Remember to support all your points with examples, facts, references to reading, etc.

Review and Revise: Exchange essays with a classmate. Using the scoring guide for Organization on page 263, score your partner's essay (while he or she scores yours). Focus on the organizational plan and use of language conventions. If necessary, rewrite your essay to improve the organizational plan and/or your use of language.

Exercise VI

English Practice

Identifying Sentence Errors

Identify the grammatical error in each of the following sentences. If the sentence contains no error, select answer choice E.

1. The mechanic repairs (A) not only (B) domestic (C) cars, but also he repairs (D) foreign cars. No error (E)

2. The clients requested (A) information on what (B) factors would effect (C) the interest that they would earn on their (D) stocks. No error (E)

3. My mother finds it peculiar that while I, (A) and most of my female friends would do (B) just about anything to get a taste of something sweet, my brother (C) and his friends wait for dinner to eat (D). No error (E)

4. Through language, stereotypes and standards are (A) communicated to those who (B) are required to listen: therefore (C), schools are a medium through which the population is controlled (D). No error (E)

5. The government, who attempt (A) to use welfare as a means of (B) helping lower economic classes, is ignoring (C) the inherent (D) problems of the system. No error (E)

Improving Sentences

The underlined portion of each sentence below contains some flaw. Select the answer choice that best corrects the flaw.

6. The first baseman forgot to take his glove to the field, and he stops in the middle of the inning to retrieve it.
   - A. and he is stopping in the middle of the inning to retrieve his mitt.
   - B. and he stopped in the middle of the inning to retrieve his mitt.
   - C. and he stops, in the middle of the inning, to retrieve his mitt.
   - D. and he stopped in the middle of the inning, retrieving his mitt.
   - E. and he is stopping in the middle of the inning, retrieving his mitt.

7. Clearing the bar at seven feet, a new high jump record was set.
   - A. A new high jump record was set, while the athlete cleared the bar at seven feet.
   - B. While clearing the bar at seven feet, a new high jump record was set.
   - C. The athlete cleared the bar at seven feet and set a new high jump record.
   - D. A new high jump record, by clearing the bar seven feet, was set.
   - E. After clearing the bar at seven feet, a new high jump record was set by the athlete.

8. The violinist was acclaimed for her performance by the audience.
   - A. For her performance the violinist was acclaimed by the audience.
   - B. The violinist was acclaimed for her performance, by the audience.
   - C. From the audience, the violinist received acclaim for her performance.
   - D. The audience acclaimed the violinist for her performance.
   - E. The audience acclaimed the performance for the violinist.

9. The college student enjoys swimming, and writing, but not to study.
   - A. The college student enjoys swimming and to write but not to study.
   - B. The college student enjoys swimming, and to write, but not to study.
   - C. The college student enjoys swimming and enjoys writing, but does not enjoy studying.
   - D. The college student enjoys to swim and to write but not to study.
   - E. The college student enjoys swimming and writing, but not studying.

10. The musical was exceptional, the cast was only mediocre.
    - A. Though the musical was exceptional, and the cast was only mediocre.
    - B. The musical was exceptional, the cast is only mediocre.
    - C. The musical was exceptional the cast was only mediocre.
    - D. The musical was exceptional, though only the cast was mediocre.
    - E. The musical, which was exceptional, but the cast was only mediocre.

Lesson Two

1. **maelstrom** (māl´ strəm) *n.* a whirlpool; turbulence; an agitated state of mind
His emotions were like a *maelstrom,* and he couldn't decide what course to follow.

2. **impotent** (im´ pə tənt) *adj.* powerless; lacking strength
Without the gun, the robber felt *impotent.*
syn: ineffective; helpless *ant: potent; powerful*

3. **emendation** (ē´men dā´ shən) *n.* a correction
The last edition of the book contains many *emendations.*
syn: improvement; amendment

4. **gloat** (glōt) *v.* to look at or think about with great satisfaction
The track team *gloated* over their latest victory.
syn: revel; crow

5. **effete** (e fēt´) *adj.* worn out; barren
Although worn down by age and a life of hard work, the man's idea was far from *effete.*
syn: exhausted; spent; sterile *ant: vital; vigorous*

6. **impale** (im pāl´) *v.* to pierce with a sharp stake through the body
The natives used sharp sticks to *impale* fish in the tide pools.

7. **bland** (bland) *adj.* mild; tasteless; dull
His *bland* manner had a calming effect on the children.
syn: smooth; agreeable *ant: exciting; thrilling*

8. **extenuate** (ek sten´ ū āt) *v.* to lessen seriousness by providing partial excuses
The jury believes that the thief's situation *extenuates* the crime of stealing food.

9. **bestial** (bes´ chəl) *adj.* savage; brutal
He took a *bestial* delight in tormenting the captive slaves.
syn: brutish; vile; cruel *ant: humane; kind*

10. **diaphanous** (dī af´ ə nəs) *adj.* very sheer and light
The *diaphanous* gown was beautiful, but Gloria wasn't sure she had the nerve to wear it.
syn: transparent; gossamer *ant: opaque*

11. **bauble** (bô´ bəl) *n.* a showy but useless thing
John had to find some kind of *bauble* to give Mary for Christmas.
syn: trinket

12. **labyrinth** **(lab´ ə rinth)** *n.* a complicated network of winding passages; a maze
The mice were made to run through a *labyrinth* in order to reach their food.

13. **impediment** **(im ped´ ə mənt)** *n.* a barrier; an obstruction
The supervisor wouldn't be an *impediment* to her advancement.
syn: obstacle; hindrance *ant: aid*

14. **shard** **(shärd)** *n.* a fragment
The doctor pulled a *shard* of glass from the girl's arm.

15. **nihilism** **(nī´ ə liz´ əm)** *n.* a total rejection of established laws
Nihilism rejects established laws and order, but it offers nothing in their place.

Exercise I

Words in Context

From the list below, supply the words needed to complete the paragraph. Some words will not be used.

bestial	**maelstrom**	**extenuate**	**impotent**	**impediment**
emendation	**impale**	**labyrinth**	**diaphanous**	**gloat**

1. Upset with declining sales, corporate headquarters appointed Loren to replace a[n] __________ manager who had been spotted on the golf course during work hours one-too-many times.

   Loren's many changes and __________ to company guidelines caused a[n] __________ in both the warehouse and the salesroom. Employees faced evaluations and new instructions that drove many to resign; however, it was all just a part of Loren's plan. The people who quit, she reasoned, were just __________ to meeting the expected monthly profit margin. The laggards usually tried to __________ their poor performance by claiming unfair wages, work hours, or treatment, but investigation showed the reasons to be false.

   Loren spent the first two weeks familiarizing herself with the __________ of shelves and palettes in the warehouse. Shreds of textiles littered parts of the packaging area; some were hefty snippets of wool, and others were __________ scraps of silk that hovered in the gust created by passing forklifts. After the first round of resignations and firings, most of the workers were intimidated by Loren's __________ management techniques.

From the list below, supply the words needed to complete the paragraph. Some words will not be used.

bauble	**bland**	**shard**	**nihilism**	**labyrinth**
effete	**gloat**	**bestial**	**impale**	

2. Most of the office personnel assumed that Devon's home life was as __________ as his uninteresting manner at work. Reserved and soft spoken, Devon sat at a desk every day filling out purchase orders and staring at the only ornamental object on his desk: a glass paperweight with a brass tag commemorating fifteen years of service—a[n] __________ presented to Devon by the company in lieu of a bonus or a raise. It must not have sentimental importance to Devon, because he did not say a word when one of the interns accidentally knocked the glass bubble to the floor, where the __________ still can be heard crunching beneath the wheels of antiquated office chairs.

   The passing years took a toll on Devon's unremarkable body. In the months following the fall of the paperweight, he developed a weary look; he had become both __________ and apathetic from the exhausting monotony of filling out purchase orders for fifteen years. Occasionally, in the break room, he listened to some of the younger workers __________ about how quickly they were promoted; most were at least ten years younger than Devon and had half the experience. A form of __________ rapidly replaced his apathy and he found himself wishing the company would simply fail, go bankrupt, and disintegrate, along with his entire world. With a sigh, he looked up at an old, yellowed postcard he had once __________ on his bulletin board with a thumbtack. It was from his brother's vacation to Hawaii—a place that seemed as out-of-reach to Devon as the planet Mars.

Exercise II

Sentence Completion

Complete the sentence in a way that shows you understand the meaning of the italicized vocabulary word.

1. You cannot *extenuate* your…
2. Nathan *impaled* an earthworm on the hook before he…
3. When Dave submitted a term paper that required *emendations*, the teacher…
4. Vicky caused a *maelstrom* of panic when she told everyone that…
5. The team must change its *effete* strategy if…
6. Heidi's friends did not want to hear her *gloat* about…
7. The crowd knew that the *impotent* boxer would not be able to…
8. The mall is a *labyrinth*, so check the map or you will…
9. People knew that Jimmy believed in *nihilism* when he…
10. Your dinner will taste *bland* if you do not…
11. *Shards* of broken taillights littered the highway after…
12. Mary scolded Bert for wasting money on useless *baubles*, such as…
13. Ashley was suspended for wearing a *diaphanous* shirt to…
14. The largest *impediment* to crossing the river is…
15. The soldier endured *bestial* treatment after…

Exercise III

Roots, Prefixes, and Suffixes

Study the entries and answer the questions that follow.

The root *somn* means "sleep."
The root *pot* means "to drink."
The root *vac* means "empty."
The root *sid* means "to sit" or "to settle."
The prefix *e–* means "out" or "completely."
The prefix *in–* means "not."
The prefix *dis–* means "not" or "apart."
The prefix *pre–* means "before" or "in front of."

1. Using *literal* translations as guidance, define the following words without using a dictionary.

A	evacuate	D.	dissenter
B.	vacate	E.	reside
C.	potation	F.	president

2. A magic drink is often called a[n] __________.

   Water from the stream will not be __________, or drinkable, until you boil it.

3. If you cannot sleep, then you might have a condition called __________.

   Somnolent music might help you to __________.

4. *Insidious* literally translates to "sitting in," but the word means "secretly working to cause harm." Explain the possible connection between the actual and literal definitions of *insidious*.

5. List as many words as you can think of that contain the root *sid*.

Exercise IV

Inference

Complete the sentence by inferring information about the italicized word from its context.

1. If Larry *gloated* about his skills after the last bowling tournament, then one can probably assume that…

2. Sometimes Nikki wakes up too early because the *diaphanous* curtains over the bedroom windows do not…

3. A storm and a flash flood *extenuated* Halley's absence from work, so he did not have to worry about…

Exercise V

Critical Reading

Below is a reading passage followed by several multiple-choice questions. Carefully read the passage and choose the best answer for each of the questions.

The following passage describes one of the worst manmade disasters in United States history. More than two thousand people died in the Johnstown Flood of 1889 when the South Fork Dam failed.

The morning of May 31st, 1889, was not an average morning for the thirty thousand citizens of Johnstown, Pennsylvania, but it was not a particularly exceptional morning, either. Heavy rains during the night had caused the Little Conemaugh River to spill over its banks, but mild flooding was not uncommon for the growing steel town. People went about their daily business among the sounds of clanging train cars, trotting horses, and clinking machinery of the iron works. All those sounds would soon be drowned in an ominous rumble from the hills north of town.

South Fork Dam, fourteen miles north of Johnstown, retained the water of Lake Conemaugh high in the Allegheny Mountains. The dam, built in 1831, created the two-mile lake, which served as a reservoir for the Pennsylvania Mainline Canal; however, railways soon rendered the canal obsolete, and the Pennsylvania Railroad purchased the canal from the state. The railroad operated parts of the canal until the dam failed in 1862 while the lake was half full. The railroad sold Lake Conemaugh to a congressman, who removed the dam's discharge system and sold it for scrap. He then sold the property to Benjamin Ruff of the South Fork Fishing and Hunting Club, and in 1879, Mr. Ruff made repairs to the dam and constructed a pleasure community around Lake Conemaugh. For ten years, the club served as a successful resort for Pittsburgh's elite, including Andrew Carnegie and Andrew Mellon.

While people in Johnstown went about their daily routines on the morning after the storm, the caretakers of the South Fork Fishing and Hunting Club scrambled to deal with a lake that was rapidly rising to dangerous levels. Everyone in the Little Conemaugh River valley, included the citizens of Johnstown, had joked about the condition of the dam for years. They speculated about the day that it would finally burst, but few actually worried about it. When the water of Lake Conemaugh approached the top of the dam, the workers in South Fork knew that it was time to worry. The 450-acre lake wanted to be free, and the **effete** dirt walls of the reservoir were not going to hold it.

After the heavy rain, approximately ten thousand cubic feet of water entered Lake Conemaugh each hour, but only six thousand cubic feet escaped over the spillway. In the morning, the lake was only two feet from the top of the dam, and it was still rising. Workers hurriedly cleaned **impediments** and debris from spillways to let more water escape, but the lake continued to rise. A team of laborers dug a trench to route water around the dam, but the ditch was too shallow to have any great effect. Inch by inch, the water neared the top of the dam, and at noon, it began to wash away the earthen structure. By two o'clock, the rushing water had cut through the top center of the dam, but most of the lake was still contained. At three o'clock, Lake Conemaugh—twenty million tons of water—burst through the center of the dam, carrying with it the destructive energy of a thousand tons of TNT.

Workers in South Fork sent telegraph warnings to Johnstown when the lake began to spill over the dam, but most of the residents dismissed them. People who actually took the warnings seriously and left for high ground were ridiculed by those who remained in town.

It took forty-five minutes for Lake Conemaugh to rush through the broken dam, and in that time it became a frothing torrent—a forty-foot wall of water that swallowed everything in its path. The wave, on a downhill course to Johnstown, grew in mass as it picked up trees, rocks, and chunks of debris. By four o'clock, the people of Johnstown noticed that the river had become strangely rapid, and in the minutes that followed, they heard a strange rumble in the distance.

The wall of water hit Johnstown at 4:07 p.m., moving at almost forty miles per hour. Neither wood nor iron slowed it down. It swept away buildings as though they were made of balsa wood. The heavy debris it carried turned the wave into a jackhammer that easily smashed through any manmade obstacle that managed to survive the initial surge. Brick walls shattered into **shards**, and steel railroad cars tumbled like children's toys. Not even the most permanent of structures proved to be heavy enough to protect people from the water. People who were swept away battled to stay afloat and alive; some were crushed by debris, and others, hiding in the attics of their homes, drowned when the wave dragged their homes from their foundations.

In ten minutes, four square miles of downtown area had been completely obliterated. Though the initial wave had passed, a swift current, twenty-feet deep, still flowed through the city. Those people lucky enough to have taken cover on solid buildings stood on rooftops and nervously watched as the **maelstrom** consumed nearby buildings. Hundreds of people were missing, and approximately five hundred were trapped in a massive pile of debris that the wave had deposited against a bridge. The twisted heap, more than forty-acres in area, contained homes, bridges, railroad cars, and machines from Johnstown and four other communities along the Little Conemaugh. People crawled from the entanglement and struggled to find high ground, but not everyone made it to safety before the debris, soaked with oil from an overturned train car, caught fire. Eighty people perished in the flames.

Two thousand, two hundred nine people died as a result of the Johnstown Flood. The destructive wave removed 99 families, 1,600 homes, and 280 businesses from the face of the earth. Unsanitary conditions, cholera, and missing family members made matters worse in the days that followed, but luckily, a little good sprouted from the destruction.

The disaster galvanized the nation, and nearly four million dollars in relief money poured into Johnstown from the United States and eighteen foreign nations. Hundreds of volunteers swarmed to the city to provide food, blankets, and temporary shelters for thousands of victims. The flood also prompted the first major disaster relief effort for the newly formed American Red Cross, which has helped countless millions since.

The story of the flood caused a media frenzy at the time, and investigations and lawsuits ensued, with most aimed at the club comprised of wealthy barons of industry. Ultimately, the dam had changed hands so many times in its 58-year existence that the club was not held responsible for the catastrophic failure. Some experts insist that had the discharge system been replaced, the damn wouldn't have failed; however, other investigators claim that the rainfall was so heavy that even the original dam would have failed. South Fork dam was never rebuilt. Regardless of where the blame belongs, the story of the Johnstown Flood will be an eternal reminder to give potential disasters their due attention before it's too late.

1A. The tone of the passage is best described as
- A. bitter and mournful.
- B. excited and nostalgic.
- C. spiteful but analytical.
- D. sober but heartening.
- E. cross and skeptical.

1B. Choose the elements of the passage that best support your answer to question 1A.
- A. indifference toward the victims
- B. tragedy and rebuilding
- C. descriptions of the destruction
- D. precise statistics about casualties and property damage
- E. blame ascribed to the private club

2A. As used in line 6, *ominous* most nearly means
- A. loud.
- B. cautious.
- C. foreboding.
- D. roaring.
- E. single.

2B. Which answer best explains how suspense is created at the beginning of the passage?
- A. Flooding is described as a normal occurrence that frequently repeats itself.
- B. The morning was abnormally quiet, despite the rain.
- C. It portrays the panic about to ensue, and it complicates it with bad weather.
- D. It uses the word *drowned*, but quickly begins a history of Johnstown.
- E. The people of the town are described as knowing what is about to happen.

3A. According to the passage, how many times has the South Fork Dam broken since 1831?
- A. zero
- B. one
- C. two
- D. three
- E. four

3B. To those who were familiar with the dam before the flood, the dam's failure was
- A. the result of underground blasting.
- B. completely unexpected.
- C. no surprise at all.
- D. merely a political opportunity.
- E. the fault of the city council.

3C. According to the passage, the South Fork Dam was made of
- A. concrete.
- B. cement.
- C. steel.
- D. earth.
- E. bakelite.

4A. Partial blame for the dam's failure, according to paragraph 2, specifically, can be attributed to
   A. heavy rain.
   B. Mr. Ruff.
   C. the removal of the discharge system.
   D. Andrew Carnegie.
   E. the Pennsylvania Railroad.

4B. Choose the reason that best supports your answer to question 4A.
   A. "[P]arts of the canal" were operated by a railroad.
   B. A congressman "removed the dam's discharge system."
   C. The area served as a "resort for Pittsburgh's elite."
   D. "[R]ailways soon rendered the canal obsolete."
   E. The dam held back a "two-mile lake."

5A. Few people evacuated the city before the flood because
   A. Johnstown was accustomed to frequent floods.
   B. the telegraph wires were down.
   C. no one took the warning seriously.
   D. the men on horses did not reach the city soon enough.
   E. the engineer at South Fork told them not to worry.

5B. What can be inferred from the following line?

   "People who actually took the warnings seriously and left for high ground were ridiculed by those who remained in town."

   A. Residents felt they would be at less risk in town.
   B. The people who left went to the South Fork Club.
   C. The people who left had probably been forced to evacuate.
   D. Most of the residents did not feel threatened.
   E. The residents were too busy working to leave.

6A. The simile in line 47, "like children's toys," primarily emphasizes
   A. the popularity of model toys in Johnstown.
   B. the overwhelming force of the surge.
   C. that most hardwood trees survived the wave.
   D. the shoddy construction of buildings in the nineteenth century.
   E. the flimsiness of the brick walls.

6B. Choose the answer that best explains the implication of the following line.

   "The heavy debris it carried turned the wave into a jackhammer that easily smashed through any manmade obstacle that managed to survive the initial surge."

   A. Construction tools in the wave spun wildly, causing additional damage to property.
   B. The heavy debris was the only thing slowing down the wave, preventing more extensive damage.
   C. Bricks were especially prone to water damage because they are lighter than metal in the wave.
   D. If the water alone failed to destroy an object, the debris the wave carried finished the job.
   E. Multiple waves hitting buildings chiseled away at the structures until they fell.

7A. Choose the line that provides the best example of the author's personifying the water.
  A. "The 450-acre lake wanted to be free…"
  B. "…most of the lake was still contained."
  C. "…laborers dug a trench to route water around the dam…"
  D. "…a lake that was rapidly rising to dangerous levels."
  E. "…the destructive energy of a thousand tons of TNT."

7B. Which phrase from the passage shows an additional example of personification?
  A. "into a jackhammer"
  B. "twisted heap"
  C. "clanging train cars"
  D. "swallowed everything"
  E. "carrying with it"

8. When the surge hit Johnstown, how long did it take to destroy the downtown area?
  A. three minutes
  B. five minutes
  C. ten minutes
  D. twenty minutes
  E. forty-five minutes

9A.. Which of the following would be the most appropriate title for this passage?
  A. Life on the Flood Plain
  B. The Johnstown Flood of 1889
  C. Preventing Looting after Disasters
  D. Recovery Efforts after the Johnstown Flood
  E. The Dangers of Heavy Rain

9B. Choose the best subtitle to attach to your answer to question 9A.
  A. A Case for Better Building Construction
  B. When Hazards are Forgotten
  C. A Tale of Tragedy
  D. Why Earthen Dams Should Be Banned
  E. Legal Murder for the Rich

10A. This passage would probably be found in a[n]
  A. engineering magazine.
  B. social studies textbook.
  C. local newspaper.
  D. book about early country clubs in the United States.
  E. American Red Cross pamphlet.

10B. The author of the passage would probably agree with which statement?
  A. The tragedy received far too much press coverage.
  B. The water was not exceptionally destructive.
  C. The dam had been damaged before the flood.
  D. There weren't enough maintenance workers at the club.
  E. Time is the best indicator of a dam's dependability.

Lesson Three

1. **adventitious** (ad´ ven tish´ əs) *adj.* accidental; nonessential
The scientists admitted that the breakthrough was an *adventitious* result of the study.
syn: incidental

2. **fecund** (fē´ kənd) *adj.* fertile; productive
The *fecund* soil produced a record number of tomatoes this year.
syn: prolific *ant: sterile*

3. **pedestrian** (pə des´ trē ən) *adj.* ordinary or dull
The crowd responded to the *pedestrian* speech with yawns.
syn: commonplace; mediocre *ant: imaginative; compelling*

4. **edify** (ed´ ə fī) *v.* to improve someone morally
The sermon was meant to *edify* the congregation.

5. **importune** (im pôr tōōn´) *v.* to ask persistently; to beg
John *importuned* his father, but could not get the car keys.
syn: appeal; badger

6. **deviate** (dē´ vē āt) *v.* to turn aside from a course; to stray
Sometimes it's better to *deviate* from the truth than to hurt someone's feelings.
syn: digress

7. **bona fide** (bō´ nə fīd) *adj.* in good faith
We made a *bona fide* offer for the property.
syn: legitimate; genuine *ant: fraudulent; phony*

8. **glower** (glou´ ər) *v.* to stare angrily
The boy *glowered* at his mother when she corrected his manners.
syn: frown; scowl *ant: grin*

9. **cataclysm** (kat´ ə kliz əm) *n.* a violent change
The earthquake in Mexico was a *cataclysm* which no one could have foreseen.
syn: disaster; catastrophe *ant: triumph; boon*

10. **obfuscate** (ob´ fus kāt) *v.* to confuse; to bewilder
The realtor tried to *obfuscate* the issue, and it was working because the confused buyer did not know if he was coming or going.
syn: muddle; obscure *ant: clarify; elucidate*

11. **antithesis** (an tith´ i sis) *n.* an exact opposite; an opposite extreme
Love is the *antithesis* of hate.
syn: converse *ant: same*

12. **chagrin** (shə grin´) *n.* embarrassment; a complete loss of courage
Joanne had never felt such *chagrin* as when she fell into the mud puddle in front of her fiancé's family.

13. **parochial** (pə rō´ kē əl) *adj.* local; narrow; limited
Because he had never traveled outside his own town, Jim had a very *parochial* view of life.
syn: provincial; narrow-minded *ant: universal; catholic*

14. **ambiguous** (am big´ yōō əs) *adj.* open to more than one interpretation
The candidate's *ambiguous* comments tended to confuse the issue even more.
syn: unclear; uncertain; vague *ant: explicit; definite*

15. **optimum** (op´ tə mum) *adj.* best; most favorable; ideal
The pilot was waiting for *optimum* conditions before setting out on the dangerous flight.

Exercise I

Words in Context

From the list below, supply the words needed to complete the paragraph. Some words will not be used.

deviate	**chagrin**	**glower**	**obfuscate**	**cataclysm**
optimum	**antithesis**	**pedestrian**	**adventitious**	

1. The __________, two-hour lecture only __________ the students. They respected the guest speaker's experience, but every time she __________ from the complex topic, she added ten __________ minutes to the harangue. The speech was the __________ of the brief overview that had been promised. The conditions of the auditorium were not __________ for long lectures; the air conditioner was broken, and the heat and poor lighting forced many of the students to fight drowsiness. One young man nodded off and woke with a start when his head struck his desk; he quickly sat up straight with a look of __________. The speaker __________ at him for a few seconds, but never stopped speaking.

From the list below, supply the words needed to complete the paragraph. Some words will not be used.

bona fide	**fecund**	**parochial**	**edify**
ambiguous	**cataclysm**	**importune**	**chagrin**

2. At the check-out line, Timmy __________ his mother to purchase a new brand of candy bar for him; however, her reaction was a[n] __________ compared to her usual tolerant reactions to Timmy's requests. Everyone stared when Lynn screamed at Timmy and told him to return the candy bar and stop whining because no, he "absolutely does not need it."

   Before she snapped in the grocery store, Lynn had concealed her anxiety for a week. The rent check was later than it had ever been, and the landlord had a[n] __________ view in financial matters. Lynn had already bought an extra week by reassuring him of her __________ intention to pay the rent with her first paycheck, but the week had passed, and she still hadn't found a job. The landlord had given her the usual speech about honoring a lease, apparently in an attempt to __________ Lynn. It was the landlord's __________ tone that really bothered her; Lynn couldn't be sure if the landlord would continue being compassionate or if he would send an eviction notice upon finding no rent payment in his mailbox that morning.

   Lynn used the last of her cash to pay for the bread and cereal. She took Timmy's hand and left the store hoping to have a[n] __________ day of job hunting.

Exercise II

Sentence Completion

Complete the sentence in a way that shows you understand the meaning of the italicized vocabulary word.

1. If you do not wait for *optimum* sailing conditions, you might…
2. Try not to *deviate* from the subject while you…
3. The *fecund* nature of the jungle…
4. The uninsured woman *importuned* the hospital to…
5. The *pedestrian* television program was not worth…
6. Todd's parents did not hide their *chagrin* after their son…
7. Sheila, covered in food, *glowered* at the waiter after he…
8. Ralph wanted a *bona fide* New York cheesecake, so he…
9. The *ambiguous* quote caused controversy because…
10. Chrissie is the *antithesis* of Ben, because she is friendly to strangers while he…
11. One *adventitious* effect that traveling has on young children is…
12. Alice thought that she could *edify* her son, but she knew that she could not when…
13. The car salesman *obfuscated* the dissatisfied customer so much that the customer…
14. A *cataclysm* caused by an asteroid striking the earth would probably…
15. Martin had a *parochial* fear of travel, so it surprised everyone when he…

Exercise III

Roots, Prefixes, and Suffixes

Study the entries and answer the questions that follow.

The root *merge* means "to plunge" or "to immerse."
The root *integr* means "whole," "intact," or "perfect."
The root *lat* means "to carry" or "to bear."
The suffixes *–ence* and *–ance* mean "the quality of [base word]-ing."
The prefix *e–* means "out" or "from."
The prefix *co–* means "together" or "with."
The prefix *trans–* means "across" or "through."

1. Using *literal* translations as guidance, define the following words without using a dictionary.

   A. submerge
   B. emergence
   C. merge
   D. integral
   E. relate
   F. collated

2. The literal meaning of *translate* is __________.

   A person who is carried upward in spirit is said to be __________.

   If someone tells you a story, you can carry it to another person and __________ it to him.

3. A person with perfect character might be said to have __________[-ity].

   You __________ something by bringing things together as a whole. If you separate the things from the whole, or if you break them up, then you __________ them.

4. List at least five words that contain the suffixes *–ance* or *–ence*.

Exercise IV

Inference

Complete the sentence by inferring information about the italicized word from its context.

1. Seek a *fecund* area in which to plant the tomatoes and corn if you want to…

2. People fell asleep during the *pedestrian* film because it was…

3. The kids went to camp to enjoy the outdoors, but the experience also had the *adventitious* effect of teaching them how to…

Exercise V

Writing

Here is a writing prompt similar to the one you will find on the writing portion of an assessment test.

Plan and write an essay based on the following statement:

> "...there was one of two things I had a right to, liberty, or death; if I could not have one, I would take de oder; for no man should take me alive; I should fight for my liberty as long as my strength lasted, and when de time came for me to go, de Lord would let dem take me."
>
> –Harriet Tubman

Assignment: If you were to identify the two most important rights, what would they be? In an essay, explain the two rights that you feel are most valuable, the importance they have in people's lives, and then speculate how society would change if those rights were taken away. Be certain to support any generalities you make with specific references to the literature you are discussing and to your experience and observation.

Thesis: Write a *one-sentence* response to the above assignment. Make certain this single sentence offers a clear statement of your position.

Example: Without the rights to both give and receive love, relationships would disintegrate, resulting in a society comprising self-serving people.

____

____

Organizational Plan: List at least three subtopics you will use to support your main idea. This list is your outline.

1. ____

2. ____

3. ____

Draft: Following your outline, write a good first draft of your essay. Remember to support all your points with examples, facts, references to reading, etc.

Review and Revise: Exchange essays with a classmate. Using the scoring guide for Development on page 264, score your partner's essay (while he or she scores yours). Focus on the development of ideas and use of language conventions. If necessary, rewrite your essay to improve the development of ideas and/or your use of language.

Exercise VI

English Practice

Improving Paragraphs

Read the following passage and then choose the best revision for the underlined portions of the paragraph. The questions will require you to make decisions regarding the revision of the reading selection. Some revisions are not of actual mistakes, but will improve the clarity of the writing.

1 Sometimes it is nice to marvel at the many products of technology. In a span of fewer than one hundred years, humans have developed antibiotics, space travel, nuclear reactors, digital communications, batteries—oh, wait: we didn't invent batteries. They've been around for quite some time—more than 2,000 years, as a matter of fact.

2 In 1936, workers excavating a 2,000-year-old village near Baghdad find a seemingly unexciting clay pot, roughly six inches tall. The **adventitious** discovery of the pot, shaped like a small vase, was casually grouped with other artifacts and placed into storage.

3 The clay pot sat untouched for two years, until the day Wilhelm Konig, a German archaeologist, made a close examination of the artifact. To his astonishment, the ancient pot contained a copper cylinder, six inches in length, through which an iron rod hung suspended. An asphalt stopper sealed the cylinder in the pot, and another piece of asphalt beneath the cylinder appeared to serve as an insulator. The iron rod showed signs of corrosion, as though, perhaps, an acidic fluid had been used as an electrolytic solution to establish a current between the copper tube and the iron rod. This was not some **ambiguous** combination of parts; Doctor Konig had just discovered a 2,000-year-old battery.

4 The battery sparked the imaginations of archaeologists all over the world. How could a civilization that knew nothing about the existence of electricity create a battery? Batteries are expensive even today. More important, why would an ancient civilization need a battery?

5 In 1940, well before scientists had finished speculating about the mysterious device, Willard Gray, a scientist at the General Electric High Voltage Laboratory in Massachusetts, decided to conduct an experiment to confirm that the clay pot was indeed a battery. He created a replica of the pot, and, using a copper sulfate solution as an electrolyte, the pot generated one-half volt. The battery was legitimate.

6 The attention of archaeologists was returned to determining the purpose of the battery. Theories put forth by the scientists primarily agreed that, based on the findings of silver-plated copper artifacts, the battery was used by the ancients for electroplating, or gilding; however, doubts were instilled about the theory because of the limited potential of the battery.

7 During the 1970s, an Egyptologist built another replica of the battery, but to test this replica, he used an electrolyte that would more likely have been available to the ancients: fresh grape juice. The replica battery reportedly generated nearly one volt. The same researcher allegedly used the replica battery to electroplate a statuette with gold, but any evidence to support the experiment has long vanished. Despite the lack of evidence, scientists still agree that the battery was probably used for plating, or gilding, metal.

8 The Baghdad Battery now sits in the Baghdad Museum with as many as twelve others like it, all dated to the vicinity of 250 B.C. Perhaps if someone had left one sitting out, the world would not have needed to wait for Alessandro Volta to invent the battery—again—in 1799. Who knows what other inventions lie buried beneath the desert sands?

9 Some scientists theorized that the ancients used the batteries for pain relief because the ancient Greeks were aware that the mysterious quality of electric eels was useful in alleviating aching feet. Others theorize that the batteries were the result of ancient Chinese acupuncture techniques because electric acupuncture is practiced in modern China. Theories even include shock-inducing, anti-theft devices that ancients might have placed inside statues.

1. Which of the following corrections would fix an error in paragraph 2?
   A. Remove the comma after "In 1936."
   B. Add *was* before *placed.*
   C. Change "was casually grouped" to "is casually grouped."
   D. Change "shaped like a vase" to "vase-shaped."
   E. Change *find* to past tense.

2. Which of the following sentences should be deleted from paragraph 4?
   A. sentence 1
   B. sentence 2
   C. sentence 3
   D. sentence 2 and sentence 3
   E. sentence 1 and sentence 4

3. Which of the following changes would best improve paragraph 6?
   A. Add details about the credentials of the theorists.
   B. Rewrite the paragraph in active voice.
   C. Include the name of Wilhelm Konig.
   D. Describe the location of the archeological site where the battery was found.
   E. Exchange paragraph 2 with paragraph 6.

4. Which of the following details would best improve the content of the passage without distracting from the topic?
   A. Briefly explain the concept of electroplating.
   B. Add another paragraph about Chinese electric acupuncture.
   C. Add a catchy title.
   D. Insert a blank space between paragraphs 3 and 4.
   E. Rewrite the passage to have a tone of skepticism.

5. Which of the following changes would best improve the conclusion of the passage?
   A. Rewrite paragraph 9.
   B. Exchange the first paragraph with the last paragraph.
   C. Place paragraph 9 to follow paragraph 4.
   D. Place paragraph 9 to follow paragraph 2.
   E. Delete paragraph 9.

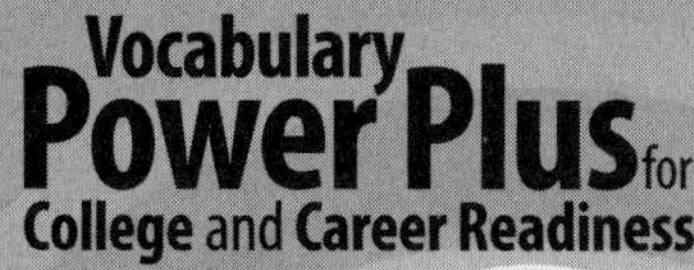

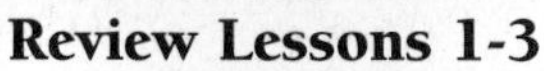

Review Lessons 1-3

Exercise I

Inferences

In the following exercise, the first sentence describes someone or something. Infer information from the first sentence, and then choose the word from the Word Bank that best completes the second sentence.

factious	**chagrin**	**diaphanous**	**impediment**
nihilism	**importune**	**obfuscated**	**extenuated**

1. If the three siblings fight over a certain toy, their mom donates the toy to charity.

   From this sentence, we can infer that the mom eliminates __________ toys if the children cannot agree over who gets to play with them.

2. The teacher excused Melissa's absence because a landslide had blocked the road to her house for two days.

   From this sentence, we can infer that the uncontrollable event __________ Melissa's absence from school.

3. The number of automobile accidents actually increased after the government mandated the unpopular safety device on new cars because the device decreased driver vision.

   From this sentence, we can infer that the new device was a[n] __________ to driving safely.

4. By the time Benny had finished his explanation of quantum theory, most of the students were completely lost.

   From this sentence, we can infer that Benny merely __________ the theory with his explanation.

5. After she forgot the song lyrics halfway through a performance, Kelly swore that she would never be embarrassed on stage again, and, indeed, she went on to have a successful singing career.

   From this sentence, we can infer that Kelly's __________ motivated her to succeed.

Exercise II

Related Words

the vocabulary words from Lessons 1 through 3 have related meanings. Complete the following ...es by choosing the word that best fits the context, based on information you infer from the use of the ...zed word. Some word pairs will be antonyms, some will be synonyms, and some will simply be words ...n used in the same context.

1. The humble prime minister rejected the __________ palace stateroom, and, instead, chose a modest, two-bedroom cottage in a *pedestrian* neighborhood on the edge of the capital city.
   A. fervent
   B. bland
   C. ambiguous
   D. opulent
   E. adventitious

2. To cover up his illegal actions, the general __________ the information in the report and ensured that no one would be able to make sense out of the *amorphous* details.
   A. gloated
   B. besieged
   C. obfuscated
   D. edified
   E. extenuated

3. The volcanic eruption was a *cataclysm* for the natural environment around the mountain; scavengers fed on __________ for weeks after the superheated air killed entire herds of deer and flocks of birds.
   A. carrion
   B. perspicacity
   C. labyrinth
   D. maelstrom
   E. shard

4. Rusty's *parochial* upbringing, which allowed for no television, trips to the mall, or any exposure to popular culture, was the __________ of his wife's childhood in which she was encouraged to learn everything about the world around her, regardless of whether she approved of it.
   A. pedestrian
   B. antithesis
   C. maelstrom
   D. nihilism
   E. boor

5. Few people visited the __________ amusement park because the rides were outdate[d] and worn out, and the staff was rendered *impotent* by the owner's refusal to invest an[y] money for repairs.
   A. optimum
   B. diaphanous
   C. effete
   D. erotic
   E. ignoble

6. Nathan *glowered* at his sister, Gigi, as she __________ about her foosball winning streak.
   A. besieged
   B. rectified
   C. deviated
   D. obfuscated
   E. gloated

7. The space shuttle __________ from its course, so the pilot fired the thrusters to *rectify* the vehicle's path of travel.
   A. glowered
   B. deviated
   C. besieged
   D. edified
   E. gloated

8. The small jet's stuck landing gear proved to be a[n] __________ that prevented the aircraft from reaching *optimum* fuel efficiency.
   A. pedestrian
   B. shard
   C. maelstrom
   D. boor
   E. impediment

9. Joie, a[n] __________ supporter of helping the homeless, *importuned* the state for a grant to construct a new shelter.
   A. fervent
   B. erotic
   C. ignoble
   D. amorphous
   E. bestial

10. Jillian claimed that the classic novel __________ her by instilling in her the idea of endeavoring to a life of success followed by *philanthropy*.
    A. glowered
    B. edified
    C. gloated
    D. besieged
    E. impaled

Exercise III

Deeper Meanings

d to replace the italicized word in each sentence. All of the possible choices for each sentence / definitions, but the correct answer will have a connotation that best suits the context. For .he words "delete," "destroy," and "obliterate," all mean "to remove or wipe out," but no one would , "I destroyed the name from the document." The correct choice will be the word with the best specific ıg and does not render the sentence awkward in tone or content. When choices seem close, look for a .n the context that makes one choice better than the other.

ote that the correct answer is not always the primary vocabulary word from the lesson.

enhance	**ephemeral**	**impediment**	**edify**	**change**
fancy	**speedy**	**alteration**	**superior**	**barrier**

1. The noisy dance club across the street proved to be a major *blockade* to Ginger's ability to study.

   Better word: ____________________

2. Bert didn't want the plain, base model of the off-road vehicle; he wanted the *opulent* model that included the optional roll-bars, big mud tires, and a winch.

   Better word: ____________________

3. Tristan hoped that his children's volunteering at the local homeless shelter would *raise* them as much as it educated them.

   Better word: ____________________

4. Moving to a new city and attending a new school proved to be a difficult *cataclysm* for Steph and Maris.

   Better word: ____________________

5. Occasionally, on a quiet day outside the nursing home, Alphonse would remember a scene from his childhood on the farm, but the *temporary* memory usually faded just as quickly as it appeared.

   Better word: ____________________

Exercise IV

Crossword Puzzle

Use the clues to complete the crossword puzzle. The answers consist of vocabulary words from Lessons 1 through 3.

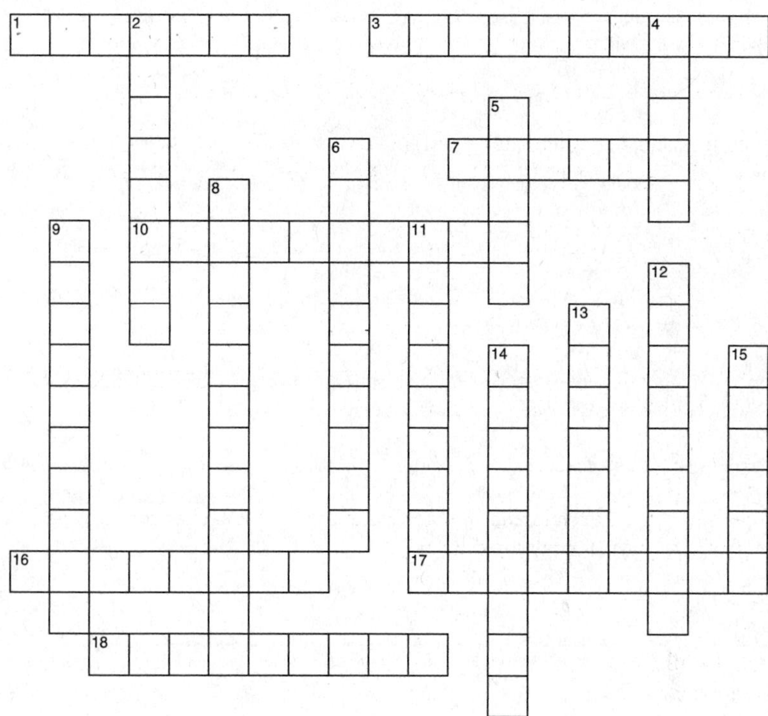

Across

1. the best of the best
3. earthquake, epidemic, volcanic eruption
7. wear the angry eyes
10. a fix
16. believing in nothing
17. to make less serious
18. good place to get lost

Down

2. Superman, in the presence of kryptonite
4. broken glass bit
5. no salt, sugar, or spices
6. see-through
8. smarts
9. love, hate, war, peace, zig, zag
11. Oh PLEASE get this one right.
12. Now it's here; now it's gone.
13. That rots.
14. whirlpool
15. trinket

Exercise V

Subject Prompts

ting prompt similar to the one you will find on the writing portion of an assessment test. Follow ions below and write a brief, efficient essay.

> The argument has been fought and, at times, won by NASA, that humankind should not focus only on solving problems on Earth before investing enormous amounts of money and labor on exploring space. The challenges of space travel, much like the challenges of a world war, often yield new technology that would not have been developed otherwise. The new technology might, as in the case of antibiotics, save millions of lives.
>
> Should the billions of dollars spent on space exploration instead be diverted to ending poverty or creating sustainable energy?
>
> Pretend that you are the governor of a state that has an above-average poverty level. Write a speech in which you argue for or against space and deep sea exploration. Include at least three reasons to support your central argument.

Thesis: Write a *one-sentence* response to the above assignment. Make certain this single sentence offers a clear statement of your position.

Example: If too much money goes to the solving of survival problems, and not enough goes to research or exploration, then the world will be stuck in the dark ages because new technology and understanding will be essentially nonexistent.

____

____

Organizational Plan: List at least three subtopics you will use to support your main idea. This list is your outline.

1. ____

2. ____

3. ____

Draft: Following your outline, write a good first draft of your essay. Remember to support all your points with examples, facts, references to reading, etc.

Review and Revise: Exchange essays with a classmate. Using the scoring guide for Organization on page 263, score your partner's essay (while he or she scores yours). Focus on the organizational plan and use of language conventions. If necessary, rewrite your essay to improve the organizational plan and/or your use of language.

Lesson Four

1. **fortuitous** (fôr tōō´ i təs) *adj.* happening by chance or accident
My father said meeting my mother was *fortuitous;* my mother said it was fate.
syn: accidental; unexpected *ant: premeditated; intentional*

2. **hedonism** (hēd´ n iz əm) *n.* the pursuit of pleasure, especially of the senses
John favors *hedonism* over self-sacrifice.

3. **celibate** (sel´ ə bit) *adj.* abstaining from intercourse; unmarried
In that religion, the priests take vows to remain impoverished and *celibate.*

4. **perfunctory** (pər fungk´ tə rē) *adj.* done without care; in a routine fashion
She greeted her guests in a *perfunctory* manner.
syn: indifferent; offhand *ant: diligent; attentive*

5. **besmirch** (bi smûrch´) *v.* to make dirty; to stain
My ex-best friend tried to *besmirch* my reputation with her vicious gossip.
syn: soil; sully; smear *ant: cleanse*

6. **demeanor** (di mē´ nər) *n.* behavior; the manner of conducting oneself
Believe me, his shy *demeanor* is just an act; he is really quite wild.
syn: deportment

7. **imperative** (im per´ ə tiv) *adj.* extremely necessary; vitally important
It is *imperative* that you leave immediately.

8. **sadistic** (sə dis´ tik) *adj.* deriving pleasure from inflicting pain on others
Donna took *sadistic* pleasure in tormenting her little sister.
syn: barbarous; perverse *ant: civilized; humane*

9. **facetious** (fə sē´ shəs) *adj.* comical; jocular; flippant
Her *facetious* comments were beginning to get tiresome.
syn: joking; witty; jocose *ant: solemn; serious*

10. **recapitulate** (rē kə pich´ ə lāt) *v.* to summarize; to repeat briefly
Television newsmen always *recapitulate* what happens at Presidential news conferences, as if the audience were incapable of understanding it.

11. **baroque** (bə rōk´) *adj.* overly decorated
The new dance club had a great light show; the *baroque* furnishings seemed right in place.
syn: ornate *ant: simple*

12. **obloquy** (äb´ lə kwē) *n.* strong disapproval; a bad reputation resulting from public criticism
His behavior brought shame to his family and *obloquy* on himself.
syn: censure; rebuke *ant: acclaim; praise*

13. **debacle** (dā bä´ kəl) *n.* a complete failure; a total collapse
After reading the reviews, the actors knew the play was a *debacle* and would close in one night.
syn: calamity; catastrophe *ant: success; triumph*

14. **quasi-** (kwā´ zī) *adj.* resembling; seeming; half
Grandfather was in only *quasi*-retirement because he couldn't give up control of the business.

15. **sacrosanct** (sak´ rō sangkt) *adj.* extremely holy
The detective's orders were to investigate everyone; no person was so *sacrosanct* that he or she was above suspicion.
syn: divine; angelic

Exercise I

Words in Context

From the list below, supply the words needed to complete the paragraph. Some words will not be used.

debacle	**hedonism**	**demeanor**	**quasi-**	**perfunctory**
besmirch	**obloquy**	**sadistic**	**imperative**	**recapitulate**

1. Advances in technology may have increased our life spans, but they also turned us into a civilization of __________ in which people are slaves to entertainment and self-satisfaction. We no longer question the __________ parenting techniques that produce children with such pathetic __________ that they prefer sitting in living rooms and playing __________ shoot-'em-up video games to going outside and experiencing the most beautiful days of the summer. It is __________ that we nurture and guide the latest generation to appreciate and embrace the beauty of the natural—the real—world. The misconception of children that success in their digital kingdoms is comparable to real, character-inspired success is one of the great __________ of the twenty-first century. Someday, the appropriate __________ will be assigned to parents who allow their own children to become __________ zombies whose best talent is playing internet role-playing-games for six hours a night—every night.

From the list below, supply the words needed to complete the paragraph. Some words will not be used.

hedonism	**recapitulate**	**besmirch**
baroque	**perfunctory**	**fortuitous**

2. The __________ interior of Mrs. Adison's house reflected her life of extravagance and world travel. We wandered through the house in amazement, and occasionally we asked Mrs. Adison to once again __________ the significance of particular items. She told us that some of the items were __________ discoveries that barely survived floods, fires, or revolutions; however, the smoke damage, water stains, and bullet holes that __________ the appearance of the artifacts only added to their intrinsic value.

From the list below, supply the words needed to complete the paragraph. Some words will not be used.

sacrosanct	**facetious**	**celibate**
obloquy	**imperative**	

3. Though four years had passed since Jake Bristol had been declared killed-in-action, his __________ wife, Georgia, refused to date, even at the urging of her family.

   "We all loved Jake," said Jake's brother, Robert, "but even the memory of my own brother is not so __________ that you should spend the rest of your life alone." Georgia did not take her eyes off the motionless porch swing.

   "Is this a proposal, Bob?" Georgia's __________ reply revealed that she wasn't as depressed as Robert had assumed.

Exercise II

Sentence Completion

Complete the sentence in a way that shows you understand the meaning of the italicized vocabulary word.

1. Lori's *demeanor* changed from angry to pleasant when…

2. People who cannot control their *hedonism* are likely to…

3. Jerry made a *fortuitous* find when…

4. No one expected to find such *baroque* furnishings in…

5. If you make a *facetious* remark during a job interview, you might…

6 In Puritan society, people were expected to remain *celibate* unless…

7. New recruits thought the drill sergeant was *sadistic*, but he was actually…

8. The neighborhood is run down and overgrown, but the *sacrosanct* house of the Jones family is…

9. Ivan has a bad injury; it is *imperative* that he…

10. The congressman experienced serious *obloquy* from his opponents because…

11. The failing grade *besmirched* Ryan's…

12. Opening the classy restaurant in the small town was a *debacle* because…

13. Pam blamed the contractors for building the home in a *perfunctory* way when she noticed…

14. Please *recapitulate* what you just said because…

15. Weary of sitting on rocks, the castaway made a *quasi*-recliner from…

Exercise III

Roots, Prefixes, and Suffixes

Study the entries and answer the questions that follow.

The root *clin* means "to lean" or "to bend."
The roots *pon* and *pos* mean "to put" or "to place."
The prefix *hyper–* means "excessive."
The root *therm* means "heat."
The prefix *com–* means "together."
The prefix *im–* means "into."
The prefix *dis–* means "apart."
The prefix *de–* means "down."

1. Using *literal* translations as guidance, define the following words without using a dictionary.

A	deposit	D.	dispose
B.	depose	E.	compose
C.	impose	F.	component

2. If your thoughts lean toward a certain activity, then you have a[n] ___________ for that activity.

   If you spend too much time leaning back on the __________, your physical fitness will __________.

3. A[n] __________ child might have trouble sitting still, and a[n] __________ judge might upset the contestants of a singing contest.

4. List all the words that you can think of that contain the root *therm*.

Exercise IV

Inference

Complete the sentence by inferring information about the italicized word from its context.

1. Martin asked the speaker to *recapitulate* the last part of the lecture because he…

2. The airline fired the mechanic for his *perfunctory* work after…

3. Hector never had a job, and his belief in *hedonism* was apparent by the way in which he…

Exercise V

Critical Reading

Below is a pair of reading passages followed by several multiple-choice questions. Carefully read the passages and choose the best answer to each of the questions.

The Love Canal incident, the subject of the following passages, was perhaps the most publicized, though not the worst, environmental catastrophe in United States history. The Love Canal has been a source of controversy for years, specifically in regard to who was responsible for the spread of contamination at the site.

Passage 1

At one time, the American dream was simply to own a home. Now, thanks to selfish industrialists, the American dream is to own a home that will not kill the homeowners.

During the 1950s, the Board of Education of Niagara Falls, New York, found the perfect site—so they thought—on which to build a new elementary school. At the center of the 16-acre property southwest of the city was the site known as the Love Canal, a partially completed canal that was dug in the 1890s by William Love, a dreamer and entrepreneur who sought to use cheap hydroelectric power to run a **quasi**-utopian model industrial city. Love's project failed, and in 1942, Hooker Electrochemical purchased the canal and dumped 20,000 tons of toxic waste in it. Hooker then capped the canal with clay and planted grass on the top. The open field looked like prime real estate to the Board of Education, which needed plenty of land to meet the demands of a rapidly growing population.

Eager to rid itself of a legal **debacle**, Hooker Chemical Corporation donated the dump and surrounding area to the school board for $1.00. The school board paid little notice to the disclaimer on the deed that released Hooker Chemical of any responsibility for future damages caused by buried chemicals; it built two elementary schools, and then sold portions of the property to housing developers.

In the years following the exchange of the Love Canal, the American dream turned into the American nightmare. Chemical vapors wafted through the streets, and strange substances surfaced in the yards. Children who played outside suffered from chemical burns and skin irritations, and residents reported abnormal numbers of miscarriages and birth defects. The families at Love Canal were living in poison.

In the late 1970s, Niagara Falls hired environmental investigators to determine the extent of the Love Canal problem. Teams confirmed the presence of many toxic chemicals in the air and in the ground around the 800 homes and 200 apartments. Black sludge oozed through basement walls, and 55-gallon drums began to surface after heavy rainfalls increased the height of the water table. In 1978, the New York Department of Health declared the Love Canal a health hazard and evacuated the homes closest to the canal. Later that year, President Carter declared the area to be a federal emergency, and another 250 families evacuated the neighborhoods adjacent to the canal. Eventually, 800 families, fearing for their lives, were relocated from their homes near the Love Canal. The homes nearest the canal now lay beneath a clay cap that was constructed in 1984 to contain the millions of gallons of toxins. An eight-foot fence encircles the poisonous field.

In the decade following the initial evacuation of the Love Canal, residents and government agencies filed nearly 1,000 lawsuits that totaled over $14 billion. As of 2000, Occidental Chemical, the company that acquired Hooker Chemical, has paid out a paltry $190 million in damages to the government—a fraction of the billions that it generates each year. Such inadequate punitive measures impart only one message to corporations: pollute as much as you want—you can afford it.

Passage 2

In 1977, when the residents of the Love Canal took to the streets to express rage over living in a former toxic waste dump, many of them blamed the local government—and rightly so. It was the government—bureaucrats enjoying the protection of sovereign immunity—that blatantly ignored the warnings of a chemical company, and then gave a **perfunctory** approval for the construction of schools and homes on top of a trench full of toxic waste.

The Love Canal, a partially dug canal just southwest of Niagara Falls, New York, was a remnant of a failed turn-of-the-century project to create an advanced industrial city. William Love abandoned the project after running low on funds, and the city of Niagara Falls took ownership of the useless, 3,000-foot trench in 1927. In 1942, Hooker Electrochemical identified the sparsely populated, clay-bottomed Love Canal area as a good location to dispose of industrial waste. Hooker purchased the land, and then the company obtained the necessary permits from Niagara Falls to legally dispose of industrial waste in the canal. From 1942 to 1953, Hooker legally buried more than 20,000 tons of industrial waste in barrels. In an age in which no dumping regulations existed, Hooker even took the courteous caution of lining the canal with clay and concrete to prevent leakage. The dump would have met standards that did not even exist until 1980—thirty years after Hooker stopped dumping and capped the canal with four feet of clay.

While Hooker prepared to close the dump in 1953, the Niagara Falls Board of Education was addressing two major problems: booming population and scarce education funds. The school board needed cheap real estate, so when it found the seemingly harmless grassy field that covered the Love Canal, it thought that it had found the perfect spot to build new schools; so perfect, in fact, that it threatened to seize the 16-acre lot through eminent domain in response to the Hooker Corporation's refusal to sell.

Hooker had two options: it could sell the land and retain the ability to warn future developers, or it could allow the city to condemn the Love Canal and thus forfeit the right to prevent future development. Hooker knew that selling a toxic waste dump to vacuous buyers was a legal time bomb, so it tried to take the ethical route of selling the land with special provisions on the deed, notably that the land be used for parks only—no construction. The board, determined to develop the toxic waste dump, rejected the deed. Hooker was forced to simplify the deed until the only remaining provision was a lengthy clause that waived Hooker for any future injuries or deaths caused by the industrial waste. Hooker even went so far as to escort school board officials to the dumpsite to physically see the chemicals for themselves. The board, apparently blind, deaf, and oblivious to the words injury and death on the deed, approved the contract and bought the land for a token $1.00. Then it started building.

The school board's first inane move was to order the construction of two schools, one of which was directly over the 20,000 tons of poison in the canal. The school ordered thousands of tons of fill to be removed from the top of the canal, and, amazingly, the contractors found chemical pits. Apparently, the school board did not bother telling the contractors that they were working in a vat of hazardous waste. The Board solved the problem by moving the school several feet to avoid the discovered chemicals.

The schools opened by 1957, and the Board of Education sought to sell adjacent land—polluted land—to developers. Hooker Chemical protested the development; it sent representatives to the board meetings to chastise the effort and once again explain that the Love Canal property was unsuitable for any type of construction—especially homes.

Hooker's warnings finally began to sink into the minds of the School Board members, but much to the wrong effect: the board did not want to fix the problem, it just wanted to unload the land and liability faster than before. In the meantime, unfortunately, city workers installed sewer lines in the Love Canal property; the excavation punched holes in the canal walls and the clay cap that contained millions of gallons of toxic sludge.

The Board of Education found developers to buy portions of the Love Canal property, and each new construction further compromised the containment ability of the dumpsite. Chemical fumes seeped into homes, and industrial waste exuded into basements. Children grew sick just playing on their own lawns. In 1978, the President of the United States declared a state of emergency at the Love Canal. In the years that followed, more than 800 families were relocated from the area. Bulldozers razed the homes nearest the canal, leaving a barren, forty-acre clay cap covering the site to this day.

Since 1978, environmental zealots and cause-of-the-week activists have wrongfully brought **obloquy** upon Hooker Chemical, portraying it as a stereotypical evil corporation that profits by intentionally poisoning its patrons; they need to find a different scapegoat because it is not big industry who fouled up the Love Canal—it was a group of bureaucrats, desperate for cheap land, who ignored repeated warnings that the property was unsuitable for development and still demanded possession of it. Ignorance at this level is inexcusable, even for bureaucrats whose poor decisions are not punishable by law.

1A. As used in the second paragraph of passage 1, the word *entrepreneur* most nearly means
  A. millionaire.
  B. attorney.
  C. governor.
  D. industrialist.
  E. visionary.

1B. Which phrase from paragraph 2 best supports your answer to question 1A?
  A. "real estate"
  B. "the perfect site"
  C. "Board of Education"
  D. "growing population"
  E. "industrial city"

2A. Choose the best title for passage 1.
  A. Corporate Irresponsibility
  B. Surviving the American Dream
  C. Niagara Falls Down
  D. The Effects of Industrial Waste in Proximity to Residential Neighborhoods
  E. The Results of Inadequate Education Budgets

2B. Choose the phrase from the passage that best supports your choice of the title for question 2A.
  A. "The open field looked like prime real estate…"
  B. "The school board paid little notice to the disclaimer…"
  C. "…the American dream turned into the American nightmare."
  D. "…Department of Health declared the Love Canal a health hazard…"
  E. "…residents and government agencies filed nearly 1,000 lawsuits…"

3A. According to passage 1, Hooker Chemical donated the Love Canal because
  A. it wanted to give back to the community.
  B. school officials were going to seize the land.
  C. it wanted to rid itself of liability for the dump.
  D. it would have looked bad to sell the dump for a profit.
  E. the company experienced layoffs.

3B. If your answer to question 3A is correct, then which statement would have to be true?
 A. The school board was basically tricked into buying the Love Canal.
 B. Hooker Chemical knew the Love Canal was extremely hazardous.
 C. The chemicals already in the canal had not yet become toxic.
 D. Hooker Chemical did not realize the risks associated with the Love Canal.
 E. Someone on the school board had been bribed into approving the purchase.

4A. According to passage 2, who is responsible for the Love Canal incident?
 A. Hooker Chemical Corporation
 B. the Board of Education
 C. the developers who built homes
 D. the city engineers
 E. the mayor of Niagara Falls

4B. The phrase "eminent domain," as it is used in line 21, means
 A. the right to take private property.
 B. a decision by vote.
 C. a tax levied on corporations.
 D. the law that forbids waste dumps on private land.
 E. a refusal to allow something to be sold.

5A. According to passage 2, which is *not* one of the ways that the chemical company tried to warn against developing the Love Canal?
 A. It added special provisions to the original deed to prevent development.
 B. It requested state intervention when the school tried to take the land.
 C. It sent representatives to board meetings.
 D. It initially refused to sell the Love Canal site.
 E. It brought school officials to the site to see the chemicals.

5B. In contrast to passage 1, passage 2 portrays Hooker Chemical's sale of the dump as a way to
 A. maintain good standing in the Niagara Falls community.
 B. retain the ability to prevent development of the land.
 C. change the name of the corporation to avoid litigation.
 D. completely sever itself from any legal consequences.
 E. obtain more time to clean up the dump before development began.

6A. As used in line 54 of passage 2, the word *razed* most nearly means
 A. burned.
 B. flattened.
 C. buried.
 D. remodeled.
 E. sold.

6B. What word below best supports your answer to question 6A?
   A. fumes
   B. dumpsite
   C. relocated
   D. nearest
   E. barren

7A. Which of the following is the best title for passage 2?
   A. The Truth about Toxic Waste
   B. Recovering Former Dumps
   C. Occidental's Accident
   D. Bureaucratic Failures
   E. Passing the Buck

7B. Which detail from passage 2 best supports your answer to question 7A?
   A. the lengthy clause in the sale contract
   B. children becoming sick
   C. the price paid for the dumping ground
   D. overcrowded schools
   E. the Love Canal's being declared a federal emergency

8A. Which of the following best describes the tone of both passages?
   A. Passage 1 is celebrative, and passage 2 is solemn.
   B. Both passages portray a tone of indifference to the subject.
   C. Passage 2 contains more supporting data than passage 1 does.
   D. Both passages have an accusatory tone.
   E. Passage 1 is fictional, while passage 2 is factual.

8B. The authors of both passages accuse a different party of engaging in which negligent action?
   A. bullying an organization into compliance
   B. attempting to dump property to avoid responsibility
   C. concealing damaging evidence of wrongdoing
   D. taking credit for solving the problem the area created
   E. ignoring the well-known dangers of toxic waste

9. Both passages describe the Love Canal property's transfer from Hooker Chemical to the school board. Which statement best describes the difference in the way the transaction is described between the two passages?
   A. Passage 1 describes Hooker as "donating" the land, versus selling it reluctantly, as in passage 2.
   B. Passage 1 claims the company paid extra to the school board to accept the deal.
   C. Only passage 2 describes the disclaimer attached to the sale.
   D. Passage 2 portrays the company as relieved to surrender the land.
   E. The school board eagerly accepts the land in passage 1, but reluctantly in passage 2.

10A. The authors of both passages would probably agree that

A. multiple agencies were responsible for the Love Canal incident.
B. Hooker Chemical should not have donated the Love Canal.
C. the Occidental Corporation should not have permitted development.
D. the Niagara Falls Board of Education lacked adequate funds.
E. Niagara Falls should have listened to the chemical company.

10B. In both passages, the residents of the Love Canal are portrayed as

A. pawns of local government.
B. victims of poor decisions.
C. greedy for cheap real estate.
D. being unconcerned about toxins.
E. too stubborn to move to safety.

10C. Only passage 2 portrays Hooker Chemical as

A. the responsible party.
B. a large corporation.
C. including a waiver on the contract.
D. worried about the dumpsite.
E. a victim.

Lesson Five

1. **imprecation** (im pri kā´ shən) *n.* a curse
Jennifer was so angry she pronounced an *imprecation* on him, his family, and all his friends.
syn: condemnation; anathema *ant: blessing*

2. **panegyric** (pan ə jir´ ik) *n.* an expression of praise
The ancient Greeks gave *panegyrics* and crowns of ivy in tribute to their heroes.
syn: tribute; extolment *ant: denunciation*

3. **nebulous** (neb´ yə ləs) *adj.* hazy; vague; uncertain
He had a *nebulous* feeling of fear all day, but he didn't understand why until the thunder started.
syn: cloudy; indistinct; obscure *ant: distinct; precise*

4. **bowdlerize** (bōd´ ler īz) *v.* to remove offensive passages of a play, novel, etc.
If the editors *bowdlerize* much more of the book, there won't be anything left to read.
syn: censor

5. **fop** (fop) *n.* an excessively fashion-conscious man
When he came in wearing a bow tie, a diamond pinky ring, and carrying a pearl-handled cane, we knew he was a *fop*.
syn: dandy

6. **elegy** (el´ ə jē) *n.* a sad or mournful poem
The reading of the *elegy* brought tears during the funeral.
syn: dirge; lament

7. **deference** (def´ ər əns) *n.* respect; consideration
In *deference* to the young widow, we moved quietly aside and allowed her to leave first.

8. **pedantic** (pə dan´ tik) *adj.* tending to show off one's learning
After one year of college, Tom lost all of his friends because of his *pedantic* behavior.
syn: bookish

9. **non sequitur** (non sek´ wi tər) *n.* something that does not logically follow
"That he would not be a good mayor because he can't control his own family is a *non sequitur*," said John.
syn: fallacy; misconception

10. **sanguine** (sang´ gwin) *adj.* cheerful; optimistic
Sally's *sanguine* personality made everyone in her company pleased to be with her.

11. **impair** (im pâr´) v. to weaken; to cause to become worse
Mother used to say that reading in poor light could *impair* your vision.
syn: damage; deteriorate *ant: enhance*

12. **quandary** (kwon´ drē) *n.* a puzzling situation; a dilemma
John was in a *quandary* deciding what his major should be.
syn: predicament

13. **ebullient** (i bŏŏl´ yənt) *adj.* enthusiastic
The *ebullient* crowd cheered as the royal family appeared.
syn: exuberant; lively *ant: dejected; dispirited*

14. **carnal** (kär´ nəl) *adj.* relating to physical appetite, especially sexual
After receiving complaints, the town council decided to remove the *carnal* statue from the park area.
syn: erotic *ant: chaste; modest*

15. **rakish** (rā´ kish) *adj.* dashingly stylish and confident
Wanting to look *rakish* for his job interview, Jeremy shined his shoes and pressed razor-edge creases into his shirt and slacks.
syn: dapper; jaunty *ant: slovenly; disheveled*

Exercise I

Words in Context

From the list below, supply the words needed to complete the paragraph. Some words will not be used.

nebulous **imprecation** **pedantic** **deference**
impair **fop** **rakish** **carnal**

1. Martin, a[n] __________ since high school, had at least nine pairs of sneakers in his closet. The __________ man wouldn't even go to the gym if he wasn't wearing crisp new workout clothes. His habit of looking in every mirror he passed in public had alienated him from his friends, and when he returned to Uniontown after earning his doctorate, his __________ conduct drove his family away. Martin never realized that his vanity __________ his social life; his __________ explanations never included any faults of his own. He reasoned that his good looks and superior intellect were a[n] __________ that he would just have to live with.

From the list below, supply the words needed to complete the paragraph. Some words will not be used.

sanguine **ebullient** **elegy** **fop**
panegyric **non sequitur** **deference**

2. All the citizens of the small town attended the viewing to show their __________ for the late Dr. Clarke. A local writer read a[n] __________ that recalled Dr. Clarke's friendly, __________ attitude and __________ approach to caring for the townspeople. He had known all of his patients by their first names, and he had made house calls at no additional expense. The children of the town remembered Dr. Clarke not only as their gentle doctor, but also as the man who occasionally stood on the bleachers during soccer matches to shout a[n] __________ for the little town's home team.

From the list below, supply the words needed to complete the paragraph. Some words will not be used.

carnal **bowdlerize** **non sequitur** **quandary** **pedantic**

3. Many of the world's greatest works of literature and drama contain violent or __________ contexts, and some groups regularly attempt to __________ these works. Whether people, specifically school-aged children, should be allowed to read such literature has been a[n] __________ of parents and educators for decades. Some people claim that exposure to immoral texts will have negative effects on young readers; however, others feel that the idea of children suffering as a result of reading books is a[n] __________.

Exercise II

Sentence Completion

Complete the sentence in a way that shows you understand the meaning of the italicized vocabulary word.

1. Finding a diamond bracelet in the parking lot created a *quandary* for Gary because he…
2. The *pedantic* teacher offered to chaperone the field trip, but the students…
3. The *rakish* young professional stood out because…
4. The coach maintained a *sanguine* attitude even though…
5. The old hermit put an *imprecation* on the entire family because…
6. Censors often *bowdlerize* novels because…
7. Out of *deference* for the fallen soldier, the honor guard…
8. Dave's *ebullient* interest in math led him to…
9. You will probably *impair* your hearing if you…
10. Superstitions are silly; it's a complete *non sequitur* to believe…
11. Some actors are regarded as *fops* because they…
12. The crowd screamed *panegyrics* when…
13. When Dawn recited the moving *elegy* during the funeral, some of the guests…
14. When the teacher sees your *nebulous* essay on the test, she will know that…
15. The piranhas went into a *carnal* frenzy when…

Exercise III

Roots, Prefixes, and Suffixes

Study the entries and answer the questions that follow.

The root *petr* means "stone."
The root *sist* means "to stand," "to stop," or "to set."
The suffix *–ous* means "full of."
The roots *viv* and *vit* mean "to live."
The root *glyph* means "to carve."
The prefix *sub–* means "under."
The suffix *–id* means "tending to."
The suffix *–al* means "pertaining to."

1. Using *literal* translations as guidance, define the following words without using a dictionary.

   A. vivid
   B. vivacious
   C. vital
   D. revitalize
   E. exist
   F. insist

2. Someone or something that has been turned to stone is __________. A[n] __________ would be a good place to find *petroglyphs*, and it would also be a good place to practice *petrology*, which is the study of __________.

3. *Subsist* literally translates to "stand under." Explain how *subsist*, which means "to maintain life," evolved from "stand under."

4. We use the term __________ to describe oils that we extract from the earth to use as fuel.

5. List as many words as you can think of that end with the suffix *–id*.

Exercise IV

Inference

Complete the sentence by inferring information about the italicized word from its context.

1. Frank called the stylish bachelor a *fop* because the man usually spent…

2. The career criminal had no *deference* for…

3. If Luke is not *ebullient* about helping you fix the car, then you should…

Exercise V

Writing

Here is a writing prompt similar to the one you will find on the writing portion of an assessment test.

Plan and write an essay based on the following statement:

> American culture positively recognizes single motherhood, while debasing single fatherhood because men do not have a positive identity as fathers outside marriage. Therefore, women often possess a certain advantage over men, creating what Barbara Dafoe Whitehead calls a "fatherhood problem." Women provide emotional ties between fathers and children, and without women and marriage, men must overcome substantial obstacles in eliminating the negative stereotype associated with unmarried fathers.

Assignment: Write an essay in which you support or refute Barbara Whitehead's assertion. Be certain to support your point with evidence and examples from literature, current events, or your own personal experience or observation.

Thesis: Write a *one-sentence* response to the above assignment. Make certain this single sentence offers a clear statement of your position.

Example: Single fathers can be positive influences and nurturing caregivers to children, but they do not have any more obstacles to overcome than single mothers, who must endure lower than average wages and long-standing stereotypes.

____

____

Organizational Plan: List at least three subtopics you will use to support your main idea. This list is your outline.

1. ____

2. ____

3. ____

Draft: Following your outline, write a good first draft of your essay. Remember to support all your points with examples, facts, references to reading, etc.

Review and Revise: Exchange essays with a classmate. Using the scoring guide for Sentence Formation and Variety on page 266, score your partner's essay (while he or she scores yours). Focus on sentence structure and the use of language conventions. If necessary, rewrite your essay to improve the sentence structure and/or your use of language.

Exercise VI

English Practice

Identifying Sentence Errors

Identify the grammatical error in each of the following sentences. If the sentence contains no error, select answer choice E.

1. Five years, three of which Shelia was out of the country, were a long time to wait.
   (A) (B) (C) (D)
   No error
   (E)

2. The third baseman's use of an illegal bat destroyed many young athletes' allusions
   (A) (B) (C)
   about the popular baseball hero. No error
   (D) (E)

3. During track season, Samantha and my statistics are usually identical. No error
   (A) (B) (C) (D) (E)

4. The club encouraged many women in the community to join, including Patricia
   (A) (B)
   and myself, even though we had only recently moved to town. No error
   (C) (D) (E)

5. To make cookies, blend two sticks of margarine with the vanilla and sugar until the
   (A) (B) (C)
   sugar has dissolved. No error
   (D) (E)

Improving Sentences

The underlined portion of each sentence below contains some flaw. Select the answer choice that best corrects the flaw.

6. At home during the summer, young adults are scrutinized by their parents, at college they are given the opportunity to make their own decisions.
   A. by their parents, but at college they are
   B. by their parents: while at college they are
   C. by their parents; but, at college, they are
   D. by parents, at college they are
   E. by his or her parents, at college he or she is

7. Fred asked, "Did Al really call me 'a monstrous, evil coach"?
   A. Fred asked, "Did Al really call me, 'a monstrous, evil coach"?
   B. Fred asked, "Did Al really call me 'a monstrous, evil coach?"
   C. Fred asked, "Did Al really call me 'a monstrous, evil coach"?'
   D. Fred asked, "Did Al really call me 'a monstrous, evil coach'?"
   E. Fred asked, "Did Al really call me 'a monstrous, evil coach?'".

8. My favorite high school teacher, who is president of the local National Education Association is also the president of the Illinois Association of Teachers of English.
   A. teacher who is president of the local National Education Association is also the president of
   B. teacher, who is president of the local, National Education Association is also the president of,
   C. teacher who is the president of the local National Education Association, is also the president of
   D. teacher, who is president, of the local National Education Association, is also the president of,
   E. teacher, who is president of the local National Education Association, is also the president of

9. I am taking graduate classes this summer, and I will be better qualified to teach collegiate-level courses this fall.
   A. I am taking graduate classes this summer, so I will be better qualified to teach collegiate-level courses this fall.
   B. This summer I am taking graduate classes, and I will be better qualified to teach collegiate-level courses this fall.
   C. I am taking graduate classes this summer, but I will be better qualified to teach collegiate-level courses this fall.
   D. Teaching collegiate-level courses this fall means that I must take graduate courses this summer.
   E. To be better qualified to teach collegiate-level courses this fall I must take graduate courses this summer.

10. Having promised to be home after work, Mrs. Thompson was irritated when her husband came in at nine o'clock.
   A. Mrs. Thompson was irritated when her husband came in at nine o'clock, having promised to be home after work.
   B. Mrs. Thompson was irritated when her husband, having promised to be home after work, came in at nine o'clock.
   C. Having promised to be home after work, Mrs. Thompson was irritated by her husband when he came in at nine o'clock.
   D. Coming in at nine o'clock, Mrs. Thompson was irritated by her husband who promised to be home after work.
   E. Mrs. Thompson was irritated by her husband, who, having promised to come home after work, came in at nine o'clock.

Lesson Six

1. **elucidate** (i lōō´ si dāt) *v.* to make clear
To *elucidate* his theory, he drew a large diagram on the board.
syn: explain; clarify *ant: obscure*

2. **banal** (bā´ nəl) *adj.* common, ordinary
His *banal* remarks quickly bored the entire class.
syn: trivial; insipid *ant: original; fresh*

3. **imminent** (im´ ə nənt) *adj.* likely to happen; threatening
Though the danger was *imminent,* the crew seemed quite relaxed.
syn: impending; approaching *ant: distant; delayed*

4. **antipathy** (an tip´ ə thē) *n.* an intense dislike
So great was her feeling of *antipathy* that she was afraid that it showed in her face.
syn: aversion *ant: affinity*

5. **scurrilous** (skûr´ ə ləs) *adj.* coarsely abusive; vulgar
The *scurrilous* patrons of the saloon were often seen shouting and fighting.
syn: indecent *ant: respectable*

6. **bedlam** (bed´ ləm) *n.* a noisy uproar; a scene of wild confusion
The concert hall was sheer *bedlam* until the rock star appeared.
syn: mayhem; chaos

7. **amoral** (ā môr´ əl) *adj.* lacking a sense of right and wrong
The *amoral* henchmen obeyed all of the boss's orders, no matter how despicable.
syn: corrupt; evil *ant: innocent; virtuous*

8. **sedulous** (sej´ ə ləs) *adj.* hard working; diligent
Everyone knew Jason would get ahead in the world because he was *sedulous* in all he undertook.
syn: studious; assiduous *ant: lazy; lax*

9. **obdurate** (äb´ də rət) *adj.* stubborn; hardhearted
The young boy was *obdurate* in his refusal to make any trade.
syn: inflexible; obstinate *ant: compliant; amenable*

10. **peruse** (pə rōōz´) *v.* to read carefully; scrutinize
Bob *peruses* the classified ads every day to try to find a part-time job.

11. **affluence** (af´ lōō əns) *n.* wealth; richness
Paul earned his fortune without relying on the *affluence* of his family.
syn: fortune

12. **parody** (par´ ə dē) *n.* a work that imitates another in a ridiculous manner
Joan's *parody* of the English teacher was funny to everyone but the English teacher.
syn: caricature; burlesque; lampoon

13. **onerous** (ōn´ er əs) *adj.* burdensome; heavy; hard to endure
The doctor had the *onerous* job of informing the family of the child's death.
syn: crushing; distressing

14. **eschew** (es chōō´) *v.* to keep away from; to avoid; to shun
The minister advised the congregation to *eschew* temptation.
ant: embrace; welcome

15. **denouement** (dā nōō män´) *n.* an outcome; result
The novel would have been exciting if it were not for the boring *denouement.*
syn: conclusion

Exercise I

Words in Context

From the list below, supply the words needed to complete the paragraph. Some words will not be used.

bedlam	**scurrilous**	**amoral**	**elucidate**
banal	**eschew**	**obdurate**	**imminent**

1. Saturday had been a[n] __________, uneventful day until the special report interrupted every television and radio broadcast in the city. A news anchorman __________ the __________ threat of an approaching tidal wave, and, in minutes, the coastal city erupted into __________. According to the experts, the 120-foot tidal wave would obliterate the city in forty minutes—not nearly enough time for an organized evacuation of three million people.

   The panic turned humans into __________ animals. In the rush to escape to the high ground beyond the peninsula, people who were once pleasant and mannerly now screamed __________ remarks at anyone preventing their fast escape. Ordinary people who had no means of transportation carjacked automobiles and threw the operators to the ground. Mobs fleeing apartment buildings trampled anyone not fast enough to keep up. There were also thousands of people who were too __________ to believe the alerts; they stayed in their homes and made futile preparations.

From the list below, supply the words needed to complete the paragraph. Some words will not be used.

onerous	**bedlam**	**eschew**
sedulous	**affluence**	**peruse**

2. Kim was a[n] __________ office manager with an impeccable record, but none of her experiences prepared her for the __________ task of firing Bill. Before the meeting, she __________ Bill's file to learn where his productivity declined. Bill was well-liked in the office, so Kim knew that Bill's coworkers would probably __________ her for firing their friend.

From the list below, supply the words needed to complete the paragraph. Some words will not be used.

scurrilous	**parody**	**affluence**
antipathy	**elucidate**	**denouement**

3. The show that we watched last night was actually a[n] __________ of a popular Shakespeare play; all the major characters were animals, and it was a comedy rather than a tragedy, unlike the original play. The plot essentially remained the same: a prince of great __________ is the target of his evil stepbrother's __________. The __________ of the new play is different because at the end of the play, the prince forgives his stepbrother instead of fighting him to the death.

Exercise II

Sentence Completion

Complete the sentence in a way that shows you understand the meaning of the italicized vocabulary word.

1. Be sure to *peruse* the contract before you…
2. The *antipathy* between the opposing teams was obvious during…
3. Casey decided to change her *banal,* daily routine by…
4. While driving in the car, dad has the habit of singing *parodies* for every song he…
5. Due to the *imminent* snowstorm,…
6. The musician was once a popular figure of *affluence*, but now she…
7. The stadium exploded into *bedlam* when the referee…
8. The job would normally take a week to complete, but Roger is a *sedulous* worker who can…
9. The judge warned Veronica to curb her *scurrilous* language or she would be…
10. Most of the novel is entertaining, but the *denouement* is…
11. If you *elucidate* your point well enough, your listeners will…
12. The *amoral* prisoner never showed…
13. Ken liked the money, but he hated his *onerous* job of…
14. Air travel is statistically safer than automobile travel, but my *obdurate* friend still…
15. In accordance with its customs, the religious community *eschewed* the man who…

Exercise III

Roots, Prefixes, and Suffixes

Study the entries and answer the questions that follow.

The root *pel* means "to push" or "to drive."
The roots *sum* and *sumpt* mean "take."
The root *celer* means "swift."
The prefix *con–* means "with" or "together."
The prefix *dis–* means "apart" or "in different directions."
The prefix *ex–* means "out" or "from."
The suffix *–ator* means "one who does."
The suffix *–ion* means "the act of."

1. Using *literal* translations as guidance, define the following words without using a dictionary.

   A. expel
   B. dispel
   C. propeller
   D. consumption
   E. sumptuous
   F. accelerator

2. Someone who moves with *celerity* is moving __________.
   The word *accelerate* means __________, but if you slow down, you __________.

3. You create a[n] __________ by taking excerpts from your career history and writing them down; however, do not __________ that someone will hire you without an interview.

4. If you drive something forward, you __________ it, but if you drive something back, you __________ it.

   A salesperson might __________ you to purchase a product, but a threat to your safety would __________ you to take cover. You will then need to __________ rumors that you ran away.

5. List as many words as you can think of that begin with the prefix *con–*.

6. List as many words as you can think of that contain the suffix *–ator*.

Exercise IV

Inference

Complete the sentence by inferring information about the italicized word from its context.

1. Tyler was accustomed to *onerous* labor, so the task of...

2. The jury could not come to a decision because one *obdurate* juror refused to...

3. Dr. Bach *elucidates* his diagnoses for patients so that they can...

Exercise V

Critical Reading

Below is a reading passage followed by several multiple-choice questions. Carefully read the passage and choose the best answer for each of the questions.

The author of the following passage describes the evolution of American handwriting and comments about the decline of the art.

The spoken word, no matter how fierce, quickly dissipates; certainly, even the finest words are at the mercy of memory. When memories die, not even the greatest speeches and stories in history can be saved. The only way to ensure the continued existence of such thought is to bond it to a medium more permanent than the fickle mind—a medium that will live ages beyond the purveyor: paper. Whether the thought is the next Magna Carta, Declaration of Independence, or a simple grocery list, it will become an artifact that archaeologists will pore over for days when they discover it beneath a scrap of plastic, fifty feet below the surface of the earth, two thousand years from today. For all you know, that little scrap featuring your penmanship—your psychological profile, essentially—will be the only relic of a lost art in the eon following the Age of Information. Think about it the next time you haphazardly scribble a note using a **banal** jumble of cursive and printed letters; is that how you really want to represent yourself to your future progeny?

The Roman Empire recognized the importance of excellent penmanship, as can be observed by the Latin carved into the many stone remnants of Roman civilization. Their simple alphabet is still the foundation of the western world's modern alphabet, but in the centuries after the fall of the Romans, the way in which letters were written varied among European cultures. As a general change, lower case letters were added to the Roman alphabet; however, specific, stylistic changes differed from region to region.

During the Dark Ages after the fall of the Roman Empire, little thought was given to good handwriting; however, little thought was given to literacy at all. Writing supplies, especially paper, were rare, expensive, and reserved for the most important documents and people.

Around the middle of the seventh century, the art of writing experienced brief standardization during the Carolingian Period, but writing soon regressed to the various gothic calligraphies that characterize medieval documents. The printing was, and is still, doubtlessly beautiful; however, the penmanship that we now regard as fine art was too tedious to standardize among the largely illiterate masses.

As commerce flourished and governments developed, so did the need for a swift method of writing. The cursive handwriting that we know today, despite its woeful decline, originated in the Renaissance, when writers discarded ornate, gothic print for expedient, connected script. Script letters, unlike printed letters, were designed specifically to connect. Prior to script, penmen had to attach handwritten letters with lines in an additional step. The Elizabethan hand, observable in William Shakespeare's sixteenth-century writings, combined elements of gothic print with script. The new, convenient script quickly spread throughout Europe, but the invention of the printing press temporarily stifled efforts to standardize a particular hand.

In the Victorian Era, a time famous for artful precision and detail, the world identified the need for clean, standardized handwriting. Enough time had passed for the Elizabethan script to evolve into copperplate, which is the roundhand forerunner of the cursive taught today. In 1848, Platt Rogers Spencer published the technique for a very refined form of roundhand script, and it became the model for American penmanship for more than 100 years. The beautiful Spencerian script augmented the beauty of the Victorian Age and made even the most mundane documents—property deeds, shipping manifests, professional certifications—cherished works of art worthy of framing. Such fine writing reflects the conscience of all the nation's earlier denizens; they lived in an era in which pride, precision, and beauty were integral parts of daily living. **Sedulous** businessmen spent considerable time practicing their handwriting, for certainly no one would take them seriously if they produced sloppy, illegible documents.

Near the late nineteenth century, a teacher and master penman named Austin Palmer noticed a need for a less **onerous** penmanship for business handwriting. Businesses had limited time to produce large amounts of writing, and, despite the existence of a Spencerian business hand devoid of flourishes and bold letters, the arm movements required for the font exhausted writers. Palmer simplified the Spencerian script, and, by 1912, over one million copies of the Palmer Method textbook had been sold. Many schools continued to teach the intricate Spencerian script until the middle of the century, but eventually, the practical Palmer style, assisted by the inventions of typewriters and copiers, brought about the **imminent** obsolescence of the Spencerian hand.

Computers, email, and other digital forms of communication are proliferating exponentially. Many people, satisfied with the monotony of mass-produced greeting cards, mini-malls, and frozen-yogurt shops, expect penmanship to go the way of candle making, and they might be right. The eloquent script of yesteryear, like classic automobiles and awe-inspiring architecture, is dying. Style and grace are not intrinsic to modern life; elements that serve only to impress or to inspire are not cost effective. Soon, no one will remember the era in which people, in order to convey their feelings, actually sat down and used their primitive hands to write letters on paper. It's probably for the better; after all, why would someone want to sign a letter by hand if he or she has a computer-generated email signature block, or maybe an avatar of a cartoon character some stranger designed to further pollute the Internet? Those are pretty original, right?

1A. As used in line 11, *progeny* most nearly means
   A. ancestors.
   B. predecessors.
   C. family.
   D. sisters and brothers.
   E. descendants.

1B. Which word from the paragraph that includes *progeny* best supports your answer to question 1A?
   A. haphazardly
   B. psychological
   C. artifact
   D. future
   E. banal

2A. The purpose of the first paragraph is to
   A. express the importance of penmanship.
   B. debunk myths about desktop publishing.
   C. explain how fine writing is disappearing.
   D. inform about the phases of handwriting.
   E. persuade people to use only computers.

2B. Choose the statement that exemplifies how paragraph 1 uses *hyperbole*, or exaggeration, in emphasizing the importance of handwriting.
   A. the suggestion that paper will last for a thousand years
   B. the repetition of important historical documents
   C. the idea that a grocery list might come to represent an entire civilization
   D. the idea of time traveling and seeing the future
   E. the assertion that scientists would study an ancient scribbled document

3A. As used in line 41, *denizens* most nearly means
   A. relatives.
   B. commanders.
   C. dwellers.
   D. totalitarians.
   E. professionals.

3B. Choose the phrase from the context of *denizens* that supports your answer to question 3A.
   A. professional certifications
   B. mundane documents
   C. fine writing
   D. practicing their handwriting
   E. beautiful Spencerian script

4A. Which answer best describes the implication of the following sentence (lines 41-42)?

"Such fine writing reflects the conscience of all the nation's earlier denizens; they lived in an era in which pride, precision, and beauty were integral parts of daily living."

   A. Fine writing reveals the conscience of England's earlier times.
   B. People in the author's time forego pride, precision, and beauty.
   C. Victorian people were very superficial.
   D. Victorian people had vivid dreams of success.
   E. Pride, precision, and beauty are mandatory elements of penmanship.

4B. The author would probably agree with which one of the following statements?
   A. Writing is not a form of art.
   B. Just getting the job done is most important.
   C. Practicing handwriting should be unnecessary.
   D. Simpler is better.
   E. Appearances are usually important.

5A. As used in line 30, the word *hand* most nearly means
   A. appendage.
   B. style.
   C. pen.
   D. drawing.
   E. assistance.

5B. According to the passage, different *hands* first began to develop when
   A. the alphabet spread among European cultures.
   B. the general population wanted to write.
   C. Platt Spencer published a book.
   D. the demand for business writing increased.
   E. computers offered several fonts to choose from.

6A. Austin Palmer created a new method of writing because
   A. he and Spencer had a professional rivalry.
   B. the Department of Education requested a simple style of writing.
   C. Spencerian writing was hard to reproduce on typewriters.
   D. schools and businesses experienced paper shortages.
   E. the Spencerian method was tiring for writers.

6B. Choose the quotation that best supports your answer to question 6A.
   A. "…schools continued to teach the intricate Spencerian script until the middle of the century…"
   B. "…the inventions of typewriters and copiers…"
   C. "…the arm movements required for the font exhausted writers."
   D. "…no one would take them seriously…"
   E. "…the world identified the need for clean, standardized handwriting."

7A. As used in line 58, *intrinsic* most nearly means
   A. avoided.
   B. essential.
   C. substituted.
   D. popular.
   E. sentimental.

7B. Choose the statement that best describes an implication from lines 58-59.
   A. Fashion trends do not apply to handwriting.
   B. Modern life is cheap and practical.
   C. Typing is expensive.
   D. No one remembers how handwriting once looked.
   E. Beautiful script requires less time than today's plain handwriting does.

8A. The last sentence of the passage can be most accurately described as an example of
   A. opinion.
   B. personification.
   C. sincerity.
   D. irony.
   E. metaphor.

8B. Which statement, according to the final two paragraphs would the author agree with?
   A. The world still reveres art and beauty, but these are digitized now.
   B. Deep down, people do not change; they will always appreciate beauty.
   C. The speed the Palmer method introduced was a good innovation.
   D. A bad, genuine signature is better than an artificial one.
   E. New generations will rediscover a love for the art of handwriting.

9. According to the passage, which of the following choices is *not* a phase in the evolution of penmanship?
   A. the development of Edwardian italic writing
   B. America adopting the Spencerian writing method
   C. standardization during the Carolingian Period
   D. changes to the Roman alphabet
   E. the introduction of the Palmer method

10A. This passage would probably be found in a[n]
   A. high school history book.
   B. arts and crafts book.
   C. encyclopedia on Europe.
   D. newspaper column.
   E. art history book.

10B. Which element of the passage best supports your answer to question 10A?
   A. optimism for change
   B. strongly expressed opinions
   C. a focus on historical eras
   D. instructions about penmanship
   E. details about designing new writing styles

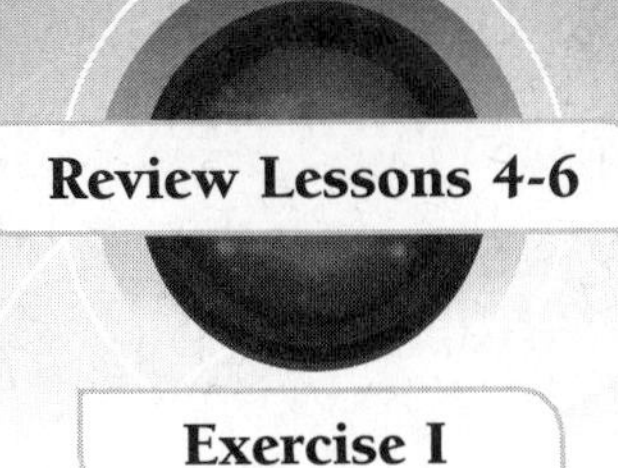

Review Lessons 4-6

Exercise I

Inferences

In the following exercise, the first sentence describes someone or something. Infer information from the first sentence, and then choose the word from the Word Bank that best completes the second sentence.

perfunctory	**deference**	**affluence**	**ebullient**
debacle	**denouement**	**demeanor**	**bedlam**

1. The guests were horrified when, at the end of the wedding ceremony, a flock of hungry seagulls seized upon the handfuls of rice thrown onto the ground, cackling loudly and soiling members of the wedding party.

   From this sentence, we can infer that the end of the wedding turned into a[n] __________.

2. A quick search of the soccer field did not produce Maggie's lost ring, but she was still sure that it was there.

   From this sentence, we can infer that a[n] __________ search for the ring was inadequate.

3. Schools were closed the day after the respected leader's death, flags were flown at half-mast, and many communities held memorial services, even though the residents had not known the deceased personally.

   From this sentence, we can infer that there was universal __________ for the late leader.

4. No one could enter the prison for three days during the riot in which several inmates and guards were killed.

   From this sentence, we can infer that the __________ during the riot caused the prison to shut down temporarily.

5. Even though Clyde hated special treatment, and would rather fail on his own than succeed with his family's wealth, he seemed to get out of every difficult situation just because of his family name.

   From this sentence, we can infer that Clyde cannot escape his family's __________.

Exercise II

Related Words

Some of the vocabulary words from Lessons 4 through 6 have related meanings. Complete the following sentences by choosing the word that best fits the context, based on information you infer from the use of the italicized word. Some word pairs will be antonyms, some will be synonyms, and some will simply be words often used in the same context.

1. None of the soldiers who survived the *bedlam* on the medieval battlefield ever forgot the __________ scene left after their victory, which was hard fought with axes, swords, and war hammers.
   A. facetious
   B. celibate
   C. carnal
   D. banal
   E. pedantic

2. After Bill's life of __________ left him broke, overweight, and emotionally bankrupt, he *eschewed* his former luxuries and lived a modest, quiet life.
   A. debacle
   B. fop
   C. antipathy
   D. hedonism
   E. parody

3. Linda's *scurrilous* insult about the coach enraged the rival fans surrounding her in the stands, all of whom considered the old man to be __________.
   A. carnal
   B. panegyric
   C. fortuitous
   D. banal
   E. sacrosanct

4. As a *parody* of an unpopular, overreaching new law, a blog posted a[n] __________ article purporting that the government had mandated the wearing of blue jeans on Fridays for all citizens.
   A. facetious
   B. baroque
   C. imperative
   D. sadistic
   E. imminent

5. The interior decorator used gilded columns and giant tapestries to transform the __________ gray restaurant dining room into a *baroque* chamber suitable for a royal palace.
   A. onerous
   B. banal
   C. scurrilous
   D. sedulous
   E. amoral

6. All of the *obloquies* during the service conveyed __________ to the deceased ambassador, whose work had saved the lives of thousands.
   A. bedlam
   B. hedonism
   C. imprecation
   D. deference
   E. parody

7. The organic chemistry teacher __________ the concept several times before the *nebulous* image became clear to the students.
   A. elucidated
   B. eschewed
   C. besmirched
   D. bowdlerized
   E. perused

8. The historian *perused* the newly discovered scrolls, and afterward, she __________ the texts for the audience of her first lecture.
   A. besmirched
   B. recapitulated
   C. eschewed
   D. impaired
   E. bowdlerized

9. John once spread gossip that *besmirched* his rival's reputation, so when the same thing happened to John, he felt that it was a[n] __________ he had brought upon himself.
   A. nebulous
   B. quandary
   C. antipathy
   D. imprecation
   E. bedlam

10. The __________ speaker suddenly changed his *demeanor* when, in the middle of his bold speech, the wind blew his toupee into the crowd.
    A. facetious
    B. sadistic
    C. rakish
    D. carnal
    E. banal

Exercise III

Deeper Meanings

Choose a word to replace the italicized word in each sentence. All of the possible choices for each sentence have similar definitions, but the correct answer will have a connotation that best suits the context. For example, the words "delete," "destroy," and "obliterate," all mean "to remove or wipe out," but no one would ever say, "I destroyed the name from the document." The correct choice will be the word with the best specific meaning and does not render the sentence awkward in tone or content. When choices seem close, look for a clue in the context that makes one choice better than the other. Note that the correct answer is not always the primary vocabulary word from the lesson.

perfunctory	**ignores**	**smart**	**eschews**	**learned**
repels	**problem**	**situation**	**crowds**	**effortless**
pedantic	**emergency**	**riots**	**lazy**	

1. Because he was freezing in the January wind, the detective's *fast* search of what appeared to be a simple crime scene failed to find the tiny shred of evidence that would later crack the case.

   Better word: ____________________

2. Since losing 150 pounds, Mike doesn't just skip the junk food, he aggressively *declines* it.

   Better word: ____________________

3. The *educated* teacher simply could not refrain from lecturing us on every item in the museum, even when the class wanted to read about the exhibits themselves.

   Better word: ____________________

4. The electricity went out just as the pumps started removing water from the sinking ship, causing a genuine *debacle* that put the crew in immediate danger.

   Better word: ____________________

5. Gene hates dealing with the *bedlam* at the shopping mall on Saturdays.

   Better word: ____________________

Exercise IV

Crossword Puzzle

Use the clues to complete the crossword puzzle. The answers consist of vocabulary words from Lessons 4 through 6.

Across

3. just can't have too much fun
4. pretty cloudy
5. way too fancy
8. nothing special
15. done without a thought
16. extremely important
17. state of having a big wallet
18. knowing more than you

Down

1. Everything goes wrong.
2. area between rock and a hard place
6. Yes! Finally! I can't wait!
7. cheery
9. a whole lot holier
10. to make worse
11. end of story
12. censor out the risky stuff
13. Clear this up for me.
14. hatred

Exercise V

Subject Prompts

Here is a writing prompt similar to the one you will find on the writing portion of an assessment test. Follow the instructions below and write a brief, efficient essay.

> Henry David Thoreau's experiment, detailed in the world-famous book *Walden*, extols the benefits of living a simple life of self-reliance and acknowledges that all people have two distinct selves—the pure, civilized self, and the wild self. In a world in which few people step foot in a forest, the wild self rarely has a chance to emerge—much to the detriment of the whole self.
>
> Do you agree with Thoreau's philosophy, or do you feel that observing nature in solitude is unnecessary to a healthy mind? Take a position and write an argument either for or against the benefits of spending time in nature. Include at least three paragraphs of supporting ideas.

Thesis: Write a *one-sentence* response to the above assignment. Make certain this single sentence offers a clear statement of your position.

Example: Nothing in civilization is made of things that were not found, or derived, from nature, so spending time in the woods is no more a natural experience than sitting under an interstate bridge.

____

____

Organizational Plan: List at least three subtopics you will use to support your main idea. This list is your outline.

1. ____

2. ____

3. ____

Draft: Following your outline, write a good first draft of your essay. Remember to support all your points with examples, facts, references to reading, etc.

Review and Revise: Exchange essays with a classmate. Using the scoring guide for Development on page 264, score your partner's essay (while he or she scores yours). Focus on the development of ideas and use of language conventions. If necessary, rewrite your essay to improve the development of ideas and/or your use of language.

Lesson Seven

1. **bovine** (bō´ vīn) *adj.* pertaining to cows or cattle
The large animal figures in the cave drawing depicted *bovine* creatures.

2. **callow** (kal´ ō) *adj.* young and inexperienced
The *callow* boy left for the war, but a cynical man returned.
syn: immature *ant: mature; sophisticated*

3. **peccadillo** (pek ə dil´ ō) *n.* a minor offense; a misdeed
Stealing tips from tables was a *peccadillo* in Bill's mind, but a major offense in the minds of the waiters.

4. **dichotomy** (dī kot´ ə mē) *n.* a division into two parts
Disagreements among board members created a *dichotomy* in the charitable organizations.

5. **macroscopic** (mak rə skop´ ik) *adj.* visible to the naked eye
On a clear night, the Milky Way appears *macroscopic.*
ant: microscopic

6. **rationalize** (rash´ ə nə līz) *v.* to make an excuse for
The boy tried to *rationalize* his absence from school.
syn: justify

7. **patent** (pat´ nt) *adj.* evident or obvious
When the electronics store saw the *patent* abuse of the game system, they refused to grant a refund.
syn: indisputable; apparent

8. **knell** (nel) *n.* a sound made by a bell, often rung slowly for a death or funeral
The *knell* of the church bell told the town that Gertrude had passed away.

9. **ferret** (fer´ it) *v.* to search or drive out
John knew the answer was in the text, but he just couldn't *ferret* it out.

10. **fatuous** (fach´ ōō əs) *adj.* foolish; inane
Her *fatuous* simpering began to grate on our nerves.
syn: silly *ant: sensible; wise*

11. **adroit** (ə droit´) *adj.* skillful; clever
He was not an *adroit* speaker, but he was a genius with numbers.
syn: dexterous; apt *ant: clumsy; awkward*

12. **affectation** (af ek tā´ shən) *n.* a phony attitude; pose
Ginger could not stand the *affectations* of the girls in the fashion clique.
syn: insincerity; sham *ant: sincerity; genuineness*

13. **laconic** (la kon´ ik) *adj.* using few words; short; concise
He was a *laconic* man who wasted few words.
syn: pithy; taciturn *ant: verbose; loquacious*

14. **quiddity** (kwid´ i tē) *n.* an essential quality
Patience is the *quiddity* of a good teacher.
syn: essence

15. **sagacious** (sə gā´ shəs) *adj.* wise; having keen perception and sound judgment
The *sagacious* old man always had the answers to moral problems.
syn: shrewd; intelligent *ant: obtuse; fatuous*

Exercise I

Words in Context

From the list below, supply the words needed to complete the paragraph. Some words will not be used.

macroscopic	**adroit**	**dichotomy**
patent	**quiddity**	**laconic**

1. The inventor's presentation of the new microprocessor was a[n] __________ between theory and application, and his __________ explanations were easy to understand. During the description of the chip's __________ components, the inventor said that the __________ of the new design was its amazing speed; the processor was over 1,000 times faster than any previous design.

From the list below, supply the words needed to complete the paragraph. Some words will not be used.

dichotomy	**sagacious**	**knell**	**affectation**
bovine	**patent**	**fatuous**	

2. The cows in the __________ pasture were marked for slaughter, and the occasional clanking cowbell reminded Dana of death __________ from a church bell. Her brother died three months ago, and any metal-on-metal sound made Dana recall the broken silence on the morning of the funeral. While at work, Dana maintained the __________ that she was fine, but her family had no trouble detecting her __________ depression. As her __________ father pointed out to the rest of the family, Dana had the closest relationship with her older brother, and she would need more time to mourn.

From the list below, supply the words needed to complete the paragraph. Some words will not be used.

rationalize	**quiddity**	**callow**	**adroit**
ferret	**fatuous**	**peccadillo**	**macroscopic**

3. Before getting fired from his warehouse job and being arrested for grand theft, Eric __________ his criminal actions as __________ that were not really hurting anyone. The __________ thief had the __________ notion that no one would notice that $17,000 in merchandise simply had vanished. In a successful effort to __________ out the thief, the __________ warehouse manager conducted secret inventories every day for two weeks.

Exercise II

Sentence Completion

Complete the sentence in a way that shows you understand the meaning of the italicized vocabulary word.

1. Don't *rationalize* your actions; you had no reason to…
2. To Susan, stealing office supplies is a *peccadillo*, but to the manager…
3. The defamed actor said the accusation was a *patent* lie that was meant to…
4. The *callow* boy wanted to hike the Appalachian trail now, but his parents told him…
5. The sergeant ordered Corporal Duncan to enter the cave and *ferret* out…
6. The *laconic* soldier guarding the gate would not…
7. The three boys did not cease their *fatuous* behavior, so the teacher…
8. The Bundy family put on an *affectation* of wealth, but everyone knew…
9. The *sagacious* oracle warned the Viking warriors…
10. The *adroit* mechanic repaired the biplane even though he…
11. Exercise is the *quiddity* of…
12. It took three weeks to drive the *bovine* herd…
13. The *adroit* thief eluded capture by…
14. At the crime scene, look for *macroscopic* evidence before you…
15. The *knelling* bells summoned…

Exercise III

Roots, Prefixes, and Suffixes

Study the entries and answer the questions that follow.

The root *tach* means "swift" or "speed."
The roots *mid*, *med*, and *meso* mean "middle."
The root *bol* means "to throw" or "to put."
The roots *prov* and *prob* mean "good" or "to test."
The prefix *meta–* means "changed."
The suffix *–meter* means "measure."
The prefix *inter–* means "among."
The prefixes *em–* and *im–* mean "in."
The prefix *sym–* means "with" or "together."
The prefix *hyper–* means "excessive."

1. Using *literal* translations as guidance, define the following words without using a dictionary.

   A. prove
   B. disapprove
   C. Mesoamerica
   D. median
   E. metabolism
   F. improve

2. A *tachometer* __________ the __________ at which an engine runs.

3. A[n] __________ meal is neither bad nor good—it is simply in the middle.

   Athletes who have better skills than beginners but fewer skills than experts are often described as being __________, or "among the middle."

4. An obstruction in a blood vessel is called a[n] __________, but if you exaggerate, or "throw" the meaning of something too far, then you have used a[n] __________.

   A skull and crossbones on a black flag could mean anything by itself, but if you see the flag flying above a ship, you might "throw" its meaning together with what it represents and realize that the design is a[n] __________ of piracy.

5. The Mars satellite will __________ the composition of the planet's surface. If someone has good chances of winning, then that person will __________ win.

Exercise IV

Inference

Complete the sentence by inferring information about the italicized word from its context.

1. The captors imprisoned Agent Sparks in a steel cage, but they also posted guards around it because the *adroit* prisoner…

2. Captain Jack, now a prisoner on his own ship, wished he had listened to the *sagacious* first mate's warning that…

3. Janice's *affectations* included speaking in a phony British accent and…

Exercise V

Writing

Here is a writing prompt similar to the one you will find on the writing portion of an assessment test.

Plan and write an essay on the following statement:

> American essayist and philosopher Ralph Waldo Emerson wrote: "A friend is Janus-faced*; he looks to the past and the future. He is a child of all my foregoing hours, the prophet of those to come, and the harbinger of a greater friend."
>
> *Janus is the Roman god of entrances and exits of life. He is pictured with two faces, one facing forward, the other behind. The month of January is named after him.

Assignment: Think of a friend, relative, or someone you know who can be described as "Janus-faced." In an essay, discuss how the person you have indicated fulfills Emerson's description of a friend. Support any generalities you make with specific examples of things that your friend has said or done, times that you've shared, or similar events.

Thesis: Write a *one-sentence* response to the above assignment. Make certain this single sentence offers a clear statement of your position.

Example: My next-door neighbor and track coach is my "Janus-faced" friend because she knows the failures and achievements of my past, and because she helps me to overcome uncertainties of the future.

____

____

Organizational Plan: List at least three subtopics you will use to support your main idea. This list is your outline.

1. ______________________________

2. ______________________________

3. ______________________________

Draft: Following your outline, write a good first draft of your essay. Remember to support all your points with examples, facts, references to reading, etc.

Review and Revise: Exchange essays with a classmate. Using the scoring guide for Word Choice on page 267, score your partner's essay (while he or she scores yours). Focus on word choice and the use of language conventions. If necessary, rewrite your essay to improve the word choice and/or use of language.

Exercise VI

English Practice

Improving Paragraphs

Read the following passage and then choose the best revision for the underlined portions of the paragraph. The questions will require you to make decisions regarding the revision of the reading selection. Some revisions are not of actual mistakes, but will improve the clarity of the writing.

[1] Small town judges are buried in seas[1]of bureaucratic paperwork, and many are working from the cramped confines of spare rooms in their own homes.

1. A. NO CHANGE
   B. are buried in oceans
   C. are drowning in seas
   D. are lost in deserts

[2] Their judicial accounts, funded by taxpayers and allocated by the town boards, are almost never enough to cover the costs of running these makeshift courts.

[3] They work part-time, and they are called upon at any hour of the day. Their[2] courts constitute the first rung of the state's legal ladder, and these elected officials are called upon to handle cases ranging from traffic **peccadillos** to first-degree murder.

2. F. NO CHANGE
   G. They're
   H. There
   J. There're

3. Which of the following changes would improve the introduction (paragraphs 1-3) of the article?
   A. Delete paragraph 1.
   B. Combine paragraphs 1, 2, and 3.
   C. Delete paragraph 2.
   D. Exchange paragraphs 2 and 3.

[4] The judges are not always reluctant to admit they are overworked and underpaid.

[5] One judge, for example, says that for his <u>$3200 hundred dollars per year,</u>[4] the state has taken away a lot of his "judgment" and swapped it for a pile of paperwork that needs to be very properly filled out and filed.

4. F. NO CHANGE
   G. $3200 per year
   H. $3200 hundred per year
   J. $3200 dollars per year

[6] He said <u>it's</u>[5] more <u>like north korea</u>[6] nowadays. The state sets all the fines and tells you how to judge the cases. Then you spend all your weekends and evenings doing the paperwork. Sometimes more than one evening a week is spent hearing cases. State requirements include two days of schooling every year, for which the only compensation is meals and mileage." A number of judges must take the day off to attend the sessions for which they are tested and "grades" handed down, just like in school.

5. A. NO CHANGE
   B. its'
   C. its
   D. that its

6. F. NO CHANGE
   G. as north korea is
   H. similar to how North Korea is
   J. like North Korea

7. The punctuation error in paragraph 6 would best be corrected by
   A. beginning the paragraph with sentence 5.
   B. omitting sentence 1.
   C. enclosing the quoted material with quotation marks.
   D. deleting the reference to a foreign nation in sentence 1.

[7] One judge has a day job as supervisor of a state campground. One of the days he must attend justice workshops is during the park's busiest month, so he loses a day's pay. "I guess I'm just fed up," he said, "and when my term is up next year, I will probably not run for re-election. I'm in my third term now, and at about eighty cents an hour, it's not <u>worth it".</u>[9] The gas money that he spends to attend the workshops is more than what the state pays him. He said he originally took the office so he could help people, but with what he terms the state "takeover" of his decisions, he does not feel he can do it anymore.

8. Which of the following sentences could be deleted from paragraph 7 without changing the intent of the paragraph?
   F. sentence 2
   G. sentence 3
   H. sentence 4
   J. sentence 5

9. A. NO CHANGE
   B. worth" it.
   C. worth it."
   D. "worth it."

[8] Another justice, on the other hand, would seek re-election for his fourth term because he finds the most highest[10] satisfaction in the work he does, which he chose to do as a means of serving his fellow human beings. He also conceded that there is a lot of paper work in the job—at least 3 to four hours[11] "in chambers" for every hour on the bench—and not easily dismissed.

10. F. NO CHANGE
    G. the more higher
    H. the most high
    J. the most

11. A. NO CHANGE
    B. 3 or 4 hour's
    C. three hours or four hours
    D. three to four hours

[9] He cited the newer judicial system as a **patent** money-raising scheme for the state. He said, that the surcharges[12] for crimes go as high as $87 for a misdemeanor, $42 for a violation of the penal law, and $25 for traffic or vehicular infractions. Is that a deterrent to committing a crime:[13] The judge didn't think so. He said that the surcharges serve as a means of generating revenue for the state.

12. F. NO CHANGE
    G. He said that "the surcharges
    H. He said: the surcharges
    J. He said that the surcharges

13. A. NO CHANGE
    B. crime!
    C. crime?
    D. crime,

14. Which of the following changes would best improve continuity within the passage?
    F. Combine paragraphs 1 and 6.
    G. Combine paragraphs 3 and 4.
    H. Combine paragraphs 4 and 5.
    J. Exchange paragraphs 4 and 5.

15. Which paragraph departs from the greater intent of the passage by including a positive element?
    A. paragraph 4
    B. paragraph 6
    C. paragraph 8
    D. paragraph 9

Lesson Eight

1. **harbinger** (här´ bin jər) *n.* an omen or a sign
To many, the black cat is a *harbinger* of bad luck.
syn: warning; portent

2. **gambol** (gam´ bəl) *v.* to frolic; to romp about playfully
The preschoolers liked to *gambol* about on the playground.
syn: play; caper; rollick

3. **quagmire** (kwag´ mīr) *n.* a swamp; a difficult or inextricable situation
The war was a political *quagmire* for three U.S. presidents.

4. **carcinogen** (kär sin´ ə jən) *n.* causing cancer
Benzene, a component of gasoline, is a *carcinogen*.

5. **grotesque** (grō tesk´) *adj.* absurd; distorted
The boy made a *grotesque* mask for Halloween.

6. **agape** (ə gāp´) *adj.* open-mouthed; surprised; agog
Even the judge was *agape* when the witness told the ridiculous story in court.
syn: astonished

7. **recondite** (rek´ ən dīt) *adj.* difficult to understand; profound
Only a few students understood the *recondite* explanation of the theory.

8. **censure** (sen´ shər) *v.* to criticize sharply
The judge *censured* the repeat offender for his criminal behavior.
syn: condemn; reproach *ant: praise; applaud*

9. **immolate** (im´ ə lāt) *v.* to kill someone as a sacrificial victim, usually by fire
Some Buddhist monks *immolated* themselves in protest of the government's policies.

10. **martinet** (mär tn et´) *n.* a strict disciplinarian; taskmaster
The teacher was a *martinet* who never made exceptions to the rules.

11. **gibe** (jīb) *v.* to scoff; to ridicule
His favorite pastime was to *gibe* at everything his wife said.
syn: jeer; taunt; sneer *ant: compliment; praise*

12. **olfactory** (ol fak´ tə rē) *adj.* pertaining to smell
If you have a cold, then your *olfactory* senses will not detect the gas leak.

13. **imperious** (im pîr´ ē əs) *adj.* domineering; haughty
The judge pronounced his findings in an *imperious* voice.
syn: overbearing; arrogant; masterful *ant: servile; submissive*

14. **neologism** (nē äl´ ə jiz əm) *n.* a new word or expression
Some writers coin *neologisms* to confuse and impress their readers.
syn: coinage

15. **hackneyed** (hak´ nēd) *adj.* commonplace; overused
"Good as gold" is a *hackneyed* expression.
syn: trite; banal *ant: fresh; imaginative*

Exercise I

Words in Context

From the list below, supply the words needed to complete the paragraph. Some words will not be used.

immolate	**agape**	**gibe**
censure	**imperious**	**martinet**

1. Janet could not contain herself when the waiter ignored her for the third time. Like a[n] __________ scolding a naughty schoolboy, Janet stood over her table and loudly __________ the waiter. Patrons, mouths __________ at surrounding tables, could not believe Janet's __________ outburst, but they were secretly happy because they, too, were upset with the poor service. Some of the patrons could not contain their chuckles when Janet angrily __________ at the manager when he appeared at the table.
   "What do I have to do—__________ myself just to get your attention? Perhaps you'd see me if I were a human torch!"
   "Please, ma'am; what is the problem here?" asked the manager.

From the list below, supply the words needed to complete the paragraph. Some words will not be used.

grotesque	**hackneyed**	**quagmire**	**gambol**
harbinger	**censure**	**recondite**	

2. While most of the second-graders innocently __________ around the playground during recess, Justin usually snuck off in search of trouble. No one—not even Justin—understood his __________ reasons for wanting to complicate Mrs. Nale's life. When asked about Justin's behavior, Mrs. Nale usually responded with the __________ expression, "Boys will be boys." Justin responded by making a[n] __________ face.

From the list below, supply the words needed to complete the paragraph. Some words will not be used.

quagmire	**censure**	**carcinogens**	**immolate**
neologism	**harbinger**	**olfactory**	**grotesque**

3. Experts fear that new strains of old diseases are __________ of the future of bioterrorism. The word *bioterrorism* is a[n] __________ that refers to the use of biological agents as terrorist weapons. By themselves, agents such as anthrax and botulism can be invisible to the naked eye and undetectable to the __________ senses. Before cities established emergency management programs, experts believed that the effective release of agents into populated areas would have caused a[n] __________ that overwhelmed every available hospital and emergency worker. Biological and chemical agents would have to be swiftly neutralized; their effects are immediate and severe, unlike those of a mild influenza or the __________ found in water or air pollution.

Exercise II

Sentence Completion

Complete the sentence in a way that shows you understand the meaning of the italicized vocabulary word.

1. A dog's *olfactory* sense is…
2. Radical supporters sometimes *immolate* themselves in order to…
3. Irene made a *grotesque* expression when she took a bite; the food was…
4. We couldn't hear the conversation, but when Will stood there looking *agape*, we knew that he…
5. One *harbinger* of danger is…
6. Jill saw her financial debt as a *quagmire* from which she could…
7. People who did not understand the *recondite* reasons for the war decided to…
8. The judge did not appreciate it when the defendant *gibed* that…
9. During recess, students *gamboled* on the playground while…
10. The editor *censured* Carol's first manuscript, so Carol decided to…
11. Leo's tutor was a *martinet* who made him…
12. Sandy didn't like to play chess with Patrick because Patrick made *imperious* remarks every time…
13. Asbestos is a *carcinogen* that can…
14. "E-mail" and "spam" are *neologisms* created to describe things that deal with…
15. *Hackneyed* expressions detract from your writing, so you should…

Exercise III

Roots, Prefixes, and Suffixes

Study the entries and answer the questions that follow.

The suffix *–ive* means "relating to" or "tending to."
The roots *ced* and *cess* mean "to yield," "to stop," "to go."
The prefix *pro–* means "for."
The prefix *ante–* means "before."
The prefix *trans–* means "across" or "through."
The root *mot* means "to move."

1. Using *literal* translations as guidance, define the following words without using a dictionary.

A	procession	D.	transitive
B.	antecedent	E.	motive
C.	process	F.	massive

2. A green light signals you to __________ through an intersection.

   Fighting must __________ if warring parties agree on a cessation of combat.

3. To communicate with someone who speaks a foreign language, you will need to send your message through a[n] __________.

   The *transcontinental* railroad ran __________ the width of the United States.

4. List as many words as you can think of that contain the root *mot.*

5. List as many words as you can think of that contain the roots *ced* or *cess.*

Exercise IV

Inference

Complete the sentence by inferring information about the italicized word from its context.

1. If the theory about hyperspace is *recondite*, then you might need to…

2. Mom says that schoolteachers used to be strict *martinets*, and now they…

3. The sudden disappearance of forest creatures is a *harbinger* of bad weather because…

Exercise V

Critical Reading

Below is a pair of reading passages followed by several multiple-choice questions. Carefully read the passages and choose the best answer to each of the questions.

Shortly before the War of 1812, Tecumseh, chief of the Shawnee, attempted to recruit other nations to his confederacy dedicated to recovering rapidly diminishing Native American homelands. Passage 1 is his purported speech to the Osage nation, which demonstrates his intent and rhetoric. Passage 2 is an account of Choctaw chief Pushmataha's retort to Tecumseh's effort to recruit the Choctaw, which shows that not all nations agreed with Tecumseh's strategy.

Passage 1

Brothers—We all belong to one family; we are all children of the Great Spirit; we walk in the same path; slake our thirst at the same spring; and now affairs of the greatest concern lead us to smoke the pipe around the same council fire!

Brothers—We are friends; we must assist each other to bear our burdens. The blood of many of our fathers and brothers has run like water on the ground, to satisfy the avarice of the white men. We, ourselves, are threatened with a great evil; nothing will pacify them but the destruction of all the red men.

Brothers—When the white men first set foot on our grounds, they were hungry; they had no place on which to spread their blankets, or to kindle their fires. They were feeble; they could do nothing for themselves. Our father commiserated their distress, and shared freely with them whatever the Great Spirit had given his red children. They gave them food when hungry, medicine when sick, spread skins for them to sleep on, and gave them grounds, that they might hunt and raise corn.

Brothers—The white people are like poisonous serpents: when chilled, they are feeble and harmless; but invigorate them with warmth, and they sting their benefactors to death.

The white people came among us feeble; and now we have made them strong, they wish to kill us, or drive us back, as they would wolves and panthers.

Brothers—The white men are not friends to the Indians: at first, they only asked for land sufficient for a wigwam; now, nothing will satisfy them but the whole of our hunting grounds, from the rising to the setting sun.

Brothers—The white men want more than our hunting grounds; they wish to kill our warriors; they would even kill our old men, women and little ones.

Brothers—Many winters ago, there was no land; the sun did not rise and set: all was darkness. The Great Spirit made all things. He gave the white people a home beyond the great waters. He supplied these grounds with game, and gave them to his red children; and he gave them strength and courage to defend them.

Brothers—My people wish for peace; the red men all wish for peace; but where the white people are, there is no peace for them, except it be on the bosom of our mother.

Brothers—The white men despise and cheat the Indians; they abuse and insult them; they do not think the red men sufficiently good to live.

The red men have borne many and great injuries; they ought to suffer them no longer. My people will not; they are determined on vengeance; they have taken up the tomahawk; they will make it fat with blood; they will drink the blood of the white people.

Brothers—My people are brave and numerous; but the white people are too strong for them alone. I wish you to take up the tomahawk with them. If we all unite, we will cause the rivers to stain the great waters with their blood.

Brothers—If you do not unite with us, they will first destroy us, and then you will fall an easy prey to them. They have destroyed many nations of red men because they were not united, because they were not friends to each other.

Brothers—The white people send runners amongst us; they wish to make us enemies that they may sweep over and desolate our hunting grounds, like devastating winds, or rushing waters.

Brothers—Our Great Father, over the great waters, is angry with the white people, our enemies. He will send his brave warriors against them; he will send us rifles, and whatever else we want—he is our friend, and we are his children.

Brothers—Who are the white people that we should fear them? They cannot run fast, and are good marks to shoot at: they are only men; our fathers have killed many of them; we are not squaws, and we will stain the earth red with blood.

Brothers—The Great Spirit is angry with our enemies; he speaks in thunder, and the earth swallows up villages, and drinks up the Mississippi. The great waters will cover their lowlands; their corn cannot grow, and the Great Spirit will sweep those who escape to the hills from the earth with his terrible reach.

Brothers—We must be united; we must smoke the same pipe; we must fight each other's battles; and more than all, we must love the Great Spirit. He is for us; he will destroy our enemies and make all his red children happy.

Passage 2

The great Shawnee orator has portrayed in vivid picture the wrongs inflicted on his and other tribes by the ravages of the paleface. The candor and fervor of his eloquent appeal breathe the conviction of truth and sincerity, and, as kindred tribes, naturally we sympathize with the misfortunes of his people. I do not come before you in any disputation either for or against these charges. It is not my purpose to contradict any of these allegations against the white man, but neither am I here to indulge in any indiscreet denunciation of him which might bring down upon my people unnecessary difficulty and embarrassment....

The distinguished Shawnee sums up his eloquent appeal to us with this direct question: Will you sit idly by, supinely awaiting complete and abject submission, or will you die fighting beside your brethren, the Shawnees, rather than submit to such ignominy?

These are plain words and it is well they have been spoken, for they bring the issue squarely before us. Mistake not, this language means war. And war with whom, pray? War with some band of marauders who have committed these depredations against the Shawnees? War with some alien host seeking the destruction of the Choctaws and Chickasaws? Nay, my fellow tribesmen. None of these are the enemy we will be called on to meet. If we take up arms against the Americans we must of necessity meet in deadly combat our daily neighbors and associates in this part of the country near our homes....

Forget not, Choctaws and Chickasaws, that we are bound in peace to the Great White Father at Washington by a sacred treaty and the Great Spirit will punish those who break their word. The Great White Father has never violated that treaty and the Choctaws have never yet been driven to the necessity of taking up the tomahawk against him or his children....

We Choctaws and Chickasaws are a peaceful people, making our subsistence by honest toil; but mistake not, my Shawnee brethren, we are not afraid of war. Neither are we strangers to war, as those who have undertaken to encroach upon our rights in the past may abundantly testify. We are thoroughly familiar with war in all its details and we know full well all its horrible consequences. It is unnecessary for me to remind you, O Choctaws and Chickasaws, veteran braves of many fierce conflicts in the past, that war is an awful thing. If we go into this war against the Americans, we must be prepared to accept its inevitable results. Not only will it foretoken deadly conflict with neighbors and death to warriors, but it will mean suffering for our women, hunger and starvation for our children, grief for our loved ones, and devastation of our homes. Notwithstanding these difficulties, if the cause be just, we should not hesitate to defend our rights to the last man, but before that fatal step is irrevocably taken, it is well that we fully understand and seriously consider the full portent and consequences of the act....

Halt, Tecumseh! Listen to me. You have come here, as you have often gone elsewhere, with a purpose to involve peaceful people in unnecessary trouble with their neighbors. Our people have had no undue friction with the whites. Why? Because we have had no leaders stirring up strife to serve their selfish, personal ambitions. You heard me say that our people are a peaceful people. They make their way, not by ravages upon their neighbors but by honest toil. In that regard they have nothing in common with you. I know your history well. You are a disturber. You have ever been a troublemaker. When you have found yourself unable to pick a quarrel with the white man, you have stirred up strife between different tribes of your own race. Not only that, you are a monarch and unyielding tyrant within your own domain. Every Shawnee man, woman, and child, must bow in humble submission to your imperious will. The Choctaws and Chickasaws have no monarchs. Their chieftains do not undertake the mastery of their people, but rather are they the people's servants, elected to serve the will of the majority. The majority has spoken on this question and it has spoken against your contention. Their decision has therefore become the law of the Choctaws and Chickasaws and Pushmataha will see that the will of the majority so recently expressed is rigidly carried out to the letter. If, after this decision, any Choctaw should be so foolish as to follow your imprudent advice and enlist to fight against the Americans, thereby abandoning his own people and turning against the decision of his own council, Pushmataha will see that proper punishment is meted out to him, which is death. You have made your choice; you have elected to fight with the British. The Americans have been our friends and we shall stand by them. We will furnish you safe conduct to the boundaries of this nation as properly befits the dignity of your office. Farewell, Tecumseh. You will see Pushmataha no more until we meet on the fateful warpath.'

1A. The intent of the first two paragraphs of passage 1 is best described as
   A. resolving differences.
   B. establishing common roots.
   C. identifying everyone involved.
   D. a desire for peace.
   E. discussing the past.

1B. Which words from the paragraphs best support your answer to question 1A?
   A. children; concern; thirst
   B. affairs; fire; destruction
   C. greatest; path; blood
   D. threatened; evil; avarice
   E. Brothers; family; friends

2A. As used in line 10, passage 1, *commiserated* most nearly means
   A. increased.
   B. accepted.
   C. avoided.
   D. pitied.
   E. rejected.

2B. In passage one, the inclusion of "father's" assistance to the white men in need serves the rhetorical purpose of
   A. increasing the depth of the betrayal.
   B. humanizing the white men.
   C. calming down the audience.
   D. putting forth a counterargument the main idea.
   E. portraying weakness.

3. Choose the best description of the organization of passage 1.
   A. descriptive narrative
   B. problem and solution
   C. chronological
   D. order of importance
   E. pros and cons

4A. Tecumseh did, in fact, ally with the British against the United States during the War of 1812, in spite of the British also being mostly "white men." Which line from the passage suggests that the British and the Americans were not the same "white men" to Tecumseh and justifies his alliance with the British?
   A. "The white men want more than our hunting grounds…"
   B. "…the white people are too strong for them alone."
   C. "He gave the white people a home beyond the great waters."
   D. "…they will first destroy us, and then you will fall an easy prey to them."
   E. "I wish you to take up the tomahawk with them."

4B. Choose the phrase used by Tecumseh that further supports your answer to question 4A. The line makes Tecumseh's relationship with the British distinct from that of his relationship with the Americans.
   A. Great Spirit
   B. poisonous serpents
   C. my people
   D. Great Father
   E. great waters

5A. Who is the person Pushmataha is referring to through the phrase "misfortunes of his people" in passage 2, line 4?
   A. a British general
   B. Tecumseh
   C. the Great White Father
   D. Pushmataha's tribesmen
   E. a fellow Chickasaw

5B. Although passage 2, as a whole, is a rebuttal of Tecumseh's arguments for war, paragraph 1 of passage 2 is dedicated to the purpose of
   A. finding common ground with Tecumseh.
   B. laying out the basis of Pushmataha's argument.
   C. providing background information for Pushmataha's decision.
   D. gaining the backing of Pushmataha's audience.
   E. establishing Tecumseh as credible and respectable.

6A. Pushmataha describes the reasons for Tecumseh's grievances against the white man as
   A. possible.
   B. already discounted.
   C. embellished for the sake of argument.
   D. fear tactics.
   E. the same treatment the Choctaw endure.

6B. In Pushmataha's example in the fourth paragraph, he provides three example of possible enemies. One is the Americans. The other two are intended to be
  A. enemies the Choctaw have always had.
  B. people who have been at peace with all tribes.
  C. enemies the Choctaw would gladly fight on behalf of the Shawnee.
  D. other enemies the Choctaw would not readily engage.
  E. enemies who cannot be defeated.

7A. The first paragraphs of passage 2, ending with "full portent and consequences of the act," can be described as respectful toward Tecumseh, but the final paragraph, which clearly changes in tone, is best described as
  A. challenging but hopeful.
  B. somber and worrisome.
  C. condemning and threatening.
  D. argumentative and clear.
  E. depressing but thoughtful.

8A. The final paragraph of passage 2 ascribes Tecumseh's true motive to
  A. his surrendering to the council.
  B. a misplaced sense of loyalty to Washington.
  C. his orders from the British king.
  D. pressure from warlike chieftains.
  E. his personal ambition.

8B. Choose the sentence that best summarizes the most important elements of the last paragraph of passage 2.
  A. Tecumseh is wrong, and any Choctaws who follow him will be killed.
  B. Pushmataha rejects Tecumseh's plans and will fight with the Americans.
  C. Tecumseh is a dictator and will bring destruction to all.
  D. Tecumseh has sided with the British and must be destroyed.
  E. A majority of Pushmataha's tribe has voted against war.

9A. Keeping in mind that the War of 1812 is pending at the time of Tecumseh's speech, Pushmataha's portrayal of Tecumseh as a "monarch" and a "tyrant" hints at which one of the following statements?
  A. Tecumseh obeys, and emulates, the British crown, or "Great Father."
  B. Pushmataha does not trust the Great White Father.
  C. The Americans have influenced Tecumseh adversely.
  D. Tecumseh, because he did not ask for a vote, is truly uncivilized.
  E. The Shawnee have been conscripted by the British Army.

9B. In contrast to Tecumseh's "tyrant" ways, Pushmataha claims that his decision to reject joining Tecumseh is the result of
  A. inspiration from the Great Spirit.
  B. self-preservation.
  C. personal conscience.
  D. the will of the majority.
  E. the way of the Choctaw.

10A. Choose the answer that best explains the differences in the intended audiences of the passages.
  A. Pushmataha is speaking only to his fellow council members.
  B. Tecumseh threatens any tribesmen who do not support him.
  C. Tecumseh is addressing various tribes; Pushmataha is addressing his own people.
  D. Pushmataha uses loyalty to make his point, but Tecumseh does not.
  E. Tecumseh speaks of potential problems in fighting, but Pushmataha does not.

10B. Both Tecumseh and Pushmataha support their respective arguments with a specific element, but Tecumseh relies on the element much more than Pushmataha. That element of Tecumseh's argument is
  A. his history with white men.
  B. religious justification.
  C. the horrors of war.
  D. the readiness to fight.
  E. actions of the white "fathers."

Lesson Nine

1. **pejorative** (pi jôr´ə tiv) *adj.* having a negative effect; insulting
Lenny resigned after overhearing his coworkers' *pejorative* remarks.
syn: disparaging; derogatory *ant: complimentary*

2. **masochist** (mas´ə kist) *n.* one who enjoys his or her own pain and suffering
Sue accused her friend of being a *masochist* because he refused to go to the doctor despite his broken toes.

3. **grandiose** (gran´ dēōs) *adj.* impressive; showy; magnificent
The young couple could not afford the *grandiose* home, so they found a smaller house.
syn: stately; imposing *ant: humble*

4. **idiosyncrasy** (id ēō sing´ krə sē) *n.* a peculiar personality trait
Hiding money in tin cans was only one of the old man's *idiosyncrasies.*
syn: eccentricity; quirk

5. **raiment** (rā´ mənt) *n.* clothing; garments
The royal *raiment* of the princess is copied by the fashion industry for the department-store market.

6. **nubile** (nōō´ bīl) *adj.* suitable for marriage in age and physical development, referring to a female
In six years, she grew from a skinny twelve-year-old to a *nubile* young woman.

7. **machination** (mak ə nā´ shən) *n.* an evil design or plan
Once again, the superhero foiled the *machinations* of the evil scientist.
syn: scheme; plot

8. **eclectic** (e klek´ tik) *adj.* choosing from various sources
The *eclectic* furnishings were from many different nations and historical periods.
syn: selective *ant: narrow*

9. **deride** (di rīd´) *v.* to ridicule; to mock
The unpopular professor *derided* students who made mistakes.
syn: scorn *ant: praise*

10. **sapient** (sā´pi ənt) *adj.* wise; full of knowledge
Everyone sought advice from the *sapient* monk who lived on the mountain.
syn: sagacious *ant: fatuous; inane*

11. **chimerical** (kə mer´ i kəl) *adj.* imaginary; fantastic
Little Tina had a *chimerical* notion that rabbits lived in trees.
syn: absurd; illusionary *ant: practical*

12. **finesse** (fi nes´) *n.* diplomacy; tact; artful management
The diplomat had the *finesse* to deal with the troublesome nation.
syn: skill; cunning *ant: tactlessness*

13. **heterogeneous** (het ər ə jē´ nēəs) *adj.* different; dissimilar
The platoon was a *heterogeneous* group of young men from various backgrounds.
syn: diverse; varied *ant: homogeneous; similar*

14. **blanch** (blanch) *v.* to whiten; to make pale
Sue's face *blanched* when she saw the charred remains of her house.

15. **hybrid** (hī´ brid) *n.* anything of mixed origin
The *hybrid* roses had the best traits of two different species.

Exercise I

Words in Context

From the list below, supply the words needed to complete the paragraph. Some words will not be used.

sapient	**idiosyncrasy**	**blanch**	**machination**
pejorative	**masochist**	**nubile**	**deride**
heterogeneous	**grandiose**	**raiment**	**finesse**

1. Dr. Quade still wore the __________ of a maximum-security prison inmate when he entered an abandoned warehouse to evade the searchlights of police helicopters. Six years of living without sunlight in an underground cell had __________ the color of his face, and the beatings and __________ treatment that he received from guards had left him with a perpetual scowl. Now, he mused, he would be free to carry out the __________ that he had planned during his confinement, but not before using his criminal __________ to steal an automobile from the nearby parking garage. The garage contained a[n] __________ collection of automobiles, but the __________ Dr. Quade chose a very dull, plain car to hotwire; a[n] __________ car could draw unwanted attention that jeopardized the escape.

   Even without keys, the mad genius was able to start the car in two minutes; however, he revealed a violent __________ by punching the dashboard when a light indicated that the car was low in fuel. The resulting cuts on his hands would have irritated a normal person, but not a[n] __________ like Dr. Quade. As he drove out of the garage, Dr. Quade allowed himself a chuckle as he __________ the system that had mistakenly thought it could keep him imprisoned.

From the list below, supply the words needed to complete the paragraph. Some words will not be used.

hybrid	**idiosyncrasy**	**deride**	**raiment**
eclectic	**nubile**	**chimerical**	

2. Robin's __________ art collection included paintings and sculptures from all over the world. Her favorite painting, *Consumption,* depicts a[n] __________ young woman in Victorian clothing standing amid a courtyard flower garden. A close look at the garden reveals poppies, a cypress tree, and tiny white butterflies, all of which are symbolic of illness or death. The artist painted the __________ scene during a tuberculosis epidemic, apparently to depict the ruthlessness of the illness. Robin calls *Consumption* a[n] __________ because the painting is simultaneously pleasing and depressing.

Exercise II

Sentence Completion

Complete the sentence in a way that shows you understand the meaning of the italicized vocabulary word.

1. The receptionist at the complaint department lacked the *finesse* to…
2. Madeline, who just turned two, has the *chimerical* notion that…
3. Mom has only knickknacks, but Tiffany's *eclectic* collection includes…
4. Luckily, Captain Freedom foiled Dr. X's evil *machinations* to…
5. Plant *hybrids*, like tangelos, are grown by combining…
6. Aaron was afraid of heights, so his face *blanched* when…
7. Don't consider yourself to be *sapient* just because you…
8. Within the jiggling block of lime gelatin was a *heterogeneous* mixture of…
9. The coach could not tolerate talented players who *derided*…
10. Once a tomboy, but now a *nubile* woman, Janice…
11. Good friends seldom allow an *idiosyncrasy* to…
12. Shouting *pejorative* remarks to the other team will not…
13. Compared to the elegant *raiment* of the Victorian era, the mass-produced clothing of modern society is…
14. Ned and Mary wanted to buy the *grandiose* mansion on the hill, but they…
15. In weather this frigid, only a *masochist* would want to…

Exercise III

Roots, Prefixes, and Suffixes

Study the entries and answer the questions that follow.

The prefix *dia–* means "across."
The roots *vad* and *vas* mean "go."
The roots *trud* and *trus* mean "thrust."
The root *verb* means "word."
The prefix *ab–* means "away" or "from."
The suffix *–gram* means "written."
The suffix *–meter* means "measure."
The root *tele* means "afar."

1. Using *literal* translations as guidance, define the following words without using a dictionary.

   A. diameter
   B. diagram
   C. speedometer
   D. invade
   E. evasive
   F. telegram

2. Literally, if you *intrude*, you __________, so the word *obtrusion* probably means __________.

   The word *abstruse* contains the root *trus*, but the word means "difficult to understand." Explain how *abstruse* might have acquired its meaning.

3. If you repeat someone word-for-word, then you quote that person __________.

   If you are __________, then you use too many words; if you commit *verbicide*, then you __________.

4. List as many words as you can think of that contain the prefix *ab–*.

5. List as many words as you can think of that contain the root *gram*.

Exercise IV

Inference

Complete the sentence by inferring information about the italicized word from its context.

1. The soldier's combat *raiment* contrasted with the native attire because it…

2. The ambassador's lack of *finesse* in dealing with the hostile forces caused…

3. Nancy did not like her employer, but she never made *pejorative* comments because she knew that it would…

Exercise V

Writing

Here is a writing prompt similar to the one you will find on the writing portion of an assessment test.

Plan and write an essay based on the following statement:

> In Henrik Ibsen's *A Doll's House,* Nora, a middle-class wife who struggles to find her identity, is confronted with what "defines" her. Responding to her husband, who has just told her that she is first a wife and then a mother, Nora states, "I don't believe in that anymore. I believe that, before all else, I'm a human being, no less than you—or anyway, I ought to try to become one. I know that the majority thinks you're right, Torvald, and plenty of books agree with you, too. But I can't go on believing what the majority says, or what's written in books."
>
> –an excerpt from *A Doll's House*, 1879

Assignment: Consider the ways in which people are expected to think, feel, or act, depending on their identities. Write an essay in which you discuss the ways in which society tries to define people. Consider how the roles imposed by society restrict or aid the lives of individuals. Discuss one or many roles that provide good examples for your thesis. Support your position with examples from literature, history, personal observations, or experiences.

Thesis: Write a *one-sentence* response to the above assignment. Make certain this single sentence offers a clear statement of your position.

Example: Just as Nora finds herself pigeonholed in the role of wife and mother in Henrik Isben's A Doll's House, *we are all categorized in some way and then stereotyped based on that category.*

____

____

Organizational Plan: List at least three subtopics you will use to support your main idea. This list is your outline.

1. ____

2. ____

3. ____

Draft: Following your outline, write a good first draft of your essay. Remember to support all your points with examples, facts, references to reading, etc.

Review and Revise: Exchange essays with a classmate. Using the Holistic scoring guide on page 268, score your partner's essay (while he or she scores yours). If necessary, rewrite your essay to correct the problems indicated by the essay's score.

Exercise VI

English Practice

Identifying Sentence Errors

Identify the grammatical error in each of the following sentences. If the sentence contains no error, select answer choice E.

1. After spending the day at the amusement park, (A) the children, who normally beg (B) to stay up past their bedtime, (C) was eager (D) to climb into their beds. No error (E)

2. After a long day at the office, (A) the chairman arrived at home (B) to find a dozen papers that needed his signature of approval (C) lying on his desk (D). No error (E)

3. During French class, (A) the students were taught (B) that the word *aimer* (C) is when you (D) like a person. No error (E)

4. Alot of people (A) who come to the United States from Asian countries (B) have (C) a hard time adjusting to Americans who wear shoes (D) when entering homes. No error (E)

5. Susie, who is notorious for finding the best bargains at the mall (A), bought the following, (B) a sweater to wear to the bonfire (C), three pairs of mittens for the parade, and suede jeans and a silk blouse (D) for the dance. No error (E)

Improving Sentences

The underlined portion of each sentence below contains some flaw. Select the answer choice that best corrects the flaw.

6. To gain a better view of the stars in the Grand Canyon, the astronomer adjusts his lens and then continued to monitor the meteor shower for his research.
   A. To gain a better view of the stars in the Grand Canyon the astronomer adjusted his lens and then continues to monitor the meteor shower for his research.
   B. While in the Grand Canyon, the astronomer adjusted his lens and then, to gain a better view of the stars, continued to monitor the meteor shower for his research.
   C. To gain a better view of the stars from the Grand Canyon, the astronomer adjusted his lens, and then continued to monitor the meteor shower for his research.
   D. In order to gain a better view of the stars in the Grand Canyon; the astronomer adjusted his lens and then continued to monitor the meteor shower for his research.
   E. Gaining a better view of the stars from the Grand Canyon, the astronomer adjusts his lens and then continued to monitor the meteor shower for his research.

7. Finding the perfect pet requires researching, planning, and to purchase the necessary supplies.
   A. research, planning, and the purchase of necessary supplies.
   B. researching, planning, and purchasing the necessary supplies.
   C. planning and researching supplies that will be necessary to purchase.
   D. supplies, in addition to research and planning.
   E. researching and planning which supplies to purchase.

8. There are more men teaching English when they are older than women.
   A. More men are teaching English when they are older than women.
   B. There are more men teaching English when they are older than women when they are older.
   C. There are more men teaching English than women when they are older.
   D. There are more men who are teaching English when they are older than women are.
   E. There are more older men teaching English than there are women.

9. A large suggestion box has been placed in the corridor outside the supervisor's office, shoppers can render their suggestions and concerns about the mall.
   A. office, where shoppers can render their suggestions and concerns about the mall.
   B. office: shoppers can render their suggestions and concerns about the mall.
   C. office. In this way, shoppers can render their suggestions and concerns about the mall.
   D. office; so that shoppers can use this to render their suggestions and concerns about the mall.
   E. office to render their suggestions and concerns about the mall, shoppers can use this.

10. The concert was finished at midnight, and no one went home.
    A. The concert was finished at midnight, moreover no one went home.
    B. The concert was finished at midnight, yet no one went home.
    C. The concert was finished at midnight, consequently, no one went home.
    D. The concert was finished at midnight, no one went home.
    E. The concert was finished at midnight, hence no one went home.

Review Lessons 7-9

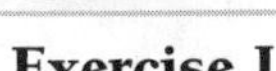

Exercise I

Inferences

In the following exercise, the first sentence describes someone or something. Infer information from the first sentence, and then choose the word from the Word Bank that best completes the second sentence.

censured	**quiddity**	**chimerical**	**imperious**
harbinger	**eclectic**	**rationalize**	**martinet**

1. The detectives all seemed to notice details that other people ignored.

   From this sentence, we can infer that paying attention to details is the __________ of a good detective.

2. Fawn likes to relax to the sound of Tuvan throat singing while she drinks Chinese gunpowder tea and reads up on the latest advances in flint knapping.

   From this sentence, we can infer that Fawn has extremely __________ interests.

3. Derek, the counselor, wanted to befriend the troubled kids, but they had a tendency to take advantage of him if he didn't enforce a strict schedule filled with boring, though consistent, activities.

   From this sentence, we can infer that Derek must be a[n] __________ to successfully handle the students in his class.

4. After quickly losing the one-on-one basketball tournament, Miles complained that the other players were not amateurs, like him, and that his new shoes did not fit well.

   From this sentence, we can infer that Miles __________ his poor performance in the tournament.

5. Janet swore that she had seen a UFO land and aliens emerge from the vessel, but not one of her friends believed her.

   From this sentence, we can infer that Janet's friends regard her UFO story as __________.

Exercise II

Related Words

Some of the vocabulary words from Lessons 7 through 9 have related meanings. Complete the following sentences by choosing the word that best fits the context, based on information you infer from the use of the italicized word. Some word pairs will be antonyms, some will be synonyms, and some will simply be words often used in the same context.

1. The __________ ninja scaled walls and rooftops with a *finesse* that took many years of training and discipline.
   A. bovine
   B. adroit
   C. sagacious
   D. grotesque
   E. eclectic

2. The newspaper opinion columnist had learned to ignore the __________ remarks in emails from readers who *derided* her because they did not agree with her opinion.
   A. macroscopic
   B. sagacious
   C. pejorative
   D. grandiose
   E. hybrid

3. A[n] __________ monk long ago offered a riddle to the traveler, and the *recondite* answer did not become clear until the travel had changed his whole perspective of life.
   A. heterogeneous
   B. grotesque
   C. macroscopic
   D. hackneyed
   E. sapient

4. Though the nation is a vastly *heterogeneous* mix of cultures, races, and ideas, political thought tends to divide the whole into a[n] __________ of "us" and "them."
   A. carcinogen
   B. harbinger
   C. dichotomy
   D. idiosyncrasy
   E. affectation

5. Anne's *sagacious* grandmother did not condemn the __________ teenagers for their inane act of vandalism because she understood their ignorance.
   A. adroit
   B. fatuous
   C. laconic
   D. patent
   E. agape

6. The ________ actress felt that any event she hosted should be a *grandiose* affair, and during such events, she ordered her staff around as though they were soldiers in boot camp.
   A. imperious
   B. grotesque
   C. hackneyed
   D. olfactory
   E. eclectic

7. The awful movie was a[n] __________ mix of *hackneyed* expressions, music, and situations found in virtually every other film in history—truly a collection of the best of the worst.
   A. sapient
   B. callow
   C. sagacious
   D. eclectic
   E. chimerical

8. Right out of college, the __________ teacher refused to become a *martinet*, no matter how troublesome her students were because it would be unfair to those who wanted to learn.
   A. macroscopic
   B. agape
   C. callow
   D. grotesque
   E. eclectic

9. Although Even spoke with a[n] __________ of confidence, his friends knew he was nervous because of his *idiosyncrasy* of laughing loudly when he is under pressure.
   A. neologism
   B. harbinger
   C. dichotomy
   D. peccadillo
   E. affectation

10. Dr. Insano __________ his latest *machinations* to seize control of the continent by reasoning that the inhabitants were too unintelligent to govern themselves.
    A. rationalized
    B. ferreted
    C. censured
    D. immolated
    E. derided

Exercise III

Deeper Meanings

Choose a word to replace the italicized word in each sentence. All of the possible choices for each sentence have similar definitions, but the correct answer will have a connotation that best suits the context. For example, the words "delete," "destroy," and "obliterate," all mean "to remove or wipe out," but no one would ever say, "I destroyed the name from the document." The correct choice will be the word with the best specific meaning and does not render the sentence awkward in tone or content. When choices seem close, look for a clue in the context that makes one choice better than the other. Note that the correct answer is not always the primary vocabulary word from the lesson.

typical	**crime**	**problem**	**hackneyed**
imperious	**show**	**intentions**	**machinations**
affectation	**failure**	**normal**	

1. Accidentally driving his car through the front of the department store was a *peccadillo* that would require Kevin to do more than simply write a check to get himself out of trouble.

   Better word: ____________________

2. Not wanting to trouble his grandma with his many worries, Luke put on a[n] *performance* of cheerfulness when he visited her this week.

   Better word: ____________________

3. This time, Dr. Insano's *ideas* revolved around his plan to turn all the city dwellers into zombies using his secret toxin.

   Better word: ____________________

4. The *tyrannical* butler seemed to become agitated when guests did not follow their usual routines.

   Better word: ____________________

5. The audience booed the stand-up comedian whose *usual* jokes had not changed at all in fifteen years.

   Better word: ____________________

Exercise IV

Crossword Puzzle

Use the clues to complete the crossword puzzle. The answers consist of vocabulary words from Lessons 7 through 9.

Across

3. the main characteristic of
6. smelly business
7. they make milk from grass
12. the tool of a phony
14. what to wear
15. wise
16. cigarettes, asbestos, radiation, etc.
17. still new at this
18. way better than you

Down

1. a mash up
2. odd trait
4. black cat; thirteen
5. all different
8. ding, dong
9. like stealing a police car
10. evil plan
11. not much for conversation
13. SO last-year

Exercise V

Subject Prompts

Here is a writing prompt similar to the one you will find on the writing portion of an assessment test. Follow the instructions below and write a brief, efficient essay.

> In 2010, the Transportation Security Administration instituted airport security measures that require pat-downs of random travelers, regardless of any suspicion of criminal intent. Now, toddlers and grandparents and convalescents are subject to intrusive hands-on searches before they are allowed to board aircraft. Detractors call it the ultimate invasion of privacy; supporters call it a necessary cost of security.
>
> Has freedom yielded to tyranny when it comes to airline travel in the United States? Where should the line be drawn? What risks, or freedoms, must be left in place in order to maintain a semblance of freedom and still be secure? Be sure to support your argument with at least three details based on examples, experiences, or your own reasoning.

Thesis: Write a *one-sentence* response to the above assignment. Make certain this single sentence offers a clear statement of your position.

Example: Airport screeners have the proper amount of authority, but they need to be permitted to use their own judgment in the screening process to avoid wasting time and alienating travelers.

____

____

Organizational Plan: List at least three subtopics you will use to support your main idea. This list is your outline.

1. ____

2. ____

3. ____

Draft: Following your outline, write a good first draft of your essay. Remember to support all your points with examples, facts, references to reading, etc.

Review and Revise: Exchange essays with a classmate. Using the scoring guide for Sentence Formation and Variety on page 266, score your partner's essay (while he or she scores yours). Focus on sentence structure and the use of language conventions. If necessary, rewrite your essay to improve the sentence structure and/or your use of language.

Lesson Ten

1. **idolatry** (ī dol´ ə trē) *n.* excessive or blind adoration; the worship of an object
The priest accused them of *idolatry* for worshipping a statue.

2. **immutable** (i myōō´ tə bəl) *adj.* unchangeable; fixed
The laws of nature are *immutable.*
syn: enduring *ant: flexible; changeable*

3. **impecunious** (im pi kyōō´ nē əs) *adj.* without money; penniless
Though *impecunious*, the man's pride prevented him from asking for help.
syn: destitute; indigent *ant: affluent; prosperous*

4. **onus** (ō´ nəs) *n.* a burden; a responsibility
When father died, Jake had the *onus* of running the farm.
syn: obligation

5. **bucolic** (byōō kol´ ik) *adj.* pertaining to the countryside; rural; rustic
The *bucolic* setting of the old inn made it a popular retreat from the city.
syn: pastoral *ant: urban*

6. **impious** (im´ pē əs) *adj.* disrespectful toward God
Some consider laughing in church to be *impious* behavior.
syn: irreligious; profane *ant: devout; pious*

7. **emanate** (em´ ə nāt) *v.* to come forth; to send forth
She tried to control her anger, but harsh words began to *emanate* from her lips.
syn: rise; emerge

8. **adulterate** (ə dul´ tə rāt) *v.* to make impure; to contaminate
The fumes from the automobiles *adulterate* the air.
syn: taint; corrupt *ant: purify; refine*

9. **garish** (gar´ ish) *adj.* tastelessly gaudy
The gypsy costumes were too *garish* for my taste.
syn: showy; glaring; flashy *ant: sedate; conservative*

10. **diadem** (dī´ ə dem´) *n.* a crown
Peter referred to his wife's blonde hair as her golden *diadem.*

11. **redolent** (red´ ə lənt) *adj.* having a pleasant odor; suggestive or evocative
The new fabric softener is advertised as being *redolent* of a spring day.
syn: aromatic *ant: acrid*

12. **sedition** (si dish´ ən) *n.* rebellion or resistance against the government
    The rebels were charged with *sedition* when they protested the new dictator.
    syn: treachery; disloyalty

13. **delineate** (di lin´ ē āt) *v.* to describe, to depict
    The politician *delineated* his disarmament proposal in great detail.

14. **gratuitous** (grə tōō´ i təs) *adj.* unnecessary or uncalled for
    He always gave *gratuitous* advice whether someone wanted it or not.

15. **caveat** (kā´ vē at) *n.* a warning
    John had so much confidence in his ability that he did not heed the old *caveat* about swimming alone.
    syn: admonition; caution

Exercise I

Words in Context

From the list below, supply the words needed to complete the paragraph. Some words will not be used.

immutable	**bucolic**	**gratuitous**	**adulterate**	**sedition**
impecunious	**delineate**	**redolent**	**emanate**	**garish**

1. Mike dreamed of leaving the loud, __________ city and returning to the __________ area where he was raised; however, his wife's opinion remained __________, and she refused to move beyond the suburbs. "Look, honey, a three-bedroom house on ten acres for half the price of our little house, and it's only an hour away; we'd actually make money if we bought it," Mike __________.

    Tara's usual opposition __________ from her mouth with little effort. "I'd rather let the smog and the crooks __________ the quality of life than the termites and mosquitoes that live in that filthy shack in the country."

    "But just imagine," Mike pleaded, "stepping outside in the morning and inhaling the air __________ of a fresh bouquet." He added __________ deep-breathing noises and satisfied "Ahhs" to make his point.

    Tara looked at him. "We would both have to sacrifice good jobs, and there's little employment out there. I really don't want to end up __________ after we've worked so hard to have nice things."

From the list below, supply the words needed to complete the paragraph. Some words will not be used.

onus	**redolent**	**diadem**	**idolatry**
caveat	**impious**	**sedition**	**bucolic**

2. The gold rush town existed solely for the __________ of the rare, yellow metal. Reverend Jerry, who arrived yesterday with the __________ of building a congregation, immediately issued __________ to the __________ establishments on Main Street, specifically the saloon and the brothel. He hoped that over time he could inspire __________ against the crooked politicians and greedy entrepreneurs that ran the boomtown; if he succeeded, Dobson City would be the __________ of the reverend's many achievements.

Exercise II

Sentence Completion

Complete the sentence in a way that shows you understand the meaning of the italicized vocabulary word.

1. *Gratuitous* handshaking is a normal routine for…
2. After the battle, the commander had the *onus* of…
3. Gina did not like spending summer in a *bucolic* setting because…
4. Dr. Ripper, the special weapons program director, *delineated* his plan to…
5. In colonial Salem, Massachusetts, people who committed *impious* acts were…
6. Some people wanted to charge the protestors with *sedition* when they…
7. Tim's mom let us borrow her car, but she included the *caveat* that if…
8. Everyone stared at Barbara's *garish* outfit when she…
9. When the neighbor's loud music *emanated* through the ceiling of the apartment, Mandy reacted by…
10. The *impecunious* family experienced a change in lifestyle when…
11. Sometimes, a fascination with television is a form of *idolatry* because we…
12. The guards took the king's *diadem* before they…
13. Leroy, who thought he was being helpful, *adulterated* the recipe by…
14. The crime boss had *immutable* authority over the town until…
15. Lisa had a broken leg, but the *redolent* flowers next to her bed helped…

Exercise III

Roots, Prefixes, and Suffixes

Study the entries and answer the questions that follow.

The roots *leg, lig,* and *lect* mean "to choose," "to read," or "to gather."
The root *neg* means "to deny."
The prefix *e–* means "out" or "from."
The prefix *re–* means "again."
The prefix *se–* means "apart."
The suffix *–ion* means "the act of."

1. Using *literal* translations as guidance, define the following words without using a dictionary.

   A. legible
   B. legion
   C. renegade
   D. negate
   E. neglect
   F. elect

2. A[n] __________ is a person who chooses specific items or types of items to gather. They often __________ items to gather by choosing the things that they need to complete whole sets.

3. The professor should know better than to __________ students for three hours without taking a break. He put forth so much information that few can __________, or *remember*, the subjects covered during the beginning of the speech.

4. If you deny a promise that you made to purchase something, you are said to __________ on the deal.

5. The word *legend* contains a root that means "to read." Explain the possible reason for the word *legend* containing the root *leg*.

Exercise IV

Inference

Complete the sentence by inferring information about the italicized word from its context.

1. As cities expand, *bucolic* areas that once featured barns and old forests are now host to…

2. You should have taken seriously my *caveat* about speeding because now you are…

3. Ernest was Blake's best friend, so when Blake died in combat, Ernest had the *onus* of…

Exercise V

Critical Reading

Below is a reading passage followed by several multiple-choice questions. Carefully read the passage and choose the best answer for each of the questions.

Alice Meynell (1847-1922), was an English poet and writer. The following passage reveals her perspective on what she describes as "decivilized" nations.

The difficulty of dealing—in the course of any critical duty—with decivilized man lies in this: when you accuse him of vulgarity—sparing him no doubt the word—he defends himself against the charge of barbarism. Especially from new soil—remote, colonial—he faces you, bronzed, with a half conviction of savagery, partly persuaded of his own youthfulness of race. He writes, and recites, poems about ranches and canyons; they are designed to betray the recklessness of his nature and to reveal the good that lurks in the lawless ways of a young society. He is there to explain himself, voluble, with a glossary for his own artless slang. But his colonialism is only provincialism very articulate. The new air does but make old decadences seem more stale; the young soil does but set into fresh conditions the ready-made, the uncostly, the refuse feeling of a race decivilizing. He who played long this pattering part of youth, hastened to assure you with so self-denying a face he did not wear war-paint and feathers, that it became doubly difficult to communicate to him that you had suspected him of nothing wilder than a second-hand (figurative) dress coat. And when it was a question not of rebuke, but of praise, even the American was ill-content with the word of the judicious who lauded him for some delicate successes in continuing something of the literature of England, something of the art of France; he was more eager for the applause that stimulated him to write poems in prose form and to paint panoramic landscape, after brief training in academies of native inspiration. Even now English voices are constantly calling upon America to begin—to begin, for the world is expectant. Whereas there is no beginning for her, but instead a fine and admirable continuity which only a constant care can guide into sustained advance.

But decivilized man is not peculiar to new soil. The English town, too, knows him in all his dailiness. In England, too, he has a literature, an art, a music, all his own—derived from many and various things of price. Trash, in the fullness of its simplicity and cheapness, is impossible without a beautiful past. Its chief characteristic—which is futility, not failure—could not be achieved but by the long abuse, the rotatory reproduction, the quotidian disgrace, of the utterances of Art, especially the utterance by words. Gaiety, vigour, vitality, the organic quality, purity, simplicity, precision—all these are among the antecedents of trash. It is after them; it is also, alas, because of them. And nothing can be much sadder that such a proof of what may possibly be the failure of derivation.

Evidently we cannot choose our posterity. Reversing the steps of time, we may, indeed choose backwards. We may give our thoughts noble forefathers. Well begotten, well born our fancies must be; they shall be also well derived. We have a voice in decreeing our inheritance, and not our inheritance only, but our heredity. Our minds may trace upwards and follow their ways to the best well-heads of the arts. The very habit of our thoughts may be persuaded one way unawares by their antenatal history. Their companions must be lovely, but need be no lovelier than their ancestors; and being so fathered and so husbanded, our thoughts may be entrusted to keep the counsels of literature.

Such is our confidence in a descent we know. But, of a sequel which of us is sure? Which of us is secured against the dangers of subsequent depreciation? And, moreover, which of us shall trace the contemporary tendencies, the one towards honor, the other towards dishonor? Or who shall discover why derivation becomes degeneration, and where and when and how the bastardy befalls? The decivilized have every grace as the antecedent of their vulgarities, every distinction as the precedent of their mediocrities. No ballad-concert song, feign it sigh, frolic, or laugh, but has the excuse that the feint was suggested, was made easy, by some living sweetness once. Nor are the decivilized to blame as having in their own persons possessed civilization and marred it. They did not possess it; they were born into some tendency to derogation, into an inclination for things mentally inexpensive. And the tendency can hardly do other than continue.

Nothing can look duller than the future of this second-hand and multiplying world. Men need not be common merely because they are many; but the infection of commonness once begun in the many, what dullness in their future! To the eye that has reluctantly discovered this truth—that the vulgarized are not *un*-civilized, and that there is no growth for them—it does not look like a future at all. More ballad-concerts, more quaint English, more robustious baritone songs, more piecemeal pictures, more colonial poetry, more young nations with withered traditions. Yet it is before this prospect that the provincial overseas lifts up his voice in a boast or a promise common enough among the incapable young, but pardonable only in senility. He promises the world a literature, an art, that shall be new because his forest is untracked and his town just built. But what the newness is to be he cannot tell. Certain words were dreadful once in the mouth of desperate old age. Dreadful and pitiable as the threat of an impotent king, what shall we name them when they are the promise of an impotent people? "I will do such things: what they are yet I know not."

1A. Through the author's use of the phrase "artless slang" in line 7, a reader can infer that
  A. the author has never left England.
  B. colonists speak in monotones.
  C. the author dislikes the colonial dialect.
  D. the passage is written for artists.
  E. the author is a professor of language.

1B. Choose the descriptive words from the context that best support your answer to question 1A.
  A. critical, bronzed
  B. voluble, articulate
  C. pattering, wilder
  D. savages, vulgarity
  E. youthfulness, ill-content

2A. As used in line 8, *provincialism* most nearly means
  A. newness.
  B. uncertainty.
  C. narrow-mindedness.
  D. over-confidence.
  E. fear of art.

2B. Lines 7-8 suggest that colonialism is
  A. equal to provincialism.
  B. preferred over provincialism.
  C. worse than provincialism.
  D. not as articulate as provincialism.
  E. sought by most provincial inhabitants.

3A. The author uses the word *decivilized* versus *uncivilized* because the decivilized people
   A. have more than normal civility.
   B. are at the height of style.
   C. never had any civilization.
   D. do not like outsiders.
   E. lost their civility.

3B. Which best paraphrases the following quotation?

   "Whereas there is no beginning for her [America], but instead a fine and admirable continuity which only a constant care can guide into sustained advance."

   A. Europeans are experts in colonization; however, most colonies reject English culture in the years following the opening of trade relations.
   B. American culture has no real beginning; it is simply a continuation of English culture, and it requires guidance in order to properly advance.
   C. No one has traced ancient American history far enough to determine when the continent was first settled.
   D. English culture is the foundation for any nation that began as a colony, except for America, which has its own native culture and atmosphere.
   E. America will fail without the help of England.

4A. Where, according to the author, can "decivilized men" be found?
   A. England and France
   B. America and France
   C. Germany and Canada
   D. West Virginia and England
   E. American and English towns

4B. Decivilized men in both the New World and the old world are prone to what behavior, according to the author?
   A. reusing old ideas and calling them original
   B. failing to explain their sources of inspiration
   C. becoming too defensive when questioned
   D. basing their art on disgraceful trend in art history
   E. creating art better than the mediocre original works

5A. In lines 28-29, "failure of derivation" refers to
   A. the failure to prevent the spread of English art.
   B. the failure to improve upon existing cultural achievements.
   C. the failure to acknowledge the history of trash.
   D. the failure to apply higher mathematics to the arts.
   E. the failure to stop the reproduction of European art and literature.

5B. Where does "trash" come from, according to the author?
   A. misguided, modern ideas
   B. the worst elements of historic art trends
   C. the corruption of valuable art
   D. new trends that have no monetary value
   E. the new World, under the guise of poetry

6A. In the third paragraph, the author suggests traveling backwards in time for the purpose of
   A. protecting artistic and literary traditions from corruption.
   B. warning ancestors about the destiny of their achievements.
   C. learning the art secrets of ancestors.
   D. persuading colonists to abstain from dabbling in art and literature.
   E. escaping a dire present time.

6B. In paragraph 3, the author offers an analogy that describes art trends in terms of
   A. time travel.
   B. stars burning out.
   C. new-world savagery.
   D. people with family trees.
   E. improving when paired with lesser thoughts.

7A. According to the fourth paragraph, why should the decivilized not be blamed for defiling civilization?
   A. Decivilized people do not know right from wrong.
   B. They never really had civilization, so they couldn't have ruined it.
   C. They began their civilization from scratch.
   D. Decivilized people are instructed by errant founding fathers.
   E. They lacked any formal education programs.

7B. Choose the quotation that best supports your answer to question 7A.
   A. "Nor are the decivilized to blame…"
   B. "Their companions must be lovely…"
   C. "…they were born…into an inclination for things mentally inexpensive."
   D. "Men need not be common merely because they are many…"
   E. "No…song…was made easy, by some living sweetness once."

8A. As used in line 46, *derogation* most nearly means
   A. an indifference toward other people.
   B. a willingness to try new things.
   C. an adaptation to austere climates.
   D. a relaxation of standards.
   E. a defense of their own ways.

8B. The implication of the word *derogation,* as it applies to the decivilized, is that they
   A. have unlimited resources.
   B. are not challenged to do better.
   C. move too slowly and thus miss the latest trends.
   D. tend to criticize what they don't understand.
   E. are hyper-aware of their delayed art movement.

9A. Which of the following best describes the tone of this passage?
   A. affectionate
   B. condescending
   C. detached
   D. friendly
   E. scathing

9B. According to the author, those who claim to have new ideas—without knowing what the ideas are—mentally resemble whom?
   A. the authors of ballads
   B. young nations seeking literary traditions
   C. the un-civilized
   D. the well-heads of the arts
   E. the very young and the very old

10A. The purpose of this passage is to
   A. belittle the traditions of colonists.
   B. explain the differences between colonies and provinces.
   C. inform about the cessation of progress in civilization.
   D. entertain through satire.
   E. argue against granting statehood to the colonies.

10B. Who is at the greatest risk of the effects of decivilization, according to the author?
   A. the uncivilized
   B. people in America or other colonies
   C. artists, authors, and musicians
   D. all of mankind
   E. royalty and those who commission works of art

Lesson Eleven

1. **desiccated** (des´ i kāt´ ed) *adj.* dried up
When she opened the old scrapbook, a *desiccated* rose fell to the floor.

2. **cessation** (se sā´ shən) *n.* a stopping; a discontinuance
There was a *cessation* in the battle, but everyone knew that the shooting would begin again.
syn: ceasing; end *ant: beginning; commencement*

3. **kinetic** (ki net´ ik) *adj.* pertaining to motion
To demonstrate *kinetic* energy, he threw a steel ball across the lab.

4. **juxtapose** (juk stə pōz´) *v.* to place side-by-side for comparison
To better understand your options, *juxtapose* the good things with the bad.
syn: measure; examine

5. **elixir** (i lik´ sər) *n.* a supposed remedy for all ailments
The old woman had a secret *elixir* that she claimed would cure a cold in a day.
syn: medicine; panacea

6. **scintillate** (sin´ til āt) *v.* to sparkle; to twinkle; to sparkle intellectually
The lights *scintillated* throughout the otherwise drab room.

7. **epitome** (i pit´ ə mē) *n.* a typical example
As she attended to the comfort of her guests, she was the *epitome* of southern hospitality.
syn: embodiment; archetype

8. **legerdemain** (lej´ ər di mān´) *n.* sleight of hand; deception
The magician's act was an extraordinary feat of *legerdemain.*

9. **lachrymose** (lak´ rə mōs) *adj.* tearful, weepy
It was time for Debbie to get over her *lachrymose* behavior and start smiling again.

10. **garrulous** (gar´ ə ləs) *adj.* talkative
We didn't think that the *garrulous* salesman would ever leave.
syn: loquacious; verbose *ant: taciturn*

11. **fetish** (fet´ ish) *n.* an object that receives respect or devotion
The totem pole was a *fetish* of the tribe.
syn: charm; talisman

12. **fissure** (fish´ ər) *n.* an opening; a groove; a split
The earthquake created *fissures* that swallowed cars and buildings.

13. **languid** (lang´ gwid) *adj.* sluggish; drooping from weakness
The hot summer day made everyone *languid.*
syn: listless; feeble; drooping *ant: robust; vigorous*

14. **defile** (di fīl´) *v.* to pollute; to corrupt
The oil spill *defiled* the entire bay.

15. **libertine** (lib´ ər tēn) *n.* one who leads an immoral life
He pretended to be righteous during the day, but he was a *libertine* at night.
syn: hedonist; glutton; epicurean

Exercise I

Words in Context

From the list below, supply the words needed to complete the paragraph. Some words will not be used.

defile fissure juxtapose cessation fetish kinetic
epitome elixir desiccated garrulous libertine

1. For months, there had been __________ arguments, sometimes even heated and angry ones, by members of the city council over the proposed casino to be built just beyond the city limits. At the __________ of the controversy over the proposal, opponents argued that a casino would __________ the city by attracting __________ and other unwanted elements. Dozens of pawn shops and payday-loan businesses would follow, so the gambling addicts could devote every last penny to their destructive __________.

   "Well, of course the idea sounds bad if you __________ legal gambling against the tiny number of criminals who might come into the city," said Mr. Taylor. "But in reality, it will be normal, everyday people who benefit from the tax revenues of the casino—not kingpins and mobsters. We are already facing a loss of revenue from the __________ of production at the local glass factory. Our __________ maintenance budget needs to be replenished, and the casino would do just that."

   Ms. Hartford spoke in response. "I know that the city is suffering, but the casino is not a[n] __________ that could instantly cure our unemployment problem. It would only make up for half of the jobs lost at the factory."

   The proposed casino had caused a[n] __________ in the council; it would take three additional meetings to make a final decision.

From the list below, supply the words needed to complete the paragraph. Some words will not be used.

legerdemain kinetic juxtapose scintillate
lachrymose languid fissure fetish

2. Madeline cried when she scratched her knee, but her __________ expression disappeared when her grandpa sat down in the swing beside her. Her eyes, still damp, __________ beneath the bright June sun, and she stared in amazement when grandpa used __________ to make it appear as though he pulled a quarter from behind Madeline's ear. Madeline smiled, jumped out of the swing, and ran to the sandbox. Grandpa, __________ from the oppressive heat, marveled at his granddaughter's constant __________ motion; Madeline appeared to have limitless energy, even on such a hot day.

Exercise II

Sentence Completion

Complete the sentence in a way that shows you understand the meaning of the italicized vocabulary word.

1. A falling brick has more *kinetic* energy than…
2. Tammy was *lachrymose* for two days after…
3. The ugly graffiti *defiled*…
4. The *desiccated* grease on the bearings of the motor caused…
5. Mr. Foster snapped when the *garrulous* students…
6. When the skiers saw that they were approaching a *fissure* in the glacier, they…
7. Using his *legerdemain*, the pickpocket…
8. The *cessation* of the riot occurred when…
9. People called Theresa the *epitome* of human compassion because she…
10. Mayor Giuliani closed the shops that attracted *libertines* to Center City because he…
11. The sequins on the prom dress *scintillated* when…
12. The senator *juxtaposed* the landfill and recent complaints from the community in order to…
13. Captain Still knew that the engine room crew was *languid* from…
14. Clive liked most classic automobiles, but his *fetish* was…
15. I knew the *elixir* was a scam because…

Exercise III

Roots, Prefixes, and Suffixes

Study the entries and answer the questions that follow.

The root *ver* means "true."
The root *fic* means "to do" or "to make."
The root *cra* means "to mix."
The root *sacr* means "sacred."
The root *idi* means "peculiar" or "one's own."
The prefix *e–* means "completely."
The prefix *pro–* means "in front of."
The suffix *–fy* means "to make."
The prefix *suf–* means "under."
The root *syn* means "together."

1. Using *literal* translations as guidance, define the following words without using a dictionary.

   A. verify
   B. very
   C. suffice
   D. sacrifice
   E. idiom
   F. idiot

2. A *veracious* person will tell the __________ while under oath so that the jury can make a good __________ about the case.

3. Explain why the word *crater* contains a root that means "to mix." If you need a starting point, consider the physical shape of a crater.

4. Doing good deeds will be __________ to your community.

   If a machine can do its job with little fuel or wasted energy, then it is said to be __________.

   A[n] __________ worker can complete a job before any of the other workers.

Exercise IV

Inference

Complete the sentence by inferring information about the italicized word from its context.

1. A *cessation* of fighting in the war-torn region allowed the residents…

2. The team asked the coach to *delineate* the complicated instructions because…

3. When Monica is in a hurry, she doesn't start conversations with her *garrulous* neighbor because…

Exercise V

Writing

Here is a writing prompt similar to the one you will find on the writing portion of an assessment test.

Plan and write an essay on the following statement:

All that is gold does not glitter,
Not all those who wander are lost;
The old that is strong does not wither,
Deep roots are not reached by the frost.

–an excerpt from J.R.R. Tolkien's *The Lord of the Rings*

Assignment: This oft-quoted poem has many shades of meaning. Write an essay in which you explain how Tolkien's poem applies to a part of your life. Support your points with evidence from your own reading, classroom studies, personal observations, and experience.

Thesis: Write a *one-sentence* response to the above statement. Make certain this single sentence offers a clear statement of your position.

Example: So many people spend their lives chasing something they think they want only to realize that they don't even know what they want.

____

____

Organizational Plan: List at least three subtopics you will use to support your main idea. This list is your outline.

1. ____

2. ____

3. ____

Draft: Following your outline, write a good first draft of your essay. Remember to support all your points with examples, facts, references to reading, etc.

Review and Revise: Exchange essays with a classmate. Using the scoring guide for Organization on page 263, score your partner's essay (while he or she scores yours). Focus on the organizational plan and the use of language conventions. If necessary, rewrite your essay to improve the organizational plan and/or your use of language.

Exercise VI

English Practice

Improving Paragraphs

Read the following passage and then answer the multiple-choice questions that follow. The questions will require you to make decisions regarding the revision of the reading selection.

1 Few substances are as useful, beautiful, and plentiful as glass; it's practical and decorative uses are practically limitless. The ancient Mesopotamians discovered glass around 3500 B.C.E., when potters, who were making glazes for pottery, accidentally combined calciferous sand with soda ash. This early technique allowed them to make a variety of glass beads, seals, and plaques. Ornamental glass had been discovered.

2 The Roman Empire turned glass manufacturing into an industry by building furnaces that increased the production and quality of glass. By 100 C.E., Roman architects were incorporating glass windows in buildings. The glass was far from flawless and transparent like the glass of the present, but the windows did allow light into otherwise dark homes.

3 Before the Roman Empire, in 1500 B.C.E., Egyptian craftsmen covered compacted sand molds with molten glass in order to form the first glass vases. The craft quickly spread throughout Mesopotamia due to Egypt's influence through trade. In 27 B.C.E., Syrian artists discovered how to blow glass, which allowed them to craft a variety of glass shapes.

4 When the Roman Empire crumbled, the glass industry diversified. Geographic regions adopted their own unique methods and styles of glassmaking; southern regions, for example, used soda ash in production, while northern areas replaced soda ash with potash—an abundant material in the forested landscapes of the north.

5 Medieval architects further developed Roman glass by dyeing it different colors, and then combining the various colors of glass to form single windows. In the eleventh century, the multi-colored glass, or stained-glass windows, filled churches and palaces and **scintillated** with exquisite light.

6 German glassmakers took glassmaking to the next step by cutting sheets from long cylinders of molten glass. The new type of glass became known as sheet glass, or crown glass. In the mid-seventeenth century, Venice lost its dominance in glassmaking when the Englishman George Ravenscroft replaced potash with lead oxide and combined it with quartz sand. The combination produced highly reflective glass. Germans added lime to potash, which resulted in yet another variation of glass. Milch glass, as it is called, had the opaque white color of porcelain.

7 As the Middle Ages faded to the Renaissance, glassmaking guilds flourished, and many laws were created to protect each region's secret technique. At the time, Venice was the center of the industry, and the laws helped the city to maintain a monopoly on glass production; however, artists in cities such as Murano were experimenting with new mixtures of glass. Murano glassmakers replaced calciferous sand with quartz sand to produce a unique, crystal-like glass.

8 In 1688, France improved the production of plate glass. Used in mirrors. By pouring molten glass onto specially designed tables and then by polishing it with felt disks, French artisans created glass that could reflect images with little or no visual distortion. The newfound plate-glass technique resulted in the creation of the famous Hall of Mirrors in the Palace of Versailles. In the eighteenth century, cut glass became popular. Crystal-like in appearance and very reflective, cut glass was used for dishes and vases, as well as exquisite glass chandeliers.

9 A **fissure** split the glass industry at the end of the nineteenth century. Some artists followed the Art Nouveau style, in which designs mirrored elements of nature. The "new" artists saw their work as explorations of artistic expressions rather than mediums of practical application. Other artists embraced the new, efficient glassmaking methods that sprang from the industrial revolution, whereby bottles, jars, and plate glass could be produced by machines at a fraction of the cost of the handmade items.

10 Today, the two divisions of glassmakers continue in the traditions of early glassmakers. New manufacturing techniques constantly increase the strength and versatility of glass, and artists continue to explore new styles that ensure glass is as pleasing to the eye as it is practical. The long history of glass, and its timeless use, ensures that it will exist for centuries to come.

1. Which of the following changes would fix a grammatical error in paragraph 1?
   A. Delete *B.C.E.*
   B. Spell *Mesopotamians* with a lower case *M*.
   C. Capitalize *ancient*.
   D. Change *it's* to *its*.
   E. Delete the first sentence.

2. Which of the following changes in paragraph order would correct the chronology of the passage?
   A. 1, 2, 3, 4
   B. 1, 3, 2, 4
   C. 3, 1, 2, 4
   D. 1, 4, 2, 3
   E. 3, 4, 1, 2

3. Which of the following changes to paragraph 7 would improve the flow of the passage?
   A. Delete paragraph 7.
   B. Describe the location of Murano.
   C. Combine paragraph 7 with paragraph 8.
   D. Begin the passage with paragraph 7.
   E. Move paragraph 7 to follow paragraph 5.

4. Which of the following describes an error in paragraph 8?
   A. sentence fragment
   B. split infinitive
   C. cliché
   D. dangling modifier
   E. improper pronoun use

5. Paragraph 8 should not
   A. include a reference to the Hall of Mirrors because it is irrelevant to the subject.
   B. be included in the passage because it detracts from the topic.
   C. include the last two sentences because they belong in a separate paragraph.
   D. begin with a prepositional phrase because it is incorrect.
   E. fail to further explain the process of making cut glass.

Lesson Twelve

1. **badinage** (bad n äzh´) *n.* playful, teasing talk
   What began as *badinage* quickly escalated to cutting insults.
   syn: chaff; joshing

2. **debauchery** (di bô´ chə rē) *n.* corruption; self-indulgence
   Sam was once wealthy, but a life of gambling and *debauchery* left him with nothing.
   syn: excess; dissipation

3. **necromancy** (nek´ rə man´ sē) *n.* magic, especially that practiced by a witch
   Puritans often executed people who had supposedly practiced *necromancy*.
   syn: black magic; conjuring

4. **blandishment** (blan´ dish mənt) *n.* flattery
   The salesman's *blandishments* did not convince me to buy the expensive watch.
   syn: overpraise; bootlicking

5. **fastidious** (fa stid´ ē əs) *adj.* hard to please; fussy
   My neighbor is a *fastidious* housekeeper.
   syn: meticulous; exacting *ant: casual; lax*

6. **halcyon** (hal´ sē ən) **adj.** calm; pleasant
   The severe windstorm interrupted the otherwise *halcyon* week.
   syn: tranquil; unruffled *ant: troubled; tumultuous*

7. **malapropism** (mal´ ə prop iz´ m) *n.* a word humorously misused
   He used a *malapropism* when he said "conspire" in place of "inspire."

8. **garner** (gär´ nər) *v.* to gather; to acquire
   During the fall harvest, extra workers were hired to *garner* the crops.
   syn: harvest

9. **kismet** (kiz´ met) *n.* destiny; fate; fortune (one's lot in life)
   She thought is was *kismet* for her to be a veterinarian until she failed her biology lab.

10. **hegira** (hi jī´ rə) *n.* flight; escape
    The flooding caused a mass *hegira* from the city.

11. **paradigm** (par´ ə dīm) *n.* a model; an example
    The class regarded Kate as a *paradigm* of good manners.

12. **ambiance** (am bē ons´) *n.* the mood or quality of
The *ambiance* of the Alaskan cabin inspired the poet much more than his cramped apartment in town did.
syn: milieu

13. **regress** (ri gres´) *v.* to move backward
If he took the job offer, Tim felt that his career might *regress* rather than move forward.

14. **bilious** (bil´ yəs) *adj.* bad tempered; cross
No one could stand being in the same room with Sam when he was in a *bilious* mood.
syn: grouchy; cantankerous *ant: pleasant*

15. **gumption** (gump´ shən) *n.* courage and initiative; common sense
It takes a lot of *gumption* to succeed in this fast-paced society.
syn: enterprise; aggressiveness; drive

Exercise I

Words in Context

From the list below, supply the words needed to complete the paragraph. Some words will not be used.

bilious	**ambiance**	**hegira**	**halcyon**
garner	**paradigm**	**blandishment**	**malapropism**
necromancy	**fastidious**		

1. It took eight years for Megan to __________ the materials that she needed to make her front lawn the __________ of landscape design. Though she is __________ about maintaining the lawn, she never allows herself to become __________ when the neighbor's playful children accidentally trample some of the flowers. The children always apologized, and the younger girl's darling use of the __________ "scrubbers" instead of "shrubs" made her far too adorable to scold.

   Deep down, Megan didn't care what people thought of her yard; she didn't construct it to receive the __________ of other gardeners. Megan just wanted a[n] __________ place in which she could relax or entertain guests. She also thought that the natural __________ would inspire her writing.

   When Megan wasn't working on her verdant courtyard, she was typing the manuscript for her first fantasy novel, a tale of sorcerers, goblins, and __________.

From the list below, supply the words needed to complete the paragraph. Some words will not be used.

gumption	**debauchery**	**garner**	**regress**	**hegira**
badinage	**kismet**	**bilious**		

2. The quality of life in Omar's homeland __________ so much that people ate roots to survive. The __________ of the crooked politicians in the former government had consumed any available relief funds. Fearing the unpredictable warlords looting villages, Omar gathered his family and joined the __________ from the war-torn region.

   The thought of a better life gave Omar the __________ to make the arduous trek with his wife and two children. The children fared well, despite the harsh conditions of the journey; at night, the __________ between the children revealed that their __________ of having to flee from a burning homeland had not entirely ruined their childhood.

Exercise II

Sentence Completion

Complete the sentence in a way that shows you understand the meaning of the italicized vocabulary word.

1. Stanley did not send Phil to meet with the investors because Phil's *bilious* manner might…
2. The *fastidious* youngster refused to eat unless the…
3. The rebels took over the island nation, but rampant *debauchery* in the new government caused…
4. After the detective *garnered* enough evidence to place the suspect at the crime scene, she…
5. Jimmy thought that football was his *kismet* in life until he…
6. Unless the depressing *ambiance* of the office changes, the employees will continue to…
7. Joe's condition *regressed* at the hospital because…
8. The bus driver was not easily distracted, but the *badinage* among the children…
9. Bernard, who was once a penniless immigrant, used his *gumption* to…
10. Molly was the *paradigm* of managers, so the executives…
11. When Bert used the *malapropism* "fire distinguisher" in place of "fire extinguisher," the English professor knew…
12. The salesperson at the expensive fashion shop used *blandishments* to…
13. The old witch practiced *necromancy* to…
14. The religious pilgrims made a *hegira* to the holy shrine because…
15. As an old man, Trey remembered the *halcyon* times…

Exercise III

Roots, Prefixes, and Suffixes

Study the entries and answer the questions that follow.

The root *greg* means "flock" or "herd."
The roots *val* and *vail* mean "to be strong" or "to be worthy."
The roots *ven*, *vent*, and *venu* mean "to come to" or "to approach."
The prefix *co–* means "with" or "together."
The prefix *e–* means "out" or "from."
The prefix *seg–* means "apart."
The prefix *a–* means "away" or "from."
The prefix *ambi–* means "both" or "around."
The prefix *in–* means "not."

1. Using *literal* translations as guidance, define the following words without using a dictionary.

   A. advent
   B. covenant
   C. ambivalent
   D. egregious
   E. invalid
   F. valiant

2. If you come to exciting places, then you might be a[n] __________-seeker. The last day of your vacation will approach rapidly, so __________ you will have to go home, but not before you purchase a[n] __________ to remind you of the trip. If you didn't enjoy the trip, then you might explore different approaches, or __________, to your next getaway.

3. __________ people enjoy the company of others; they often congregate on the weekend for dinner or conversation.

   Concrete mixed with rocks is a[n] __________ solution because you could break it up and __________ the rocks from the concrete if you wanted to.

4. The brave soldier received a medal for __________ in combat after his battalion __________ over the enemy forces.

Exercise IV

Inference

Complete the sentence by inferring information about the italicized word from its context.

1. Autumn needed to *garner* information about her family's history, and she began the task by...

2. Brianna feels that her *kismet* in life is to be a doctor, so she is going to...

3. When Jared leaves empty pizza boxes on the living room floor, his *fastidious* roommate...

Exercise V

Critical Reading

Below is a pair of reading passages followed by several multiple-choice questions. Carefully read the passages and choose the best answer to each of the questions.

The first passage, adapted from English writer-philosopher John Stuart Mill's 1859 essay "On Liberty," emphasizes the importance of individuality among tyrannical majorities. The second passage, from 1776, is an excerpt from Adam Smith's book, The Wealth of Nations. *Adam Smith's philosophies helped to inspire the creation of America's free-market capitalist economy. In this passage, the Scottish philosopher explains that the division of labor is a product of self-interest—the natural force that drives all human activity.*

Passage 1

In sober truth, whatever homage may be professed, or even paid, to real or supposed mental superiority, the general tendency of things throughout the world is to render mediocrity the ascendant power among mankind. In ancient history, in the middle ages, and in a diminishing degree through the long transition from feudality to the present time, the individual was power in himself; and if he had either great talents or a high social position, he was a considerable power. At present, individuals are lost in the crowd. In politics, it is almost a triviality to say that public opinion now rules the world. The only power deserving the name is that of masses, and of governments while they make themselves the organ of the tendencies and instincts of masses. This is as true in the moral and social relations of private life as in public transactions. Those whose opinions go by the name of public opinion, are not always the same sort of public: in America, they are the whole white population; in England, chiefly the middle class. But they are always a mass, that is to say, collective mediocrity. And what is still greater novelty, the mass do not now take their opinions from dignitaries in Church or State, from ostensible leaders, or from books. Their thinking is done for them by men much like themselves, addressing them or speaking in their name, on the spur of the moment, through the newspapers. I am not complaining of all this. I do not assert that anything better is compatible, as a general rule, with the present low state of the human mind. But that does not hinder the government of mediocrity from being mediocre government. No government by a democracy or a numerous aristocracy, either in its political acts or in the opinions, qualities, and tone of mind which it fosters, ever did or could rise above mediocrity, except in so far as the sovereign Many have let themselves be guided (which in their best times they always have done) by the counsels and influence of a more highly gifted and instructed One or Few. The initiation of all wise or noble things, comes and must come from individuals; generally at first from some one individual. The honor and glory of the average man is that he is capable of following that initiative; that he can respond internally to wise and noble things, and be led to them with his eyes open. I am not countenancing the sort of "hero-worship" which applauds the strong man of genius for forcibly seizing on the government of the world and making it do his bidding in spite of itself. All he can claim is freedom to point out the way. The power of compelling others into it, is not only inconsistent with the freedom and development of all the rest, but corrupting to the strong man himself. It does seem, however, that when the opinions of masses of merely average men are everywhere become or becoming the dominant power, the counterpoise and corrective to that tendency would be the more and more pronounced individuality of those who stand on the higher eminences of thought. It is in these circumstances most especially that exceptional individuals, instead of being deterred, should be encouraged in acting differently from the mass. In other times there was no advantage in their doing so, unless they acted not only differently, but better. In this age, the mere example of non-conformity, the mere refusal to bend the knee to custom, is itself a service. Precisely because the tyranny of opinion is such as to make eccentricity a reproach, it is desirable, in order to break through that tyranny, that people should be eccentric. Eccentricity has always abounded when and where strength of character has abounded; and the amount of eccentricity in a society has generally been proportional to the amount of genius, mental vigor, and moral courage which it contained. That so few now dare to be eccentric marks the chief danger of the time.

Passage 2

Division of labor, from which so many advantages are derived, is not originally the effect of any human wisdom which foresees and intends that general opulence to which it gives occasion. It is the necessary, though very slow and gradual, consequence of a certain propensity in human nature...to truck, barter and exchange one thing for another.

In almost every other race of animals, each individual animal, when it is grown up to maturity, is entirely independent, and in its natural state has the occasion for the assistance of no other living creature.

But man has almost constant occasion for the help of his brethren, and it is in vain for him to expect it from their benevolence only. He will be more likely to prevail if he can interest their self-love in his favor and show them that it is for their own advantage to do for him what he requires of them.

It is not from the benevolence of the butcher, the brewer or the baker that we expect our dinner, but from their regard to their own interest. We address ourselves not to their humanity, but to their self-love, and never talk to them of our own necessities, but of their advantages.

As it is by treaty, by barter, and by purchase that we obtain from one another the greater part of those mutual good offices which we stand in need of, so it is this same trucking disposition which originally gives occasion to the division of labor. In a tribe of hunters or shepherds, a particular person makes bows and arrows, for example, with more readiness and dexterity than any other. He frequently exchanges them for cattle or venison with his companions; and he finds at last that he can in this manner get more cattle and venison than if he himself went to the field to catch them.

From a regard to his own interest, therefore, the making of bows and arrows grows to be his chief business, and he becomes a sort of armorer. Another excels in making the frames and covers of their little huts or movable houses. He is accustomed to be of use in this way to his neighbors, who reward him in the same manner with cattle and venison, till at last he finds it his interest to dedicate himself entirely to this employment, to become a sort of house carpenter. In the same manner a third becomes a smith or a brazier; a fourth, a tanner or dresser of hides or skins.

And thus, the certainty of being able to exchange all that surplus part of the produce of his own labor, which is over and above his own consumption, for such parts of the produce of other men's labor as he may have occasion for, encourages every man to apply himself to a particular occupation, and to cultivate and bring to perfection whatever talent or genius he may possess for that particular species of business.

1A. As used throughout the first passage, *mediocrity* most nearly means
   A. of no exceptional quality.
   B. out-of-tune.
   C. of a boring nature.
   D. unintelligent.
   E. of no origin.

1B. Which phrase from passage 1 best supports your answer to question 1A?
   A. "break through that tyranny"
   B. "All he can claim is freedom"
   C. "public opinion now rules the world"
   D. "refusal to bend the knee to custom"
   E. "individuals are lost in the crowd"

2A. According to the first passage, it is inevitable that people will
   A. allow democratic governments to turn socialist.
   B. elect intelligent, independent government representatives.
   C. allow themselves to be imprisoned.
   D. allow themselves to be governed by mediocre people making dull decisions.
   E. make foolish decisions about their own futures.

2B. The answer to questions 2A, in the author's opinion, is a result of
   A. the rise of a growing upper class.
   B. the decrease of power and importance of the individual.
   C. strong people outnumbering the weak people.
   D. medieval ideas of government.
   E. the separation of church and state.

3A. The author of the first passage probably believes that
   A. people should avoid any form of government.
   B. the government should consist of two or three people at most.
   C. the decision of one wise individual is preferable to one made by a group of ordinary people.
   D. it is unethical to produce so much of a product that there is a surplus.
   E. wise individuals generally make better decisions than groups of wise individuals, but if the group gets too small, it makes mediocre decisions.

3B. A democratic government is not in danger of becoming *mediocre*, according to passage 1, because
   A. governments are run by individuals.
   B. only talented groups of people make up the government.
   C. governments naturally tend to tyranny.
   D. democratic governments can vote representatives out if necessary.
   E. governments of many are naturally mediocre.

4A. According to passage 1, the "honor and glory of the average man" is
   A. his ability to follow wise and noble ideas.
   B. his desire to be remembered.
   C. his readiness to accept public opinion.
   D. his penchant for intelligent conversation.
   E. his many technological achievements through hard work.

4B. The author contends that the masses don't think for themselves; however, because of a prolific news media, the thinking is, at least, done by
   A. the leaders of non-governmental organizations.
   B. governments who control the media.
   C. their equals—like-minded average people.
   D. books about government.
   E. their children.

5A. "Division of labor" probably refers to
   A. the shortening of the work week to forty hours.
   B. separating men and women in the workplace.
   C. individuals choosing careers based on their own needs or talents.
   D. ensuring that workers can do any job in a manufacturing process.
   E. the effects that labor unions have on industry.

5B. Select the answer that does not exemplify the idea of "division of labor."
   A. a talented artist designing all the duck-themed plates at a plate factory.
   B. doing all the activities necessary to survive on one's own.
   C. hiring a landscaper to design a new front-yard hedge arrangement.
   D. shipping tires from a tire factory to be placed on cars at a car factory.
   E. selling homemade crafts on the Internet.

6A. As used in lines 4 and 16 of passage 2, the terms "truck" and "trucking" probably refer to
   A. shipping goods.
   B. insider trading.
   C. using oxcarts to move goods.
   D. farming.
   E. making deals.

6B. Which statement best exemplifies the advantage provided by "trucking" and the subsequent division of labor?
   A. "…he can in this manner get more cattle….than if he himself went to the field to catch them."
   B. "We address ourselves not to their humanity, but to their self-love…"
   C. "But man has almost constant occasion for the help of his brethren…"
   D. "…each individual animal, when it is grown up…is entirely independent…"
   E. "He is accustomed to be of use…"

6C. The author of passage 2 suggests that workers should have specific jobs because
- A. some people cannot perform certain tasks.
- B. implications of never learning how to do a good job at one thing would lead to failed businesses and broken families.
- C. they want raises whenever they have to learn new things.
- D. workers, in general, are not intelligent enough to be good at five or six different jobs.
- E. workers will perfect their skills at specific jobs, which benefits everyone.

7A. Which of the following choices best expresses the opposite of the following sentence?

"It is not from the benevolence of the butcher, the brewer or the baker that we expect our dinner, but from their regard to their own interest."

- A. There are no benevolent people in the services industry.
- B. Butchers, bakers, and brewers provide their services out of charity; they rarely do it to help themselves.
- C. Butchers and bakers just want to make money, so they'll sell anything.
- D. Butchers, bakers, and brewers must rarely enjoy what they are doing.
- E. Good blue-collar workers drive the success of a free economy.

7B. The implication of your answer to question 7A is that human beings are best motivated by
- A. greed.
- B. fear of harm.
- C. job security.
- D. self-interest.
- E. forced charity.

8. Passage 2 includes the example of commerce in a primitive tribe because
- A. it supports the author's assertion that bartering is a product of human nature.
- B. it supports the author's assertion that the division of labor is a natural human tendency.
- C. it supports the idea that mankind will never change in behavior.
- D. the example provides comic relief to the passage.
- E. primitive tribes were very proficient at manufacturing.

9A. Which of the following choices best describes the most important difference between the passages?
- A. The author of the first passage identifies a problem and responds to it, while the author of the second passage simply explains a theory.
- B. The first passage is written in third-person point of view, while the second passage is in first-person.
- C. The passages have opposite topics.
- D. The first passage uses no examples in support of its topic.
- E. Only the first passage suggests the importance of the individual.

9B. Which of the following best describes the difference in tone between the passages?
   A. Passage 2 is more condemning than passage 1 is.
   B. Passage 1 is entirely positive, and passage 2 is negative.
   C. Neither of the passages has a title.
   D. Passage 1 is mildly disparaging, while passage 2 is constructive.
   E. Passage 1 is about government, while passage 2 is about economy.

10. Mill, the author of passage 1, prescribes "eccentricity" as the best weapon against "tyranny of opinion," in which new ideas are scorned. How would Adam Smith, of passage 2, feel Mill's solution would work in economic matters?
   A. Smith would agree that eccentricity is necessary for mediocre thoughts.
   B. Smith would reject the idea because people must think the same way to do business.
   C. Smith would support the idea because the division of labor is based on individuals doing what they do best.
   D. Smith would reject eccentricity because people should not be allowed to accumulate too much wealth.
   E. Smith's division of labor requires government, which is necessarily mediocre and does not support eccentricity.

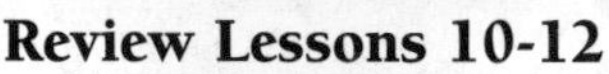

Review Lessons 10-12

Exercise I

Inferences

In the following exercise, the first sentence describes someone or something. Infer information from the first sentence, and then choose the word from the Word Bank that best completes the second sentence.

emanates	**juxtaposes**	**caveat**	**ambiance**	**languid**
kismet	**garnered**	**gratuitous**	**adulterated**	

1. No one at the party wanted any corn chips after a toddler, covered with paste, gravel, and cookie crumbs, ran her hands through the bowl several times, fascinated by the texture of the chips.

   From this sentence, we can infer that the toddler __________ the corn chips.

2. The company's advertisement portrayed their idealized customer as suave and sophisticated, and their competitor's typical customer as foolish and slovenly.

   From this sentence, we can infer that the advertisement __________ two types of fictional customers in order to make one appear preferable to the other.

3. A new restaurant opened in the former colonial prison, replete with barred cells, dark, gloomy corridors, and the courtyard in which the gallows once stood.

   From this sentence, we can infer that the __________ of the restaurant would be best suited for Halloween parties.

4. The crowd was so excited that the concert could not be heard over the applause, which never seemed to stop.

   From this sentence, we can infer that __________ ruined the concert.

5. Christina, who would become the flight engineer on the third Mars mission, knew from childhood that one day she would be an astronaut, and found little interest in anything that didn't involve space travel.

   From this sentence, we can infer that Christina regarded space travel as her __________ in life.

Exercise II

Related Words

Some of the vocabulary words from Lessons 10 through 12 have related meanings. Complete the following sentences by choosing the word that best fits the context, based on information you infer from the use of the italicized word. Some word pairs will be antonyms, some will be synonyms, and some will simply be words often used in the same context.

1. Nuclear scientists intentionally *adulterated* the plutonium with heavy elements that rendered it useless for making atomic bombs, and then sealed it in heavy steel containers so that the highly radioactive, toxic metal could not __________ the storage site.
   A. delineate
   B. defile
   C. scintillate
   D. emanate
   E. garner

2. At the age of sixty-two, Dr. Van Helsing lost his __________ to hunt vampires, so he began training a successor to whom he could pass the *onus* of the hazardous job.
   A. diadem
   B. sedition
   C. gumption
   D. cessation
   E. fetish

3. Just one year after winning the lottery, Vick's __________ and excess left him more *impecunious* than he had been before he won the millions.
   A. elixir
   B. epitome
   C. fissure
   D. debauchery
   E. diadem

4. Lucas sought a *halcyon* week in the __________ farm country up north, but instead, he spent two days trapped in his snowbound car after a sudden snowstorm left him stranded in the mountains.
   A. immutable
   B. garish
   C. garrulous
   D. languid
   E. bucolic

5. The __________ team leader assembled everyone and *delineated* each of their roles in the project, leaving no doubt as to who would do which job, and when.
   A. redolent
   B. impecunious
   C. gratuitous
   D. fastidious
   E. impious

6. Whispers of __________ immediately followed the dictator's proclamation that his changes to the election laws were *immutable.*
   A. diadem
   B. elixir
   C. sedition
   D. epitome
   E. debauchery

7. Stan's *bilious* sister, Shelly, said Stan could borrow her new car, but she added the __________ that he would suffer great harm if he returned the car to her with any damage.
   A. caveat
   B. kismet
   C. sedition
   D. cessation
   E. fetish

8. The manager established a *paradigm* at the company in which hard work and dedication is rewarded with pay bonuses and __________ vacation time upwards of 40 days.
   A. bucolic
   B. garish
   C. kinetic
   D. gratuitous
   E. bilious

9. The tribal chiefs agreed to a[n] __________ of fighting as long as neither side *regressed* to the behaviors that had started the war in the first place.
   A. necromancy
   B. paradigm
   C. cessation
   D. diadem
   E. elixir

10. Sean's __________ coworker was friendly, but her unending *badinage* got on his nerves when he wanted to concentrate on his work.
   A. gratuitous
   B. redolent
   C. bilious
   D. immutable
   E. garrulous

Exercise III

Deeper Meanings

Choose a word to replace the italicized word in each sentence. All of the possible choices for each sentence have similar definitions, but the correct answer will have a connotation that best suits the context. For example, the words "delete," "destroy," and "obliterate," all mean "to remove or wipe out," but no one would ever say, "I destroyed the name from the document." The correct choice will be the word with the best specific meaning and does not render the sentence awkward in tone or content. When choices seem close, look for a clue in the context that makes one choice better than the other. Note that the correct answer is not always the primary vocabulary word from the lesson.

soiled	**picky**	**voiced**	**dead**	**neurotic**
bilious	**meticulous**	**sad**	**wailing**	**adulterated**
languid	**warlike**	**showed**		

1. The camper's noisy car stereo *infected* the peaceful, natural sounds of the woodland valley.

   Better word: ____________________

2. After a 12-hour shift shoveling coal, the *slow* miners emerged from the earth and achingly walked the dirt road toward town as the sun set.

   Better word: ____________________

3. Dale was a truly *grumpy* man who thought that arguing was the only good alternative to complaining.

   Better word: ____________________

4. Gavin is a very *strange* eater; he won't touch his dinner if the different foods touch on the plate.

   Better word: ____________________

5. Mark *delineated* his choice of dessert to the waiter at the diner.

   Better word: ____________________

Exercise IV

Crossword Puzzle

Use the clues to complete the crossword puzzle. The answers consist of vocabulary words from Lessons 10 through 12.

Across

4. getting worse
7. pose for comparison
12. like cows, a tractor, and windmill
13. It's on you, not on us.
15. to contaminate
16. just doesn't shut up
17. black magic
18. what traitors do

Down

1. how sad movies make me
2. never even close to happy
3. It'll happen someday.
5. smelly and nice
6. That outfit looks great on you!
8. breaking ground
9. super-cheap
10. card tricks
11. It might clog your sciences.
14. bowing down for the wrong things

Exercise V

Subject Prompts

Here is a writing prompt similar to the one you will find on the writing portion of an assessment test. Follow the instructions below and write a brief, efficient essay.

> Most schools have dress codes, but few public schools require uniforms. Even private schools sometimes relax uniform codes for simpler neat, casual dress codes.
>
> At the center of the uniform debate is the principle of individual expression versus discipline and effective learning. Uniforms equalize appearance, mitigating embarrassment over tattered or out of style clothing or egoistic pursuits of expensive garments. Opponents claim that uniforms infringe upon students' individuality, at least visually, and uniforms create an expense for parents who already pay taxes for public school.
>
> Argue whether or not you believe uniforms should be mandatory in school environments. Base your argument on personal experience, observations, or your own reasoning. Include at least three supporting ideas.

Thesis: Write a *one-sentence* response to the above assignment. Make certain this single sentence offers a clear statement of your position.

Example: Uniforms are unnecessary in schools, but dress codes—even strict ones—are certainly necessary to prevent a few students from distracting everyone else.

____

____

Organizational Plan: List at least three subtopics you will use to support your main idea. This list is your outline.

1. ____

2. ____

3. ____

Draft: Following your outline, write a good first draft of your essay. Remember to support all your points with examples, facts, references to reading, etc.

Review and Revise: Exchange essays with a classmate. Using the scoring guide for Word Choice on page 267, score your partner's essay (while he or she scores yours). Focus on word choice and the use of language conventions. If necessary, rewrite your essay to improve the word choice and/or use of language.

Lesson Thirteen

1. **salutary** (sal´ yə ter ē) *adj.* healthful; wholesome
The country air had a *salutary* influence on the child's chronic cough.
syn: beneficial *ant: pernicious*

2. **empathy** (em´ pə thē) *n.* an understanding of another's feelings
The same thing happened to me once, so I felt *empathy* for the person whose car broke down on the interstate.
syn: appreciation; compassion

3. **redundant** (ri dun´ dant) *adj.* repetitious; using more words than needed
Saying that a person is a rich millionaire is *redundant.*
syn: wordy; excessive; unnecessary *ant: essential*

4. **impinge** (im pinj´) *v.* to encroach; to trespass
Do not *impinge* on your neighbors by walking in uninvited.
syn: infringe; intrude

5. **brevity** (brev´ i tē) *n.* briefness; a short duration
The *brevity* of the candidate's speech surprised everyone.
syn: terseness; conciseness *ant: lengthiness*

6. **nirvana** (nər vä´ nə) *n.* a condition of great peace or happiness
After work, Irene sought *nirvana* through meditation.

7. **animosity** (an ə mos´ i tē) *n.* hatred
There was more *animosity* between the opposing teams' fans than between the teams themselves.
syn: ill-will; hostility *ant: friendliness; congeniality*

8. **despicable** (des´ pi kə bəl) *adj.* contemptible; hateful
Only a *despicable* cad would behave so horribly.
syn: vile; base *ant: laudable; worthy*

9. **harlequin** (här´ lə kwən) *n.* a clown
The king summoned the *harlequin* to entertain the dinner guests.

10. **savant** (sə vänt´) *n.* a person of extensive learning; an eminent scholar
Einstein was a *savant* who will always be remembered for $E = MC^2$.

11. **obsequious** (əb sē´ kwē əs) *adj.* excessively submissive or overly attentive
The waiter's *obsequious* behavior annoyed the patrons at the expensive restaurant.
syn: servile; fawning *ant: domineering; haughty*

12. **offal** (ô´ fəl) *n.* garbage; waste parts
No one wanted the task of carrying the *offal* from the butcher shop to the trash container.

13. **hoi polloi** (hoi´ pə loi´) *n.* the common people; the masses
The *hoi polloi* of ancient Rome loved to watch the Christians fight the lions.

14. **lascivious** (la siv´ ē əs) *adj.* lustful or lewd
His *lascivious* smile disgusted the other people in the room.
syn: wanton; obscene *ant: wholesome; decent*

15. **cataract** (kat´ ə rakt) *n.* a large waterfall
Because of the *cataract* in that part of the river, you can't put a canoe in the water.

Exercise I

Words in Context

From the list below, supply the words needed to complete the paragraph. Some words will not be used.

cataract **harlequin** **hoi polloi** **salutary** **nirvana**
empathy **animosity**

1. Paul was never very sociable, so when he tired of the __________ of the city, he sought __________ in the peace of the wilderness. At least once a week, he took a[n] __________ hike on the trail behind his house until he reached Toby Creek. A drastic change in elevation there created a sparkling __________, and the noise of the falling water seemed to flush away any __________ that Paul had generated during the week.

From the list below, supply the words needed to complete the paragraph. Some words will not be used.

obsequious **lascivious** **brevity** **savant**
harlequin **empathy** **despicable** **offal**

2. The __________ ruler had no __________ for the citizens who could not afford to pay higher taxes; she ordered them to be imprisoned. Fearing the queen's wrath, the servants responded to her every wish in a[n] __________ manner. The __________ dreaded entertaining her because he feared that his wit might offend her; after all, the queen had beheaded the previous jester for making a[n] __________ joke that she felt was too vulgar for her court. Though the queen was a self-proclaimed __________, most of the jester's jokes went right over her head. The __________ of her reign can be attributed to her assassination.

From the list below, supply the words needed to complete the paragraph. Some words will not be used.

hoi polloi **redundant** **offal**
savant **impinge** **lascivious**

3. Weary after working a twelve-hour shift at the seafood processing plant, Sal used the forklift to move drums of fish __________ reserved for fisherman to use as chum. The task was nearly finished, but Sal felt work was __________ on his family life, and he spilled four hundred gallons of rotting fish parts onto the loading dock. Sal didn't know what would be worse: cleaning up the disgusting mess or enduring another __________ lecture from his boss about losing concentration.

Exercise II

Sentence Completion

Complete the sentence in a way that shows you understand the meaning of the italicized vocabulary word.

1. The war was long over, but the *animosity* between the two nations still caused…

2. Flash cards and practice problems are *salutary* ways for students to…

3. The *despicable* pirate forced the prisoners to…

4. The *hoi polloi* did not really notice the new legislation until…

5. The audience members appreciated the *brevity* of the professor's conclusion because they…

6. When Kyle's parents noticed his *obsequious* behavior, they knew that…

7. The rafters began drifting toward the *cataract* in the river ahead, so they…

8. Some networks refuse to broadcast *lascivious* programs because…

9. Logan, who knew what it was like to lose friends, expressed his *empathy* for Kim during…

10. The *savant* impressed everyone with her ability to…

11. The pig farmer used the *offal* from the dinner table to…

12. The *harlequin* danced and juggled batons in an attempt to…

13. Many thought that the new seatbelt law *impinged* their…

14. Shawna had just finished working a double shift at the plant, so she felt as if she had reached *nirvana* when she finally…

15. The editor fixed the *redundant* sentence by…

Exercise III

Roots, Prefixes, and Suffixes

Study the entries and answer the questions that follow.

The root *anim* means "feeling," "spirit," or "life."
The roots *sec* and *sect* mean "cut."
The root *cand* means "to shine."
The suffix *–id* means "tending to."
The root *magn* means "great."
The prefix *un–* means "one."
The suffix *–ence* means "of."

1. Using *literal* translations as guidance, define the following words without using a dictionary.

   A. reanimate
   B. magnanimous
   C. candidate
   D. candescence
   E. intersect
   F. bisect

2. The literal meaning of *unanimous* is __________.

   There is __________ between two people who dislike each other, but *animation* is the act of __________.

3. An *incandescent* light bulb is __________, but the word *candid* comes from the same root, and it means "pure" or "sincere." Describe the probable evolution of the word *candid.*

4. List as many words as you can think of that contain the root *sect.*

5. List as many words as you can think of that contain the root *anim.*

Exercise IV

Inference

Complete the sentence by inferring information about the italicized word from its context.

1. Max knew that the clothing shop was hurting for business because the *obsequious* salesman would not…

2. The *redundant* phrase, "2:00 a.m. in the morning," should be rewritten to omit "in the morning" because…

3. Charlie had genuine *empathy* for the troubled youths because he, too, had grown up in…

Exercise V

Writing

Here is a writing prompt similar to the one you will find on the writing portion of an assessment test.

Plan and write an essay based on the following statement:

> We shall never understand the natural environment until we see it as being an organism. Land can be healthy or sick, fertile or barren, rich or poor, lovingly nurtured or bled white. Our present attitudes and laws governing the ownership and use of land represent an abuse of the concept of private property. Today you can murder land for private profit. You can leave the corpse for all to see and nobody calls the cops.
>
> –Paul Brooks, *The Pursuit of Wilderness,* 1971

Assignment: In a well-organized essay, refute or defend the quotation. Consider the time in which it was written, and whether or not it is as relevant today. Support your position by discussing examples from current events, classroom studies, science, technology, or your own personal observations and experience.

Thesis: Write a *one-sentence* response to the above assignment. Make certain this single sentence offers a clear statement of your position.

Example: While his observation that the natural environment is like a living organism is accurate enough, Paul Brooks is overdramatic in his assessment of our current laws regarding the use and protection of the world's resources and habitats.

____

____

Organizational Plan: List at least three subtopics you will use to support your main idea. This list is your outline.

1. ____
2. ____
3. ____

Draft: Following your outline, write a good first draft of your essay. Remember to support all your points with examples, facts, references to reading, etc.

Review and Revise: Exchange essays with a classmate. Using the scoring guide for Development on page 264, score your partner's essay (while he or she scores yours). Focus on the development of ideas and the use of language conventions. If necessary, rewrite your essay to improve the development of ideas and/or your use of language.

Exercise VI

English Practice

Identifying Sentence Errors

Identify the grammatical error in each of the following sentences. If the sentence contains no error, select answer choice E.

1. Uninterested students commonly exhibit (A) one or more of the following symptoms: (B) withdrawal, rebelliousness, (C) restlessness, and they are tired. (D) No error (E)

2. I did not enjoy speech class (A) today because my teacher (B) was very critical to my (C) presentation. (D) No error (E)

3. Generalizing (A) is easier than (B) grounding one's (C) thoughts in reality. (D) No error (E)

4. The politician declared, (A) "I promise that (B) I will never (C) except a bribe!" (D) No error (E)

5. Whenever Sharon (A) visits her grandmother in the hospital, (B) she seems to be (C) a little happier than the last time. (D) No error (E)

Improving Sentences

The underlined portion of each sentence below contains some flaw. Select the answer choice that best corrects the flaw.

6. Ringing loudly, John reached over his head and hit the alarm clock.
   A. Ringing loudly, the alarm clock was reached over John's head.
   B. John reached over his head and hit the alarm clock, ringing loudly.
   C. John reached over his head and hit the loudly ringing alarm clock.
   D. The alarm clock was ringing loudly. John reached over his head and hit the loud clock and turned the alarm clock off.
   E. Because the alarm clock was ringing loudly and John reached over to hit it.

7. When Pratt rushed into the cottage, he was as white as a ghost, and it was crystal clear that he had been playing with fire when he fed the wild animal.
   A. pale with fear, and it was obvious that he had taken a risk when he fed the wild animal.
   B. as white as a ghost, making it crystal clear that he should not have played with fire by feeding a wild animal.
   C. terrified because it was crystal clear that feeding the wild animal was like playing with fire.
   D. white as a ghost when it dawned on him that he should not have been feeding a wild animal.
   E. he was pale as a ghost. It became crystal clear he had actually been feeding a wild animal that could have killed him. That was like playing with fire.

8. Today's politicians frequently give speeches about problems concerning the environment and world peace and terrorism.
   A. pollution and world peace, and terrorism.
   B. pollution, world peace, and terrorism.
   C. pollution, with world peace, with terrorism.
   D. pollution, world, peace, terrorism.
   E. the problems of pollution, followed by world peace and terrorism.

9. The cat lay quite motionless in front of the cupboard. Waiting silently for the mouse to emerge.
   A. The cat, lying quite motionless in front of the cupboard, waiting silently for the mouse to emerge.
   B. The cat lay, quite motionless, in front of the cupboard. Waiting silently for the mouse to emerge.
   C. The cat lay quite motionless. It was in front of the cupboard. It was waiting silently for the frightened mouse to come out.
   D. Waiting silently for the mouse to emerge, the cat lay quite motionless in front of the cupboard.
   E. The cat was lying quite motionless in front of the cupboard. Waiting silently for the mouse to emerge.

10. The rock concert was the most bizarre event I have ever witnessed. Especially since the lead guitarist destroyed his most priceless guitar as part of the show.
   A. The rock concert was the most bizarre event I have ever witnessed, especially since the lead guitarist destroyed his most priceless guitar as part of the show.
   B. The rock concert was a bizarre event. The lead guitarist destroyed his priceless guitar as part of the show.
   C. The rock concert was a bizarre event since the lead guitarist destroyed his very priceless guitar as part of the show.
   D. The rock concert was the most bizarre event I have ever witnessed, especially since the lead guitarist destroyed his priceless guitar as part of the show.
   E. The rock concert was an event I had never witnessed before especially since the lead guitarist destroyed his most priceless guitar as part of the show.

Lesson Fourteen

1. **recoil** (ri koil´) *v.* to retreat; to draw back
   Liz *recoiled* from the harsh words as though she had been struck.

2. **orthography** (ôr thog´ rə fē) *n.* correct spelling
   Anne's excellent spelling grades are testament to her grasp of *orthography*.

3. **endemic** (en dem´ ik) *adj.* confined to a particular country or area
   Once it had been *endemic* to Africa, but now it is becoming a world-wide epidemic.
   syn: native; indigenous *ant: alien; foreign*

4. **aggrandize** (ə gran´ dīz) *v.* 1. to increase the range of; to expand
   2. to make appear larger
   Much of what they did was not intended to aid their country, but to *aggrandize* their own positions.
   The advertisement *aggrandizes* the new product by making it appear as though everyone owns one.
   (1) syn: enlarge; augment; enrich *ant: decrease; diminish*
   (2) syn: exaggerate; embellish *ant: belittle; devalue*

5. **saturnine** (sat´ er nīn) *adj.* gloomy; sluggish
   The hostess's *saturnine* attitude caused the party to end early.
   syn: sullen; morose *ant: genial*

6. **paleontology** (pā lē ən tol´ ə jē) *n.* a science dealing with prehistoric life through the study of fossils
   The expert in *paleontology* dated the skeleton to 2000 B.C.

7. **shibboleth** (shib´ ə lith) *n.* a word or pronunciation that distinguishes someone as of a particular group
   Pronouncing "creek" as "crick" is a *shibboleth* of people in mid-Atlantic states.

8. **bombast** (bom´ bast) *n.* impressive but meaningless language
   Please, professor, spare the *bombast*; just give me the facts.

9. **panache** (pə nash´) *n.* self-confidence; a showy manner
   The actor always exhibited great *panache,* so his first appearance on the talk show didn't make him the least bit nervous.
   syn: charisma; spirit

10. **mendacious** (men dā´ shəs) *adj.* lying; false; deceitful
    Everyone knew the politician was *mendacious,* yet the voters kept reelecting him.
    syn: duplicitous *ant: truthful*

11. **obviate** (ob´ vē āt) *v.* to prevent; to get around
They delayed the release of the film in order to *obviate* a barrage of criticism.
syn: circumvent

12. **paroxysm** (par´ ək siz əm) *n.* a sudden outburst; a fit
The class stopped its *paroxysm* of laughter and went silent as soon as the principal walked into the room.
syn: outburst; commotion

13. **deign** (dān) *v.* to lower oneself before an inferior
"After what she did to me, I would not *deign* to say hello to her," said Mary about her former best friend.
syn: stoop; condescend

14. **flaunt** (flônt) *v.* to show off
Some people *flaunt* their wealth by buying islands.
syn: boast; exhibit *ant: conceal*

15. **elicit** (i lis´ it) *v.* to draw forth; to call forth
The attorney tried to *elicit* a response from his client, but the man remained silent.
syn: evoke; extract *ant: cover; suppress*

Exercise I

Words in Context

From the list below, supply the words needed to complete the paragraph. Some words will not be used.

recoil	**bombast**	**paleontology**	**panache**	**flaunt**
elicit	**shibboleth**	**aggrandize**	**obviate**	**endemic**

1. When Dr. Carter is not fulfilling his duties as the professor of __________ at Ganton College, he is in the jungles of South America supervising excavations of ancient creatures. During the last dig, Dr. Carter __________ when a poisonous snake tried to bite him. Now he wears tall boots and gloves to __________ the risk of dangerous animals __________ to the region. He will definitely __________ the need for such safety measures. Some of the incoming scientists will accuse him of self-__________, despite the fact that the sociable doctor always avoids using too much __________ when speaking about safety; he'll __________ his amazing findings when he returns to the campus at the end of the summer. He can put his __________ to better use in the classroom.

From the list below, supply the words needed to complete the paragraph. Some words will not be used.

shibboleth	**obviate**	**mendacious**	**deign**
orthography	**saturnine**	**paroxysm**	**endemic**

2. Baker __________ to give a semi-friendly nod to his Nazi captors, and he immediately suffered the consequences. Baker then endured the loud __________ of his cellmates: "What was that? What, are you working for them, too?"

   He understood their paranoia. Just weeks before, a[n] __________ rebel captive had revealed the escape plan to the guards. The prisoners, including Baker, had to abandon months of secrecy and labor that went into the construction of the tunnel. They had not yet regrouped; most of the __________ prisoners simply lay in their cells, defeated.

   Baker sat against the wall and thought about his capture. He had misused the __________ that the Nazis used to identify foreign spies, and the lack of __________ on his forged travel documents instantly signaled that he was not the German officer he claimed to have been. They must need information, he reasoned, or they would have executed him by now.

Exercise II

Sentence Completion

Complete the sentence in a way that shows you understand the meaning of the italicized vocabulary word.

1. To *obviate* a surprise attack, the lieutenant sent a scout ahead to…
2. Bill *recoiled* when he saw that the person on the news broadcast was…
3. The duke was not well-liked among his subjects because he never *deigned* to…
4. Save your *bombast* for the presentation and…
5. If you show too much *panache* at the interview, you might…
6. The *endemic* species of squirrel is found only in…
7. Helen promised that if Kelly had another *paroxysm* when she heard the word "no," Helen would…
8. What she did was wrong, but it should not *elicit* the…
9. Charlie worked for thirty years to buy his Corvette, and he *flaunted* it by…
10. The *mendacious* thief used forged credentials to…
11. The *saturnine* children just stared out the window and said that they…
12. The queen *aggrandized* her power and influence by…
13. The *paleontology* class visited the museum to observe the…
14. Attention to *orthography* is especially important on your college application because…
15. The suspicious soldier at the entry gate misspoke the *shibboleth*, so the guard refused to…

Exercise III

Roots, Prefixes, and Suffixes

Study the entries, and answer the questions that follow.

The root *mon* means "to advise," "to remind," or "to warn."
The roots *volv* and *volut* mean "to roll" or "to turn."
The root *ambulare* means "to walk."
The suffix *–ance* means "state of" or "quality of."
The prefix *per–* means "through" or "completely."
The prefix *e–* means "from" or "out."
The prefix *de–* means "down" or "thoroughly."

1. Using *literal* translations as guidance, define the following words without using a dictionary.

   A. revolve
   B. devolve
   C. evolve
   D. premonition
   E. monster
   F. demonstrate

2. A[n] __________ might remind you that you should be in class, and an *admonishment* should __________ you to improve your behavior.

3. If an injured person cannot walk, then he might need a[n] __________ to transport him to a doctor. If you *perambulate* a tunnel, then you ______________ it.

4. A *volume* is a collection of documents. Using what you know about the history of paper, explain why *volume*, which uses the root *vol*, "to roll," came to mean "a collection of documents."

Exercise IV

Inference

Complete the sentence by inferring information about the italicized word from its context.

1. The owners of the store had record profits, so they plan to *aggrandize* their share of the market even more by…

2. The amnesia victim had no memory of his identity, so a hypnotist tried to *elicit* clues from the man's subconscious that…

3. On the raft, Irene *obviated* the danger of drowning by…

Exercise V

Critical Reading

Below is a reading passage followed by several multiple-choice questions. Carefully read the passage and choose the best answer for each of the questions.

The following article details the exploits of the obscure Joshua Norton—a bankrupted businessman who, in 1859, declared himself Emperor of the United States. The city of San Francisco humored the eccentric Norton, and for twenty-one years, he "ruled" the United States, sometimes with the assistance of his two dogs: Bummer and Lazarus.

America's short history is so full of interesting characters that some of them naturally get overlooked—even rulers as prestigious as Norton I, Emperor of the United States and Protector of Mexico.

Joshua Norton was born an Englishman around the year 1819, but his family soon moved to South Africa and grew wealthy as traders. By the time Norton turned thirty, news of gold discoveries in California had spread around the world, and Norton, like many young entrepreneurs, relocated to San Francisco hoping to make his fortune in the rapidly growing city. Norton had quite a running start, too; he arrived in San Francisco with forty-thousand dollars in hand—an amount that would render Norton a millionaire in today's dollar value.

Norton did not find riches in gold, but he did find wealth in rice. The large population of Chinese immigrants in San Francisco ensured a high demand for the grain, and in four years, Norton had banked nearly one-quarter million dollars. When a famine in China caused the price of rice to skyrocket, Norton cleverly decided to **aggrandize** his position by purchasing all of the rice in the city; unfortunately, immediately after Norton spent his last penny acquiring what he thought was the only ship of rice in the city, many more ships arrived—all loaded with rice. The value of rice fell, plunging well below what it had been before the famine, and Norton was financially ruined.

Norton spent the next three years in court trying to recoup his losses and retain his property. He lost every case, and the trauma took a toll on Norton's wit. He vanished for a year, and then, in 1857, Norton returned as a different man, apparently obsessed with the bureaucratic inadequacies of the nation; however, no one knew just how obsessed—some say "delusional"—Norton had become.

In the year 1859, Joshua Norton proclaimed himself Norton I, Emperor of the United States. A San Francisco newspaper printed the very formal decree, which also summoned representatives of all states to assemble at a San Francisco music hall to discuss the Emperor's modifications to national legislation; however, the latter never occurred because Norton decided to abolish the United States Congress before the meeting day arrived.

Angered by the rebellious government's unwillingness to desist operations, Norton issued another decree, this time ordering the commanding general of the United States Army, by name, to assemble a force and "clear the Halls of Congress." Strangely, neither Congress nor General Scott responded to the Emperor's **bombast**, so in 1860, Norton used his imperial authority to disband the Union entirely. Along the way, the Emperor also assumed the duty of Protector of Mexico, but he retained the position for only a decade before deciding that not even an Emperor as clever as Norton was capable of protecting Mexico.

During his reign, the regal Norton forewent the traditional minutiae of ruling an empire to instead be close to his many beloved subjects. Each day he marched with **panache**, sans entourage, though the streets of San Francisco, inspecting the many properties and processes of his capital city. Citizens recognized him immediately, for each day he **flaunted** the Emperor's regalia: a blue military uniform complete with gold epaulets, a beaver hat with a feather plume, and a battered sword. Sometimes Norton simply enlightened his subjects on matters of state, and, on at least one occasion, the wise Emperor was known to have intervened in order to quell a riot.

For most of his reign, Emperor Norton retired each night in the imperial suite of his estate—a barren, closet-sized room in a boardinghouse; however, Norton's spartan accommodations did not reflect the services that his loyal subjects provided for him. During the reign of Norton, all established eateries welcomed the Emperor to partake of complimentary dinners and lunches. Theaters and music halls reserved seats for the sovereign, and public officials often acknowledged their benevolent ruler.

Occasionally, matters of such importance would arise that Norton was compelled to issue more edicts, and the major city newspapers were more than happy to humor the Emperor, rather than **recoil** from his declarations. The Civil War (1861–1865) was of great concern to Norton, and he issued several decrees addressing the violent conflict. Other edicts dealt with matters of diplomacy or responded to various injustices of Norton's concern. In an effort to resolve political skirmishes, Norton, in 1869, officially eliminated both the Democratic and Republican parties. Three years later, he outlawed the word "'Frisco," because it "has no linguistic or other warrant," according to the official decree. Violators of the "High Misdemeanor" were to pay a fine of twenty-five dollars.

The reign of Emperor Norton I lasted until January 8, 1880, when the kindly monarch collapsed during his daily duties. People immediately reacted to save the aging sovereign, but no one could help. The newspaper headlines on the following day read "Le Roi est Mort"—"The king is dead."

The good Emperor left an estate valued at approximately ten dollars, but more importantly, he left a priceless impression on his many subjects. An estimated ten thousand people lined the streets in order to pay homage to their fallen monarch during the funeral, and the City of San Francisco paid for Norton's burial. Norton is now at peace, but his story will **elicit** humor and wonder in the imagination of anyone who happens to catch a glimpse of an old photograph portraying the bizarre but munificent Norton the First.

1A. The author of the passage uses Norton's title of Emperor
- A. as criticism of the current president.
- B. as a way to demonstrate the silliness of politics.
- C. to reflect the actual title Norton assumed.
- D. as an acknowledgment of Norton's delusion.
- E. because it will ridicule and satirize Norton.

1B. Joshua Norton was born in
- A. South Africa.
- B. San Francisco.
- C. England.
- D. Germany.
- E. Mexico.

2A. Norton lost his fortune because
- A. he was never a competent businessman.
- B. the price of rice plunged.
- C. in his madness, he forgot the location of his assets.
- D. he bought a cargo ship, and then the bank foreclosed on him.
- E. he had to pay tribute to the State of California for his title.

2B. From the details of Norton's business failure, you can properly infer that
   A. shipping is a very unstable market.
   B. the price of rice is driven by the price of rice in China.
   C. Norton was not an expert in the rice trade.
   D. perishables cannot stay fresh at port for longer than a few days.
   E. if there is an abundance of an item, it is worth less.

3A. The way in which Norton's starting fortune is described in paragraph 2 suggests that
   A. a dollar in Norton's time was worth much more than a dollar today.
   B. Norton probably paid for his rice with gold.
   C. too much money made Norton careless.
   D. a dollar today is much more valuable than it was in Norton's time.
   E. Norton's investment was foolish because rice is inexpensive.

3B. In which year did Norton lose his fortune?
   A. 1849
   B. 1851
   C. 1853
   D. 1857
   E. 1859

4A. As used in line 19, *wit* most nearly means
   A. perspective.
   B. behavior.
   C. neurotic.
   D. judgment.
   E. sanity.

4B. Which words from the paragraph including the word *wit* best support your answer to question 4A?
   A. obsessed; different man
   B. trying; recoup
   C. property; vanished
   D. losses; lost
   E. trauma; bureaucratic

5A. In 1860, the commanding general of the U.S. Army was
   A. Scott.
   B. Macarthur.
   C. Patton.
   D. Byron.
   E. Norton.

5B. Even though he ignored Norton's "orders," the general was instructed to
- A. abolish the United States government.
- B. put Washington, D.C., under emergency rule.
- C. remove the United States Congress from its offices.
- D. impose martial law in all of San Francisco.
- E. move the capital of Mexico to Southern California.

6A. As used in line 35, "traditional minutiae" probably refers to
- A. diplomatic influence.
- B. time limits for meeting with subjects.
- C. punishing rebels of the empire.
- D. day-to-day duties.
- E. uniform and apparel.

6B. Which choice best explains Norton's real reason for forgoing the traditional minutiae of running his empire?
- A. He felt that emperors can do as they please.
- B. There were no actual duties.
- C. Norton did not want to deal with the duties of a bureaucracy.
- D. The emperor handled responsibilities at his house.
- E. He was more comfortable associating with his "subjects."

7. Which of the following was not a detail in one of Norton's imperial orders?
- A. supporting the North in the Civil War
- B. abolishing two major political parties
- C. removing Congress with military force
- D. prohibiting the use of the word *Frisco*
- E. dissolving the Union

8A. As it is used in line 43, *spartan* most nearly means
- A. warlike.
- B. elaborate.
- C. wood.
- D. old-fashioned.
- E. plain.

8B. The word from the context that best supports your answer to question 8A is
- A. barren.
- B. imperial.
- C. suite.
- D. boardinghouse.
- E. closet-sized.

9A. The tone of this passage is best described as
   A. satiric and bitter.
   B. farcical but respectful.
   C. exaggerated but impersonal.
   D. angry but admiring.
   E. distant and understanding.

9B. According to the passage, the people of San Francisco regard Norton as
   A. a respected leader who turned misfortune into success.
   B. an important lesson in investment risks and overworking.
   C. a harmless but entertaining man and pillar of the community.
   D. a weird oddity, not worthy of their time or efforts.
   E. an important symbol of their city, despite his peculiarities.

10A. The primary purpose of this passage is to
   A. persuade readers that San Francisco has a quaint history.
   B. explain how a failed financial career can ruin someone's mental health.
   C. entertain readers with humorous accounts of Norton's exploits.
   D. inform about an interesting character in American history.
   E. explain how personalities were different in the nineteenth century.

10B. the passage is best suited for
   A. a psychology magazine.
   B. a textbook on failed business ventures.
   C. a magazine article about San Francisco.
   D. a San Francisco human interest web page.
   E. an article about people with obsessive-compulsive disorders.

Lesson Fifteen

1. **hallow** (hal´ ō) *v.* to make holy
   We cannot *hallow* this field, for the men who died here made it holy.
   syn: bless; consecrate *ant: desecrate*

2. **aesthetic** (es thet´ ik) *adj.* pertaining to beauty
   The house was cheap, but it lacked any *aesthetic* qualities.
   syn: artistic *ant: displeasing; unattractive*

3. **empirical** (em pîr´ i kəl) *adj.* based on practical experience rather than theory
   Her theory sounded logical, but the *empirical* data did not support it.
   syn: observable *ant: theoretical*

4. **hermetic** (hər met´ ik) *adj.* tightly sealed
   That medicine should be packed in *hermetic* containers.
   syn: airtight

5. **querulous** (kwer´ ə ləs) *adj.* complaining; grumbling
   The *querulous* child on the plane annoyed the other passengers.
   syn: fretful; peevish *ant: complacent; satisfied*

6. **egregious** (i grē´ jəs) *adj.* remarkably bad; outrageous
   His remark was so *egregious* that it shocked everyone at the party.
   syn: flagrant; gross *ant: moderate*

7. **foment** (fō ment´) *v.* to stir up; to incite
   At the convention, people were hired to *foment* disruptions during the senator's speech.
   syn: instigate; arouse *ant: quell; curb*

8. **germane** (jər mān´) *adj.* relevant; fitting
   Make sure that all of your answers are *germane* to the questions.
   syn: appropriate; pertinent; suitable *ant: irrelevant*

9. **flaccid** (flas´ id) *adj.* flabby
   The retired athlete's muscles became *flaccid* after years without exercise.
   syn: weak; feeble *ant: solid; taut*

10. **ratiocinate** (rash i os´ ə nāt) *v.* to reason; to think
    Because alcohol had dulled his mind, he was no longer able to *ratiocinate* clearly.

11. **orifice** (ôr´ ə fis) *n.* mouth; opening
    The cavity in his tooth felt like a giant *orifice*, but it actually was quite small.

12. **chaff** (chaf) *n.* worthless matter
    "Give me just the facts," the professor said. "Separate the wheat from the *chaff.*"
    syn: rubbish

13. **meretricious** (mer i trish´ əs) *adj.* attractive in a cheap, flashy way
    She was naturally beautiful, so no one knew why she wore such *meretricious* looking clothing.
    syn: gaudy; showy; tawdry *ant: restrained; tasteful*

14. **perdition** (pər dish´ ən) *n.* damnation; ruin; hell
    The sermon was about the sins that lead to *perdition.*

15. **hospice** (hos´ pis) *n.* a shelter for travelers, orphans, or the ill or destitute
    The new *hospice* for cancer patients opened in July.

Exercise I

Words in Context

From the list below, supply the words needed to complete the paragraph. Some words will not be used.

aesthetic	**orifice**	**ratiocinate**	**meretricious**
hospice	**flaccid**	**chaff**	

1. Low hemlock branches hid the __________ of the cave and kept the rain out. The cave didn't compare to the __________ in which Ben had spent the previous night, but it was still a better alternative to sleeping in the open. As the sun sank behind the wood line, Ben sat on a decaying log and __________ about his next move. He was penniless and lost, and while the __________ scenery of the old forest was nice to look at, it didn't provide the food that Ben would need to survive. The temperature was dropping, and his __________, Italian-leather jacket looked sporty but provided little warmth.

From the list below, supply the words needed to complete the paragraph. Some words will not be used.

hallow	**perdition**	**egregious**	**hospice**
foment	**empirical**	**querulous**	**meretricious**

2. She had always __________ her son as an angel who could do no wrong, so Mrs. Patterson nearly fainted when she read about her son's __________ crime in the police report of the local newspaper. As usual, her __________ son, Tom, blamed everyone else for his crime—his friends, the police, the storeowner, etc. Tom's mother had __________ knowledge about the fate of criminals; Tom's father had regularly __________ trouble, and he died in prison. Mrs. Patterson feared that if Tom didn't redeem himself by abandoning his criminal ways, his life also would end in __________.

From the list below, supply the words needed to complete the paragraph. Some words will not be used.

germane	**chaff**	**orifice**	**hermetic**
flaccid	**hallow**		

3. Dedicated to toning her __________ arms and legs, Rita started jogging three days a week. Every night, she took a multivitamin from a[n] __________ sealed container. She considered this absolutely __________ to her fitness goals. She saw too many people rely on pills or protein powders or similar __________ when they really just needed to get up and exercise.

Exercise II

Sentence Completion

Complete the sentence in a way that shows you understand the meaning of the italicized vocabulary word.

1. If you *ratiocinate* too long about how to get to the theater, you will…
2. The town *hallowed* the site of the tragic accident; no one was allowed to…
3. The *hermetic* vials were stored in a safe because…
4. The elderly man was moved to a *hospice* after…
5. Since Dirk thought that he was already headed for *perdition*, he…
6. Johnny's parents grounded him for his *egregious* behavior after he…
7. A state with *aesthetic* mountain scenery will attract tourists because…
8. People could hear calls for help, but the *orifice* was…
9. Maggie's parents told her to change her *meretricious* behavior if she wanted to…
10. The *querulous* passenger refused to…
11. Terri's *flaccid* excuse for not studying was…
12. Include only *germane* information when you take an essay test, or else you will…
13. Tina could not stand all the *chaff* on television, so she…
14. The *empirical* data showed the prototype jet would need…
15. Max liked to *foment* arguments at the dinner table by…

Exercise III

Roots, Prefixes, and Suffixes

Study the entries and answer the questions that follow.

The root *equ* means "equal."
The roots *flect* and *flex* mean "bend."
The suffix *–ity* means "quality of."
The root *nox* means "night."
The suffixes *–able* and *–ible* mean "able to be."
The prefix *sub–* means "secretly."
The root *fug* means "flee."
The root *cent* means "center."

1. Using *literal* translations as guidance, define the following words without using a dictionary.

   A. inflection
   B. flexible
   C. equitable
   D. equinox
   E. subterfuge
   F. centrifuge

2. When you are too cold or too hot, your body will shiver or perspire in order to achieve a state of __________.

3. A suit of armor might __________ the blows of an enemy's sword, but the armor has stiff joints that make the wearer unable to bend, or __________.

4. One who flees from the law is a[n] __________, and one who flees from harm is a[n] __________.

   A *fugue* (or a *round*, such as "Row-Row-Row Your Boat") is a musical composition in which a theme begins in one voice, and is then imitated and built upon by different successive voices at various times throughout the propagation of the melody. Explain the possible reasoning for the word *fugue* having a root that means "to flee."

5. List all the words that you can think of that contain the root *cent*.

Exercise IV

Inference

Complete the sentence by inferring information about the italicized word from its context.

1. Dr. Paxton gathered *empirical* data during the accelerated plant-growth experiment by...

2. Some of the protestors at the World Bank meeting were actually concerned about policies that affect underdeveloped nations, but others went to *foment* trouble by...

3. The concussion impaired the man's ability to *ratiocinate*, judging by the way in which he...

Exercise V

Writing

Here is a writing prompt similar to the one you will find on the writing portion of an assessment test.

Plan and write an essay based on the following statement:

None are so deaf as those who will not hear.
Of those whose vision's dim where'er they be,
None are so blind as those who will not see."

–a book of proverbs compiled in 1876

Assignment: In an essay, explain the proverb's relevance to the present world. Provide at least one example for each of the proverb's two assertions, that "none are so deaf..." and "none are so blind...." Support your claim using evidence from your reading, studies, personal observations, and experiences.

Thesis: Write a *one-sentence* response to the above assignment. Make certain this single sentence offers a clear statement of your position.

Example: If true blindness and deafness is an inability to see or hear painful truths, then many modern Americans are both blind and deaf.

____

____

Organizational Plan: List at least three subtopics you will use to support your main idea. This list is your outline.

1. ____

2. ____

3. ____

Draft: Following your outline, write a good first draft of your essay. Remember to support all your points with examples, facts, references to reading, etc.

Review and Revise: Exchange essays with a classmate. Using the scoring guide for Sentence Formation and Variety on page 266, score your partner's essay (while he or she scores yours). Focus on sentence structure and the use of language conventions. If necessary, rewrite your essay to improve the sentence structure and/or your use of language.

Exercise VI

English Practice

Improving Paragraphs

Read the following passage and then choose the best revision for the underlined portions of the paragraph. The questions will require you to make decisions regarding the revision of the reading selection. Some revisions are not of actual mistakes, but will improve the clarity of the writing.

[1] Proper care of the teeth and gums is essential for a healthy lifestyle. Ignoring[1] in-depth maintenance of the teeth and surrounding structures can lead to many avoidable problems. Incomplete chewing of food can lead to indigestion and the probability that food is not being properly absorbed, this ultimately results in malnutrition. Teeth function as the nutrition procurement system of the body, and they are also an early warning system of disease. The fact is, properly maintaining the mouth[3] is the first step to a lifetime of proper nutrition.

1. A. NO CHANGE
   B. a healthy lifestyle; while ignoring
   C. a healthy lifestyle and ignoring
   D. a healthy, life style. Ignoring

2. Which of the following changes would repair a structural error in paragraph 1?
   F. Hyphenate *nutrition procurement system.*
   G. Combine the first two sentences using a colon.
   H. Change *essential for* to *essential to.*
   J. Place a semicolon after *absorbed.*

3. A. NO CHANGE
   B. The fact is, that properly maintaining the mouth
   C. The fact is that, properly maintaining the mouth
   D. Properly maintaining the mouth

[2] As the ultimate in perfectly designed food processors, the mouth handles all nutrients prior to ingestion. Saliva, working in conjunction with teeth, is the first agent to work on the digestion of food. The normal pH of saliva is slightly acidic; but[4] it can be neutralized with an alkaline mouthwash such as baking soda and water. Cleaning the teeth also after meals[5] helps to maintain the proper pH level of the mouth.

4. F. NO CHANGE
   G. acidic; and
   H. acidic, but
   J. acidic therefore

5. A. NO CHANGE
   B. Also: cleaning the teeth after meals
   C. Cleaning the teeth also after meals
   D. Cleaning the teeth after meals also

[3] As procurement officers, teeth are designed to <u>grab, tearing, and to grind</u>[6] fueling substances that empower the body to do work. For the teeth to be <u>effective</u>[7] as blenders providing sustenance for the body, they need to be properly aligned. The grinding teeth the upper and lower molars fit face to face on every plane so that when <u>it comes</u>[8] together, they are in exact alignment to mash food into a digestible form. If nature <u>has not saw</u>[9] to their precise alignment, an orthodontist may be called in to make suitable adjustments. Designer braces are available for those who can afford them. Thanks to dental technology, braces and retainers are no longer an inconvenient or unsightly way <u>to insure</u>[10] proper alignment.

6. F. NO CHANGE
   G. grab, to tear, and grinding
   H. grab, tear, and to grind
   J. grab, tear, and grind

7. A. NO CHANGE
   B. effecting
   C. affective
   D. affecting

8. F. NO CHANGE
   G. it gets
   H. they are gotten
   J. they come

9. A. NO CHANGE
   B. has not seen
   C. has not saw
   D. had not seen

10. F. NO CHANGE
    G. to ensure
    H. so as to assure
    J. that censures

11. If you had to delete a sentence in paragraph 3, which would be the most appropriate choice?
    A. sentence 2
    B. sentence 3
    C. sentence 4
    D. sentence 5

12. Which sentence in paragraph 1 should be moved to paragraph 3?
    F. sentence 1
    G. sentence 2
    H. sentence 3
    J. sentence 4

13. Which of the following suggestions would correct a flaw in the third paragraph?
    A. Add hyphens to *face to face.*
    B. Capitalize *orthodontist.*
    C. Insert commas around *the upper,* as well as *the lower molars.*
    D. Change *nature* to read *Mother Nature.*

[4] Proper care of the teeth includes brushing up and down to remove tiny food particles and bacteria. Flossing can be helpful when teeth are so close together that a brush cannot clear the spaces in-between. If <u>through</u>[14] maintenance is applied to the teeth every day, they should never need replacement. Your own teeth are <u>most unique</u>[15] to you, and dentures are not nearly as good.

14. F. NO CHANGE
    G. thought
    H. threw
    J. thorough

15. A. NO CHANGE
    B. most important
    C. more unique
    D. unique

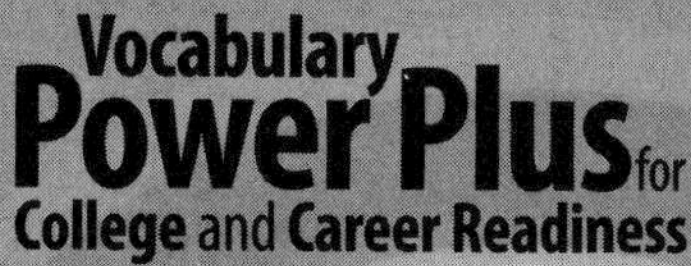

Review Lessons 13-15

Exercise I

Inferences

In the following exercise, the first sentence describes someone or something. Infer information from the first sentence, and then choose the word from the Word Bank that best completes the second sentence.

elicit	**hallowed**	**redundant**	**meretricious**
deign	**obviated**	**fomented**	**endemic**

1. The television show received poor ratings because the characters explained every little detail in the story rather than allowing viewers to figure things out on their own, especially the obvious details.

   From this sentence, we can infer that it is __________ to portray events on television while describing what is being betrayed.

2. Kip refused to drive his mom's old, rusted minivan until he found himself unable to afford the payments on his muscle car, which he was forced to sell before asking his mom for use of the van again.

   From this sentence, we can infer that Kip must __________ to drive an ugly car or get used to walking.

3. A food shortage and two natural disasters within a month created hardships that made it easy for the rebel leader to rally people in an uprising against the king.

   From this sentence, we can infer that the rebel leader __________ the public into outrage against the king.

4. It is the tradition of the people to treat the burial ground with respect, which means never constructing any buildings above it or harvesting lumber near the graves.

   From this sentence, we can infer that the living have __________ the burial grounds.

5. The beautiful flower can grow only in the unique ecosystem found in a single mountain range in South America.

   From this sentence, we can infer that the flower is __________ only to the mountain range.

Exercise II

Related Words

Some of the vocabulary words from Lessons 13 through 15 have related meanings. Complete the following sentences by choosing the word that best fits the context, based on information you infer from the use of the italicized word. Some word pairs will be antonyms, some will be synonyms, and some will simply be words often used in the same context.

1. While searching for information __________ to her essay topic, Ashley found only *redundant* articles, all based on the same scientific study and concluding the same thing.
   A. despicable
   B. obsequious
   C. saturnine
   D. egregious
   E. germane

2. The *mendacious* criminal's most __________ offense was his armed robbery of a charity for terminally ill children.
   A. empirical
   B. aesthetic
   C. redundant
   D. egregious
   E. endemic

3. Following a *paroxysm* of boos, the stadium crowd turned __________ after a referee's bad call put the home team at a severe disadvantage.
   A. obsequious
   B. querulous
   C. endemic
   D. flaccid
   E. hermetic

4. The calligrapher felt that the *orthography* of a letter was secondary to the __________ appeal of the words on the page.
   A. despicable
   B. redundant
   C. aesthetic
   D. salutary
   E. endemic

5. After the death of her friend, the __________ woman simply needed *empathy*, not pity.
   A. hermetic
   B. saturnine
   C. meretricious
   D. obsequious
   E. aesthetic

6. Having had plenty of quiet time to __________ in his prison cell, the double agent concocted a plan to *obviate* his pending transfer to the labor camp, where he would surely die.
   A. ratiocinate
   B. flaunt
   C. impinge
   D. foment
   E. elicit

7. Clad in a[n] __________ heap of gold chains and oversized rings, the cartel leader directed his *bombast* toward the drug enforcement agents arresting him, promising them that he would rise to the top again.
   A. despicable
   B. redundant
   C. meretricious
   D. flaccid
   E. salutary

8. In spite of what diet gurus and vitamin salesmen told Travis, *empirical* evidence convinced him that __________ habits of eating small meals and exercising daily would work much better.
   A. saturnine
   B. salutary
   C. aesthetic
   D. endemic
   E. egregious

9. The *lascivious* character's attempts to find love were amusing on television; however, in the real world, such behavior would be considered __________ as well as downright creepy.
   A. querulous
   B. hermetic
   C. flaccid
   D. egregious
   E. saturnine

10. As a way to__________ his own public image, the politician started rumors that *fomented* the public, turning them against the incumbent governor.
   A. impinge
   B. obviate
   C. recoil
   D. ratiocinated
   E. aggrandize

Exercise III

Deeper Meanings

Choose a word to replace the italicized word in each sentence. All of the possible choices for each sentence have similar definitions, but the correct answer will have a connotation that best suits the context. For example, the words "delete," "destroy," and "obliterate," all mean "to remove or wipe out," but no one would ever say, "I destroyed the name from the document." The correct choice will be the word with the best specific meaning and does not render the sentence awkward in tone or content. When choices seem close, look for a clue in the context that makes one choice better than the other. Note that the correct answer is not always the primary vocabulary word from the lesson.

aggrandize	**crazed**	**flaunt**	**reveal**	**evil**	**hostile**
despicable	**querulous**	**change**	**impinged**	**visited**	

1. If you *show* your recent winnings by waving money around, you'll probably attract the wrong kinds of friends.

   Better word: ____________________

2. Josh didn't mind the neighbors' building a new barn, but he became angry when he realized the end of the new structure *trespassed* on his own property by at least ten feet.

   Better word: ____________________

3. The con artist's *mean* scheme involved "selling" empty homes whose owners were out of town, and then fleeing after collecting the down payments.

   Better word: ____________________

4. The *outraged* lady could never simply enjoy a meal at a restaurant without arguing about the food, service, or even the carpet on the floor.

   Better word: ____________________

5. The gubernatorial candidate hoped that getting in the news for his controversial remarks on spending less on aid to cities would *grow* his image as an innovator.

   Better word: ____________________

Exercise IV

Crossword Puzzle

Use the clues to complete the crossword puzzle. The answers consist of vocabulary words from Lessons 13 through 15.

Across

1. to expand
5. sticks to the subject
7. over and over and over and over
11. more unwanted garbage
12. sealed up
15. Send in the clown.
17. like first-hand experience of the real thing
18. Niagara Falls

Down

2. finally: total peace
3. just horrible
4. study of buried, ancient things
6. I understand how you feel.
8. all over this one place
9. A picturesque home has this quality.
10. the worst possible outcome
13. jump back out of danger
14. pie hole
16. saying a bunch of nothin'

Exercise V

Subject Prompts

Here is a writing prompt similar to the one you will find on the writing portion of an assessment test. Follow the instructions below and write a brief, efficient essay.

> Few people questioned graphic video game violence when conflicts were straightforward, good-versus-evil battles. The antihero has since found his or her way into video games and is often as evil as those he or she intends to destroy or avenge. Heroes now, in popular games, may inflict virtual violence on anyone or anything. Fights between good and evil have evolved into fights between evil characters and more evil characters. Players now have the option to fantasize the part of the criminal, or tyrant; quite often, the primary role is, indeed, that of a criminal character.
>
> What, if any, effect does this type of role playing have upon the psychology of the gamers? Should violent games be regulated? Write a letter explaining your opinion to the Federal Communications Commission (FCC) or to your local congressperson. Take a clear side and include your recommendations on what needs to be, or doesn't need to be, put into action. Consider the ever-changing types of heroes and primary characters in the games. Base your argument on your own observations and experience, and include at least three supporting details.

Note: If you are not familiar enough with video games, apply this topic to film or literature.

Thesis: Write a *one-sentence* response to the above assignment. Make certain this single sentence offers a clear statement of your position.

Example: Video game violence is pure fantasy, like the fantasy found in books or films, and the only controls should be to ensure that young children are not exposed to portrayals of extreme violence.

____

____

Organizational Plan: List at least three subtopics you will use to support your main idea. This list is your outline.

1. ____

2. ____

3. ____

Draft: Following your outline, write a good first draft of your essay. Remember to support all your points with examples, facts, references to reading, etc.

Review and Revise: Exchange essays with a classmate. Using the Holistic scoring guide on page 268, score your partner's essay (while he or she scores yours). If necessary, rewrite your essay to correct the problems indicated by the essay's score.

Lesson Sixteen

1. **recant** (ri kant´) *v.* to withdraw or disavow a statement or opinion
The suspect *recanted* his confession, so the police had to release him.

2. **impalpable** (im pāl´ pə bəl) *adj.* unable to be felt; intangible
He was aware of some *impalpable* fear as he entered the room.
syn: imperceptible; indiscernible

3. **salient** (sā´ lē ənt) *adj.* significant; conspicuous; standing out from the rest
The judge advised the attorney to stick to the *salient* facts of the case.
syn: important

4. **specious** (spē´ shəs) *adj.* deceptive or misleading
The *specious* advertisement depicts the run-down resort as a heavenly place.
syn: false *ant: accurate*

5. **salacious** (sə lā´ shəs) *adj.* obscene; lustful
The minister denounced the movie because of its *salacious* nature.
syn: lecherous *ant: chaste*

6. **fiscal** (fis´ kəl) *adj.* pertaining to finances
December is the accountant's busiest month because it is the end of the *fiscal* year.
syn: economic; budgetary

7. **recreant** (rek´ rē ənt) *n.* a coward; a traitor
Benedict Arnold is one of the most famous *recreants* in history.

8. **palliate** (pal´ ē āt) *v.* to ease; to lessen; to soothe
She became a nurse to *palliate* suffering, but all she had done so far was record patients' temperatures.
syn: alleviate; excuse *ant: intensify; exacerbate*

9. **jocular** (jok´ yə lər) *adj.* humorous; lighthearted
Dad's *jocular* manner faded when he started preparing the taxes.
syn: joking; witty; amusing *ant: solemn; morose*

10. **malleable** (mal´ ē ə bəl) *adj.* capable of being changed; easily shaped
The sculptor wanted to keep the clay *malleable* until he was sure of the final design.
syn: workable *ant: rigid; inflexible*

11. **affinity** (ə fin´ i tē) *n.* an attraction to
The young man had an *affinity* for fast cars and easy money.
syn: partiality; fondness *ant: aversion*

12. **regale** (ri gāl´) *v.* to delight with something pleasing or amusing
John *regaled* the crowd for hours with his stories of Scotland.
syn: entertain; amuse *ant: anger; depress; annoy*

13. **miscreant** (mis´ krē ənt) *n.* a vicious person
The police were looking for the *miscreant* in all of the local hangouts.
syn: villain; criminal; knave

14. **sentient** (sen´ shənt) *adj.* conscious; capable of feeling or perceiving
They didn't know if the girl in the coma was *sentient,* but they continued to hold her hand and talk to her.
syn: alert; alive; cognizant

15. **flout** (flout) *v.* to ridicule; to show contempt for
He broke the rules and *flouted* all authority, and now he has to pay.
syn: mock; scoff *ant: esteem; revere*

Exercise I

Words in Context

From the list below, supply the words needed to complete the paragraph. Some words will not be used.

salient	**miscreant**	**flout**	**affinity**
recant	**salacious**	**jocular**	

1. The actor was a[n] __________ who regularly __________ the law. Tabloid reporters followed him around all day, hoping to catch his __________ behavior on film. He had a[n] __________ for dive bars in bad neighborhoods. The reporters paid for any __________, negative information on him.

From the list below, supply the words needed to complete the paragraph. Some words will not be used.

palliate	**flout**	**specious**	**fiscal**
recant	**sentient**		

2. When a teacher sent a note of concern about Sara's imaginary friend, Sara's mother, Beth, realized that it might be time to have a talk about it; Sara was, after all, old enough for her behavior to cause concern. Beth __________ the talk by taking Sara for ice cream, and then asked Sara if she understood that her imaginary friend was not a[n] __________, living being.

   "Of course, mom," Sara replied. I was just messing with some of the kids at school; they fall for anything." Relieved, Beth realized that Sara's __________ friend was just a joke.

From the list below, supply the words needed to complete the paragraph. Some words will not be used.

jocular	**fiscal**	**affinity**	**recreant**
malleable	**impalpable**	**regale**	**specious**

3. The two __________ who had run away from the battle were engaged in __________ conversation when the search team surprised them. The cowards had stolen the battalion's treasury and __________ themselves with the thought of securing their __________ futures. They had planned to melt the __________ gold coins into bars and sell them on the black market. The weight of leg irons, however, helped them to snap out of their __________ dream.

Exercise II

Sentence Completion

Complete the sentence in a way that shows you understand the meaning of the italicized vocabulary word.

1. The surgeon *palliated* the patient's fears by...
2. Rachel *flouted* the rules at the rock concert, so the guards...
3. Teenagers with *malleable* beliefs are susceptible to cults because...
4. When the police cornered the *miscreant* in the alley, he...
5. The engine and wheels are *salient* parts of...
6. Greg did not understand the *impalpable*, sad meaning of the poem, and he...
7. The senator *recanted* his controversial statement because it...
8. Brandon brought a *salacious* magazine to class, so the teacher...
9. The *recreant* was temporarily happy to have escaped the fighting, but when the other soldiers found him, he...
10. Helen *regaled* the family by telling them about...
11. The husband and wife spy team made *specious* comments about...
12. It is good to see Jason in such a *jocular* mood for a change; he is usually...
13. Caleb has an *affinity* for Cajun food, but Allison prefers to...
14. Stormtech, a huge corporation, uses its vast *fiscal* powers to...
15. The crash victim was *sentient*, but she could not...

Exercise III

Roots, Prefixes, and Suffixes

Study the entries and answer the questions that follow.

The root *derm* means "skin."
The root *fer* means "to bear" or "to carry."
The prefix *in–* means "into" or "against."
The prefixes *suf–*, *sub–*, and *sus–* mean "under" or "secretly."
The prefix *epi–* means "upon," "over," or "above."
The prefix *de–* means "down" or "off."
The suffix *–al* means "pertaining to."
The suffix *–itis* means "inflammation of."

1. Using *literal* translations as guidance, define the following words without using a dictionary.

A.	tendinitis	D.	fertile
B.	suffer	E.	infer
C.	epicenter	F.	subdermal

2. An inflammation of the skin is a form of __________, and the best doctor to treat it is a[n] __________.

3. Literally, *transfer* means __________ __________.

   If a reading passage carries a thought to an outside idea, then the passage __________ to that idea.

   If you need to put off a payment until next month, you might ask the bank to __________ the payment until you have money.

4. List as many words as you can think of that contain the root *fer*.

5. List as many words as you can think of that end with the suffix *–al*.

Exercise IV

Inference

Complete the sentence by inferring information about the italicized word from its context.

1. The FBI reviewed the company's *fiscal* activities after investigators...

2. The arthritic artist preferred sculpting *malleable* clay to chiseling hard granite because the clay is...

3. Brook did not like crowds, but she had such an *affinity* for the band that she took herself to...

Exercise V

Critical Reading

Below is a pair of reading passages followed by several multiple-choice questions. Carefully read the passages and choose the best answer to each of the questions.

The first passage is an excerpt from the final chapter of Leo Tolstoy's novella, The Death of Ivan Ilych *(1886). In this passage, Ivan, an uninteresting bureaucrat on his deathbed, comes to terms with the spiritless life that he lived. The second passage is an excerpt from a chapter of* Sketches by Boz, *a collection of stories by Charles Dickens, first published in 1836. Chapter Twelve, "A Visit to Newgate," is Dickens's creative account of a visit to Victorian London's dreadful Newgate Prison. In this excerpt from the chapter, Dickens observes a condemned prisoner awaiting execution.*

Passage 1

For three whole days, during which time did not exist for him, he struggled in that black sack into which he was being thrust by an invisible, resistless force. He struggled as a man condemned to death struggles in the hands of the executioner, knowing that he cannot save himself. And every moment he felt that despite all his efforts he was drawing nearer and nearer to what terrified him. He felt that his agony was due to his being thrust into that black hole and still more to his not being able to get right into it. He was hindered from getting into it by his conviction that his life had been a good one. That very justification of his life held him fast and prevented his moving forward, and it caused him most torment of all.

Suddenly some force struck him in the chest and side, making it still harder to breathe, and he fell through the hole and there at the bottom was a light. What had happened to him was like the sensation one sometimes experiences in a railway carriage when one thinks one is going backwards while one is really going forwards and suddenly becomes aware of the real direction.

"Yes, it was not the right thing," he said to himself, "but that's no matter. It can be done. But what is the right thing?" he asked himself, and suddenly grew quiet.

This occurred at the end of the third day, two hours before his death. Just then his schoolboy son had crept softly in and gone up to the bedside. The dying man was still screaming desperately and waving his arms. His hand fell on the boy's head, and the boy caught it, pressed it to his lips, and began to cry.

At that very moment Ivan Ilych fell through and caught sight of the light, and it was revealed to him that though his life had not been what it should have been, this could still be rectified. He asked himself, "What *is* the right thing?" and grew still, listening. Then he felt that someone was kissing his hand. He opened his eyes, looked at his son, and felt sorry for him. His wife came up to him and he glanced at her. She was gazing at him open-mouthed, with undried tears on her nose and cheek and a despairing look on her face. He felt sorry for her too.

"Yes, I am making them wretched," he thought. "They are sorry, but it will be better for them when I die." He wished to say this but had not the strength to utter it. "Besides, why speak? I must act," he thought. With a look at his wife he indicated his son and said: "Take him away...sorry for him...sorry for you too...." He tried to add, "Forgive me," but said "Forego" and waved his hand, knowing that He whose understanding mattered would understand.

And suddenly it grew clear to him that what had been oppressing him and would not leave him was all dropping away at once from two sides, from ten sides, and from all sides. He was sorry for them, he must act so as not to hurt them: release them and free himself from these sufferings. "How good and how simple!" he thought. "And the pain?" he asked himself. "What has become of it? Where are you, pain?"

He turned his attention to it.

"Yes, here it is. Well, what of it? Let the pain be."

"And death...where is it?"

He sought his former accustomed fear of death and did not find it. "Where is it? What death?" There was no fear because there was no death.

In place of death there was light.

"So that's what it is!" he suddenly exclaimed aloud. "What joy!"

To him all this happened in a single instant, and the meaning of that instant did not change. For those present his agony continued for another two hours. Something rattled in his throat, his emaciated body twitched, then the gasping and rattle became less and less frequent.

"It is finished!" said someone near him.

He heard these words and repeated them in his soul.

"Death is finished," he said to himself. "It is no more!"

He drew in a breath, stopped in the midst of a sigh, stretched out, and died.

Passage 2

We entered the first cell. It was a stone dungeon, eight feet long by six wide, with a bench at the upper end, under which were a common rug, a bible, and prayer-book. An iron candlestick was fixed into the wall at the side; and a small high window in the back admitted as much air and light as could struggle in between a double row of heavy, crossed iron bars. It contained no other furniture of any description.

Conceive the situation of a man, spending his last night on earth in this cell. Buoyed up with some vague and undefined hope of reprieve, he knew not why—indulging in some wild and visionary idea of escaping, he knew not how—hour after hour of the three preceding days allowed him for preparation, has fled with a speed which no man living would deem possible, for none but this dying man can know. He has wearied his friends with entreaties, exhausted the attendants with importunities, neglected in his feverish restlessness the timely warnings of his spiritual consoler; and, now that the illusion is at last dispelled, now that eternity is before him and guilt behind, now that his fears of death amount almost to madness, and an overwhelming sense of his helpless, hopeless state rushes upon him, he is lost and stupefied, and has neither thoughts to turn to, nor power to call upon, the Almighty Being, from whom alone he can seek mercy and forgiveness, and before whom his repentance can alone avail.

Hours have glided by, and still he sits upon the same stone bench with folded arms, heedless alike of the fast decreasing time before him, and the urgent entreaties of the good man at his side. The feeble light is wasting gradually, and the deathlike stillness of the street without, broken only by the rumbling of some passing vehicle which echoes mournfully through the empty yards, warns him that the night is waning fast away. The deep bell of St. Paul's strikes—one! He heard it; it has roused him. Seven hours left! He paces the narrow limits of his cell with rapid strides, cold drops of terror starting on his forehead, and every muscle of his frame quivering with agony.

Seven hours! He suffers himself to be led to his seat, mechanically takes the bible which is placed in his hand, and tries to read and listen. No: his thoughts will wander. The book is torn and soiled by use—and like the book he read his lessons in, at school, just forty years ago! He has never bestowed a thought upon it, perhaps, since he left it as a child: and yet the place, the time, the room—nay, the very boys he played with, crowd as vividly before him as if they were scenes of yesterday; and some forgotten phrase, some childish word, rings in his ears like the echo of one uttered but a minute since. The voice of the clergyman recalls him to himself. He is reading from the sacred book its solemn promises of pardon for repentance, and its awful denunciation of obdurate men. He falls upon his knees and clasps his hands to pray. Hush! what sound was that? He starts upon his feet. It cannot be two yet. Hark! Two quarters have struck;—the third—the fourth. It is! Six hours left. Tell him not of repentance! Six hours' repentance for eight times six years of guilt and sin! He buries his face in his hands, and throws himself on the bench.

Worn with watching and excitement, he sleeps, and the same unsettled state of mind pursues him in his dreams. An insupportable load is taken from his breast; he is walking with his wife in a pleasant field, with the bright sky above them, and a fresh and boundless prospect on every side—how different from the stone walls of Newgate! She is looking—not as she did when he saw her for the last time in that dreadful place, but as she used when he loved her—long, long ago, before misery and ill-treatment had altered her looks, and vice had changed his nature, and she is leaning upon his arm, and looking up into his face with tenderness and affection—and he does NOT strike her now, nor rudely shake her from him. And oh! how glad he is to tell her all he had forgotten in that last hurried interview, and to fall on his knees before her and fervently beseech her pardon for all the unkindness and cruelty that wasted her form and broke her heart! The scene suddenly changes. He is on his trial again: there are the judge and jury, and prosecutors, and witnesses, just as they were before. How full the court is—what a sea of heads—with a gallows, too, and a scaffold—and how all those people stare at HIM! Verdict, 'Guilty.' No matter; he will escape.

The night is dark and cold, the gates have been left open, and in an instant he is in the street, flying from the scene of his imprisonment like the wind. The streets are cleared, the open fields are gained and the broad, wide country lies before him. Onward he dashes in the midst of darkness, over hedge and ditch, through mud and pool, bounding from spot to spot with a speed and lightness, astonishing even to himself. At length he pauses; he must be safe from pursuit now; he will stretch himself on that bank and sleep till sunrise.

A period of unconsciousness succeeds. He wakes, cold and wretched. The dull, gray light of morning is stealing into the cell, and falls upon the form of the attendant turnkey. Confused by his dreams, he starts from his uneasy bed in momentary uncertainty. It is but momentary. Every object in the narrow cell is too frightfully real to admit of doubt or mistake. He is the condemned felon again, guilty and despairing; and in two hours more will be dead.

1A. In paragraph 1 of the first passage, "being thrust into that black hole" is a metaphor for

A. repentance.
B. the inability to remember.
C. falling asleep.
D. surrendering to death.
E. justifying one's life.

1B. The source of Ivan's first internal struggle with death is best described as

A. a need to confront his family.
B. the torture he must endure from his nurse.
C. his belief that his life had been good.
D. a deep fear of confined spaces and darkness.
E. his unfinished confession of a crime.

2A. Which of the following best paraphrases this sentence from lines 28-29 of the first passage?

"He tried to add, 'Forgive me,' but said 'Forego' and waved his hand, knowing that He whose understanding mattered would understand."

A. It didn't matter if his family understood him because God would not understand.
B. Ivan never really cared for his family, so it did not matter if they failed to understand him.
C. God understood him, and that fact, unlike his family's lack of understanding, mattered.
D. He knew that God understood him, which mattered more than his family's contempt for him.
E. What Ivan understood did not matter, unlike what his family or God understood.

2B. Which statement, in support of your answer to question 2A, best describes Ivan's lack of concern about his last words?
A. Ivan had never been emotionally close to his family.
B. Ivan knew his son could grasp his (Ivan's) meaning.
C. Even on his deathbed, Ivan is cold toward his wife.
D. Ivan had given up on trying to fix his relationship.
E. Ivan's apology released him from any earthly concerns.

3A. The first passage is best described as
A. a depiction of the last few hours of Ivan Ilych's life.
B. a sketch of Ivan Ilych before his execution.
C. an account of Ivan Ilych's perception of his impending death.
D. Tolstoy's attempt to depict a universal reaction to dying.
E. the details of a dream of Ivan Ilych, Tolstoy's creation.

3B. What is Ivan Ilych's reaction to his earlier fear of death?
A. He wants to feel the fear again but cannot.
B. He no longer has the fear he had before.
C. He experiences the fear once again.
D. He longs to be rid of the fear because it pains him.
E. He substitutes love for family for the fear of death.

4A. What has "fled" in paragraph 2 of the second passage?
A. the prisoner's imagination
B. the will to seek redemption
C. the prisoner's hopes of escape
D. the prisoner's fears of death
E. the hours preceding the execution

4B. How is your answer to question 4A an element shared by both passages?
- A. Both men imagine that they have led good lives.
- B. The rules of time do not apply to those about to die.
- C. The look of Ivan's deathbed is identical to the bed in the prison cell.
- D. Both men find redemption through acceptance before they die.
- E. Light is used as symbolic of hope to both of the dying men.

5A. According to paragraph 3 of the second passage, the prisoner is
- A. 28 years old.
- B. 33 years old.
- C. 40 years old.
- D. 48 years old.
- E. 56 years old.

5B. The prisoner's age is included for the purpose of
- A. accurate reporting and truth.
- B. portraying him as less pitiable.
- C. showing how little time he spent repenting.
- D. showing his mortality.
- E. portraying him as someone finally accepting God.

6A. Which of the following best states the implication of this line from passage 2 (lines 42-43)?

"…she is leaning upon his arm, and looking up into his face with tenderness and affection—and he does NOT strike her now, nor rudely shake her from him."

- A. The prisoner does not understand why he cannot strike his wife.
- B. The prisoner used to physically abuse his wife.
- C. The prisoner and his wife do not usually get along.
- D. The prisoner has a terrible temper.
- E. The prisoner and his wife have not seen each other for years.

6B. Choose the quotation that provides the best support for your answer to question 6A.
- A. "…looking up into his face with tenderness and affection…"
- B. "…how glad he is…to fall on his knees before her…"
- C. "She is looking…as she used when he loved her…"
- D. "…unkindness and cruelty that wasted her form and broke her heart!"
- E. "…people stare at HIM! Verdict, 'Guilty.' "

7A. As used in line 57 of the second passage, *stealing* most nearly means
- A. taking without permission.
- B. leaving.
- C. forging.
- D. creating a metallic shine.
- E. creeping.

7B. The light described in the final paragraph of passage 2 can be said to symbolize
   A. fantasy.
   B. reality.
   C. hope.
   D. death.
   E. guilt.

8A. One emotion that the central characters of both passages feel is
   A. remorse for hurting their families.
   B. awe for the unknown.
   C. remorse for their own situations.
   D. arrogance toward death.
   E. fear of not repenting.

8B. What feeling does the prisoner harbor that seems contrary to his guilt?
   A. hope for escape.
   B. need for love.
   C. anger over his trial.
   D. embarrassment.
   E. pride.

9A. Which of the following best describes the difference in the situation between the main characters in each of the passages?
   A. Ivan handles death much better than the prisoner does.
   B. The prisoner does not exhibit any regret, while Ivan apologizes.
   C. Ivan is physically dying, while the prisoner is waiting to be killed.
   D. Ivan's death is a nonfiction account, while Dickens's story is exaggerated.
   E. The prisoner is willing to accept death as punishment, but Ivan dreams of escaping from death.

9B. Which choice best describes the relationship between the narrator and the prisoner of passage 2?
   A. The prisoner is telling his own story.
   B. The narrator of passage 2 does not know the prisoner's internal thoughts.
   C. The narrator is fictional, while the prisoner is real.
   D. The prisoner is a character in the narrator's story.
   E. The narrator is the prisoner's warden.

10. Which of the following is a major theme shared by both passages?
   A. accepting one's fate
   B. mistreatment of the dying
   C. family communication
   D. the benefits of optimism
   E. the power of religion

Lesson Seventeen

1. **avuncular** (ə vung´ kyə lər) *adj.* similar to an uncle
Martin was not related to the children, but he had an *avuncular* role in raising them.

2. **desultory** (des´ əl tôr ē) *adj.* wandering from subject to subject
He gave his talk in such a *desultory* fashion that it was hard to understand.
syn: disconnected; rambling

3. **hector** (hek´ tər) *v.* to bully; to pester
If you don't take a stand, that bully will *hector* you for the rest of the year.
syn: badger; browbeat

4. **beguile** (bi gīl´) *v.* to deceive; to charm; to enchant
Scarlet O'Hara tried to *beguile* all the eligible men she met.
syn: charm; fool *ant: irritate; bore*

5. **hiatus** (hī ā´ təs) *n.* a pause or gap
If you take a *hiatus* from your studies, you might forget the things you have learned.
syn: intermission; break

6. **insolence** (in´ sō lens) *n.* disrespectful arrogance; rudeness
Certain Greek warriors were known for their *insolence* toward enemies in battle.
syn: offensiveness; contempt *ant: humility; respect*

7. **nonentity** (non en´ ti tē) *n.* a person or thing of little importance
"I'm right here!" she yelled, "but you treat me as a *nonentity*."
syn: cipher; nobody

8. **coalesce** (kō ə les´) *v.* to blend; to merge
The citizens overcame their differences and *coalesced* to rebuild the town after the hurricane.
syn: mix; unite; combine *ant: separate; divide*

9. **lambent** (lam´ bənt) *adj.* softly bright or radiant; flickering lightly over a surface
The *lambent* flames cast shadows throughout the cabin.
syn: glowing; lucid

10. **sibilant** (sib´ ə lənt) *adj.* a hissing sound
The guide stopped moving when he heard the *sibilant* sound of a snake.

11. **rebuke** (ri byōōk´) *v.* to scold; to blame
The professor *rebuked* his students for not studying for the exam.
syn: admonish; reprimand *ant: praise; laud*

12. **pandemic** (pan dem´ ik) *adj.* general; widespread
The Center for Disease Control announced that the disease has become *pandemic.*

13. **ennui** (än wē´) *n.* boredom; a weariness resulting from a lack of interest
The speaker sensed the *ennui* of the audience, so he told a joke.
ant: excitement; interest

14. **ergo** (ûr´ gō) *conj.* therefore
I am broke; *ergo,* I can't pay the rent this week.
syn: consequently; hence

15. **pecuniary** (pi kyōō´ nē er´ ē) *adj.* pertaining to money; financial
Jill faced many *pecuniary* troubles after losing her job.
syn: monetary

Exercise I

Words in Context

From the list below, supply the words needed to complete the paragraph. Some words will not be used.

ennui	**hiatus**	**ergo**	**pandemic**
avuncular	**rebuke**	**sibilant**	

1. Bill, a hazardous-materials cleanup technician, kept his cool when he heard the __________ sound of air escaping from his breathing apparatus. His air was running out, but he had to close the valve on the chemical tank before __________ contamination forced the city to evacuate. As he struggled to turn the valve, Bill __________ himself for not inspecting his equipment more often. Six months earlier, an injury had forced Bill to take a[n] __________ from his career, and the __________ of doing nothing had been more painful to him than the chemical burn. Since the injury, Bill had taken on a[n] __________ role to the rookies on his team, offering his mistakes as lessons for them to stay safe in the field.

From the list below, supply the words needed to complete the paragraph. Some words will not be used.

nonentity	**pecuniary**	**ergo**	**beguile**	**hector**
ennui	**desultory**	**hiatus**	**coalesce**	**insolence**

2. Anne's __________ worries made it hard for her to concentrate on her roommate's __________ rambling. Disrespectful bill collectors __________ Anne every day, and she knew that her next check would not stop their __________. She gazed at the __________ patterns of light that the aquarium cast on the floor, while allowing moneymaking ideas to __________ in her head. Anne had already tried to __________ her boss into letting her work more hours, but the company regarded college students as __________ who did not warrant full-time jobs. She needed to make enough money to pay for the next semester; __________, Anne would have to find a better job.

Exercise II

Sentence Completion

Complete the sentence in a way that shows you understand the meaning of the italicized vocabulary word.

1. Jazz was conceived in the United States, but its *pandemic* growth...

2. Adam wanted to teach again, but the *hiatus* in his career was so long that...

3. During the company strike, some of the picketers *hectored* the people who continued...

4. The *lambent* moonlight reflected on the surface of...

5. When the bank saw that Cole had had *pecuniary* troubles in the past, it refused to...

6. Major Battles responds to *insolence* in the ranks by...

7. To Leslie, the board meeting was two hours of *ennui*, and it would be difficult for her to...

8. While discussing colleges, Alexa's parents said that her boyfriend is a *nonentity* and that he should not influence...

9. I will not go out to dinner with you; *ergo*,...

10. The vacuum cleaner salesman *beguiled* the couple into believing...

11. The suspect's *desultory* alibi convinced the police that...

12. Lucas *rebuked* the dog, but...

13. Matthews is an *avuncular* friend to the children; sometimes he takes them...

14. The auto-body repair shop *coalesced* all its records so that...

15. When Courtney heard the *sibilant* noise coming from the tire, she knew that...

Exercise III

Roots, Prefixes, and Suffixes

Study the entries and answer the questions that follow.

The root *lud* means "to play" or "to mock."
The root *grav* means "heavy."
The root *son* means "sound" or "to sound."
The root *und* means "wave," "to surge," or "to flood."
The prefix *ab–* means "to flow."
The prefix *inter–* means "between" or "among."

1. Using *literal* translations as guidance, define the following words without using a dictionary.

A.	elude	D.	sonic
B.	ludicrous	E.	gravity
C.	illusion	F.	undulate

2. The __________ to the play consisted of a narrator describing the setting before the curtain opened. An orchestra played musical __________ between acts while the theater crew rearranged the stage.

3. A[n] __________ situation has heavy consequences, and if you __________ the problem, then you will add to it.

4. The alphabet consists of sounds that we call vowels and __________.
If the members of a chorus all sing together, then they are said to be singing in __________.

   William Shakespeare is famous for his drama and his __________, or poems consisting of fourteen lines.

5. A[n] __________ essay is flooded with extra words, and its unnecessary length might __________ readers.

Exercise IV

Inference

Complete the sentence by inferring information about the italicized word from its context.

1. The cockroach is a *pandemic* insect; most of the people on Earth would probably be able to...

2. The student's typical *insolence* finally crossed the line and got her into trouble when ...

3. Tim believed that his thoughts were too *desultory* for him to become a pharmacist; he worried that he might fill the wrong prescription because he...

Exercise V

Writing

Here is a writing prompt similar to the one you will find on the writing portion of an assessment test.

Plan and write an essay based on the following statement:

> Author Anna Quindlen wrote in *How Reading Changed My Life*, "I did not read from a sense of superiority, or advancement, or even learning. I read because I loved it more than any other activity on earth."

Assignment: Consider the importance Quindlen attaches to reading. Is the act of reading truly that important, or do equally valid substitutes exist, especially in the media-rich modern world? In an essay, discuss your position on reading and why it should, or should not, be a top priority for everyone. Include examples and support based on your own life, reading, or observations.

Thesis: Write a *one-sentence* response to the above assignment. Make certain this single sentence offers a clear statement of your position.

Example: Of course reading is a beneficial activity, but the only way to truly learn, and improve, is by taking action at some point and using the knowledge one has gained.

____

____

Organizational Plan: List at least three subtopics you will use to support your main idea. This list is your outline.

1. ______________________________

2. ______________________________

3. ______________________________

Draft: Following your outline, write a good first draft of your essay. Remember to support all your points with examples, facts, references to reading, etc.

Review and Revise: Exchange essays with a classmate. Using the scoring guide for Word Choice on page 267, score your partner's essay (while he or she scores yours). Focus on word choice and the use of language conventions. If necessary, rewrite your essay to improve your word choice and/or your use of language.

Exercise VI

English Practice

Identifying Sentence Errors

Identify the grammatical error in each of the following sentences. If the sentence contains no error, select answer choice E.

1. By the time Joe finally (A) got a job he (B) had applied to more than (C) fifty companies (D). No error (E)

2. Has the coach chose (A) the new uniforms (B) for the soccer team (C) yet? (D) No error (E)

3. Anyone (A) who is seeking articles lost at the theater (B) may check (C) lost and found for their items (D). No error (E)

4. Dave is so ill (A) that he has done (B) nothing but lay (C) on the bed all day (D). No error (E)

5. Young people, (A) like you and I, (B) have so many career options available that it (C) is hard to (D) make a selection. No error (E)

Improving Sentences

The underlined portion of each sentence below contains some flaw. Select the answer choice that best corrects the flaw.

6. The thief ran up behind her, <u>grabs the woman's purse,</u> and ran around a corner before anyone could see his face.
   A. grabbed the woman's purse
   B. grabs the women's purse
   C. grabbed the womens' purse
   D. grabs the purse of the woman
   E. grabbed the womans'

7. Jane has excellent qualifications not only as a scientist, <u>but she knows a lot about management, too.</u>
   A. and she wants to be a manager, too.
   B. but also in the skills of management.
   C. but also as a manager.
   D. but in management, as well.
   E. but also in managing.

8. Lucy baked <u>chocolate chip cookies to give her friends with walnuts</u>.
   A. walnuts with chocolate chip cookies to give her friends.
   B. chocolate chip cookies with walnuts.
   C. chocolate chip cookies for her friends to give.
   D. to give her friends, chocolate chip cookies with walnuts.
   E. chocolate chip cookies with walnuts to give her friends.

9. Our boss called <u>a meeting in relation to</u> the sales project.
   A. a meeting about
   B. a discussion session in relation to
   C. to tell us to meet to talk about
   D. a meeting in which we were to discuss
   E. about

10. Monk Pond <u>is much more shallower than</u> Goodman's Lake.
   A. contains less depth than
   B. is shallower than
   C. does not have the depth of
   D. is much more shallow than
   E. is much less deep than

Lesson Eighteen

1. **contiguous** (kən tig´ ū wəs) *adj.* making contact or touching at some point; side by side
   New Jersey and New York are *contiguous* states because they share a common boundary.
   syn: adjoining; abutting *ant: separated; detached*

2. **apotheosis** (ə pä thē ō´səs) *n.* the finest example
   The British Parliament has become the *apotheosis* of parliamentary government and serves as a model for many other nations around the world.
   syn: epitome; archetype

3. **proletariat** (prō lə ter´ ē ət) *n.* the working class or lower class
   While many of the rich lived in the hills surrounding the town, the *proletariat* lived in the valley near where they worked.

4. **malfeasance** (mal fēz´ əns) *n.* poor conduct or wrongdoing, especially on the part of a public official
   The *malfeasance* of the congressman caused an investigation into his personal conduct.
   syn: corruption; crookedness

5. **vociferous** (vō si´ fə rəs) *adj.* marked by noise; loud
   The *vociferous* yelling of the crowd seemed to inspire the team toward victory.
   syn: boisterous; clamorous

6. **incendiary** (in sen´ dē er ē) *adj.* causing to excite or inflame
   The speaker was not invited back because his *incendiary* behavior caused a riot.
   syn: instigative; inciting

7. **platonic** (plə tä´ nik) *adj.* marked by the absence of romance or physical attraction
   Gayle and Robert's *platonic* friendship was based on similar interests and not on romantic interest.

8. **prurient** (prur´ ē ənt) *adj.* given to lustful or lewd thoughts
   Sean's weak willpower often led him to *prurient* activities that were of a questionable nature.
   syn: obscene

9. **auspicious** (o spi´ shəs) *adj.* signaling favorable or promising results
   The dark clouds were an *auspicious* sign that rain would fall on the withered fields.
   syn: encouraging

10. **sang-froid** (sän frwa´) *n.* calmness; composure or cool self-possession
The speaker maintained his *sang-froid* despite the heckler's comments.
syn: aplomb; self-confidence *ant: uneasiness; perturbation*

11. **tenacious** (tə nā´ shəs) *adj.* strongly held; not easy to separate
No one could break the child's *tenacious* grip on the doll.
syn: clinging; resolute *ant: weak*

12. **flagellate** (flaj´ ə lāt) *v.* to whip; to lash
The boy's father never struck him, but he *flagellated* him verbally.
syn: flog

13. **refractory** (ri frak´ tə rē) *adj.* unmanageable or difficult to control; willful
The *refractory* group of boys refused to stop joking with each other during class.
syn: defiant; provocative *ant: obedient; conforming*

14. **inimitable** (i ni´ mə tə bəl) *adj.* cannot be imitated
The actress was famous for her *inimitable* techniques.
syn: incomparable; unparalleled

15. **pontificate** (pän ti´ fə kāt) *v.* to speak in a pretentiously dignified or dogmatic way
The prosecutor *pontificated* about the defendant's considerable criminal record.
syn: orate; sermonize

Exercise I

Words in Context

From the list below, supply the words needed to complete the paragraph. Some words will not be used.

tenacious	**inimitable**	**auspicious**	**platonic**
vociferous	**pontificate**	**proletariat**	

1. The economist, famous for his __________ style of speaking, claimed the shrinking __________ and growing middle class was a[n] __________ sign that the nation's economy was maturing properly. In addition, despite __________ cries to the contrary, he insisted that the nation would need to break its __________ dependence on fossil fuels and develop new forms of technology.

From the list below, supply the words needed to complete the paragraph. Some words will not be used.

refractory	**malfeasance**	**sang-froid**	**flagellate**
contiguous	**platonic**	**vociferous**	

2. For the third morning in a row, Heidi looked outside her kitchen window only to see the neighbor's cow __________ itself with its tail to keep mosquitoes at bay. The pasture is __________ with Heidi's property, and Mark, the cow's owner, never checks the fence for damage. In the previous year, Mark's __________ goats ate every shrub on Heidi's lawn before Mark decided that owning them wasn't worth the expense. Though the neighbors had once had a[n] __________ friendship, Heidi was struggling to maintain her __________ in dealing with Mark every time one of his animals destroyed her property.

From the list below, supply the words needed to complete the paragraph. Some words will not be used.

pontificate	**malfeasance**	**contiguous**	**apotheosis**
incendiary	**proletariat**	**prurient**	

3. Thousands of citizens phoned the network with __________ remarks about the __________ halftime show that featured scantily-clad dancers. Some considered the show to be a[n] __________ of the head of the network, and others described the show as the __________ of a declining culture. Talk show hosts and political speakers __________ about the display for weeks after the game.

Exercise II

Sentence Completion

Complete the sentence in a way that shows you understand the meaning of the italicized vocabulary word.

1. On the tour of the castle, the guide *pontificated* about…

2. Ashley has only *platonic* relationships with coworkers because she believes that…

3. When people in the town revealed the teacher's *prurient* night life, the administration decided to…

4. Julia kept a *tenacious* grip on her purse whenever she…

5. The buggy driver *flagellated* the horses in an attempt to…

6. When the owners of the steel mills refused to raise wages, the *proletariat*…

7. Your sculpture is not exactly the *apotheosis* of fine art, so stop complaining about the way I…

8. The *auspicious* blossoms on the orange trees gave the farmers hope that the frost had not…

9. Nicole hated walking the *refractory* pack of dogs down the street because they…

10. Ethan could no longer stand his neighbor's *vociferous* parties, so he…

11. A fireman who loses his *sang-froid* while fighting a fire may…

12. Texas, being the largest of the *contiguous* forty-eight states, is…

13. Allison did not bother to curb her *incendiary* remarks in her letter to…

14. The governor denied any *malfeasance* on her behalf, but the investigating committee…

15. The artist's *inimitable* style makes her work impossible to…

Exercise III

Roots, Prefixes, and Suffixes

Study the entries and answer the questions that follow.

The root *mut* means "to change."
The root *oper* means "to work."
The root *pet* means "to seek" or "to go toward."
The prefix *in–* means "against" or "not."
The prefix *per–* means "through" or "completely."
The prefix *com–* means "together."

1. Using *literal* translations as guidance, define the following words without using a dictionary.

   A. petition
   B. impetus
   C. transmute
   D. perpetual
   E. cooperate
   F. operation

2. A change to something is a[n] __________, and things that cannot be changed are said to be __________.

   Members of a parole board might meet together and decide to change, or __________, an inmate's prison sentence.

3. Opposing teams __________ by going, or working, toward a goal, and this act of going toward something together is called a[n] __________.

   When you lift weights for exercise, each act of going again is called one __________.

4. List as many words as you can think of that begin with the prefix *in–* as it is defined in this exercise.

Exercise IV

Inference

Complete the sentence by inferring information about the italicized word from its context.

1. The auditor suspected that the city treasurer was guilty of *malfeasance* when he discovered that the treasurer had…

2. Marty was still comatose, but the doctor said that movement of his fingers was an *auspicious* sign that Marty would probably…

3. Danielle considers the painting to be the *apotheosis* of contemporary art, but Kurt…

Exercise V

Critical Reading

Below is a reading passage followed by several multiple-choice questions. Carefully read the passage and choose the best answer for each of the questions.

The following passage, entitled "The American Invasion," is one of Oscar Wilde's many astute observations of life during the Victorian period. In this essay, the famous satirist and dramatist comments on the spread of American culture to London, including such elements as Buffalo Bill's Wild West Show and the appearance of Cora Brown-Potter, an American of high society, who abandoned class expectations to become an actress.

A terrible danger is hanging over the Americans in London. Their future and their reputation this season depend entirely on the success of Buffalo Bill and Mrs. Brown-Potter. The former is certain to draw; for English people are far more interested in American barbarism than they are in American civilization. When they sight Sandy Hook they look to their rifles and ammunition; and, after dining once at Delmonico's, start off for Colorado or California, for Montana or the Yellow Stone Park. Rocky Mountains charm them more than riotous millionaires; they have been known to prefer buffaloes to Boston. Why should they not? The cities of America are inexpressibly tedious. The Bostonians take their learning too sadly; culture with them is an accomplishment rather than an atmosphere; their "Hub," as they call it, is the paradise of prigs. Chicago is a sort of monster-shop, full of bustle and bores. Political life at Washington is like political life in a suburban vestry. Baltimore is amusing for a week, but Philadelphia is dreadfully provincial; and though one can dine in New York one could not dwell there. Better the Far West with its grizzly bears and its untamed cowboys, its free open-air life and its free open-air manners, its boundless prairie and its boundless mendacity! This is what Buffalo Bill is going to bring to London; and we have no doubt that London will fully appreciate his show.

With regard to Mrs. Brown-Potter, as acting is no longer considered absolutely essential for success on the English stage, there is really no reason why the pretty bright-eyed lady who charmed us all last June by her merry laugh and her nonchalant ways, should not—to borrow an expression from her native language—make a big boom and paint the town red. We sincerely hope she will; for, on the whole, the American invasion has done English society a great deal of good. American women are bright, clever, and wonderfully cosmopolitan. Their patriotic feelings are limited to an admiration for Niagara and a regret for the Elevated Railway; and, unlike the men, they never bore us with Bunker Hill. They take their dresses from Paris and their manners from Piccadilly, and wear both charmingly. They have a quaint pertness, a delightful conceit, a native self-assertion. They insist on being paid compliments and have almost succeeded in making Englishmen eloquent. For our aristocracy they have an ardent admiration; they adore titles and are a permanent blow to Republican principles. In the art of amusing men they are adepts, both by nature and education, and can actually tell a story without forgetting the point—an accomplishment that is extremely rare among the women of other countries. It is true that they lack repose and that their voices are somewhat harsh and strident when they land first at Liverpool; but after a time one gets to love those pretty whirlwinds in petticoats that sweep so recklessly through society and are so agitating to all duchesses who have daughters. There is something fascinating in their funny, exaggerated gestures and their petulant way of tossing the head. Their eyes have no magic nor mystery in them, but they challenge us for combat; and when we engage we are always worsted. Their lips seem made for laughter and yet they never grimace. As for their voices they soon get them into tune. Some of them have been known to acquire a fashionable drawl in two seasons; and after they have been presented to Royalty they all roll their R's as vigorously as a young equerry or an old lady-in-waiting. Still, they never really lose their accent; it keeps peeping out here and there, and when they chatter together they are like a bevy of peacocks. Nothing is more amusing than to watch two American girls greeting each other in a drawing-room or in the Row. They are like children with their shrill staccato cries of wonder, their odd little exclamations. Their conversation sounds like a series of exploding crackers; they are exquisitely incoherent and use a sort of primitive, emotional language. After five minutes they are left beautifully breathless and look at each other half in amusement and half in affection. If a stolid young Englishman is fortunate enough to be introduced to them he is amazed at their extraordinary vivacity, their electric quickness of repartee, their inexhaustible store of curious catchwords. He never really understands them, for their thoughts flutter about with the sweet irresponsibility of butterflies; but he is pleased and amused and feels as if he were in an aviary. On the whole, American girls have a wonderful charm and, perhaps, the chief secret of their charm is that they never talk seriously except about amusements. They have, however, one grave fault—their mothers. Dreary as were those old Pilgrim Fathers who left our shores more than two centuries ago to found a New England beyond the seas, the Pilgrim Mothers who have returned to us in the nineteenth century are drearier still.

Here and there, of course, there are exceptions, but as a class they are either dull, dowdy or dyspeptic. It is only fair to the rising generation of America to state that they are not to blame for this. Indeed, they spare no pains at all to bring up their parents properly and to give them a suitable, if somewhat late, education. From its earliest years every American child spends most of its time in correcting the faults of its father and mother; and no one who has had the opportunity of watching an American family on the deck of an Atlantic steamer, or in the refined seclusion of a New York boarding-house, can fail to have been struck by this characteristic of their civilization. In America the young are always ready to give to those who are older than themselves the full benefits of their inexperience. A boy of only eleven or twelve years of age will firmly but kindly point out to his father his defects of manner or temper; will never weary of warning him against extravagance, idleness, late hours, unpunctuality, and the other temptations to which the aged are so particularly exposed; and sometimes, should he fancy that he is monopolizing too much of the conversation at dinner, will remind him, across the table, of the new child's adage, "Parents should be seen, not heard." Nor does any mistaken idea of kindness prevent the little American girl from censuring her mother whenever it is necessary. Often, indeed, feeling that a rebuke conveyed in the presence of others is more truly efficacious than one merely whispered in the quiet of the nursery, she will call the attention of perfect strangers to her mother's general untidiness, her want of intellectual Boston conversation, immoderate love of iced water and green corn, stinginess in the matter of candy, ignorance of the usages of the best Baltimore Society, bodily ailments, and the like. In fact, it may be truly said that no American child is ever blind to the deficiencies of its parents, no matter how much it may love them.

Yet, somehow, this educational system has not been so successful as it deserved. In many cases, no doubt, the material with which the children had to deal was crude and incapable of real development; but the fact remains that the American mother is a tedious person. The American father is better, for he is never seen in London. He passes his life entirely in Wall Street and communicates with his family once a month by means of a telegram in cipher. The mother, however, is always with us, and, lacking the quick imitative faculty of the younger generation, remains uninteresting and provincial to the last. In spite of her, however, the American girl is always welcome. She brightens our dull dinner parties for us and makes life go pleasantly by for a season. In the race for coronets she often carries off the prize; but, once she has gained the victory, she is generous and forgives her English rivals everything, even their beauty.

Warned by the example of her mother that American women do not grow old gracefully, she tries not to grow old at all and often succeeds. She has exquisite feet and hands, is always *bien chaussée et bien gantée* and can talk brilliantly upon any subject, provided that she knows nothing about it.

Her sense of humor keeps her from the tragedy of a grand passion, and, as there is neither romance nor humility in her love, she makes an excellent wife. What her ultimate influence on English life will be it is difficult to estimate at present; but there can be no doubt that, of all the factors that have contributed to the social revolution of London, there are few more important, and none more delightful, than the American Invasion.

1A. Paragraph 1 portrays the English visitors to America as eager to
   A. enjoy the luxuries of the wealthy cities.
   B. forego civilization for the wilder areas.
   C. cavort with millionaires accessible in New York.
   D. visit each American city and witness the political scene.
   E. avoid the tourist traps of the American "West."

1B. Reread this sentence from paragraph 1: "Better the Far West with its grizzly bears and its untamed cowboys, its free open-air life and its free open-air manners, its boundless prairie and its boundless mendacity!" *Mendacity* means "falseness" or "lies." Which statement best rephrases Wilde's line while maintaining his intent?
   A. Lying is permissible and encouraged in the American West.
   B. Cowboys lie about the West, grizzlies, manners, and prairies.
   C. The idea of the "Far West" is an unlimited fantasy.
   D. Untruths about the Far West are primarily about Nature.
   E. No one knows for sure what happens in American West.

2A. Why does Wilde bring up Mrs. Brown-Potter, but then discusses her only briefly?
   A. She is meant to be a symbol of American women.
   B. She is a well-known example of American actresses.
   C. She has been to England previously and knows the country.
   D. She was a big hit on the British stage and shows that Americans can act.
   E. She provides a concrete example of America that Wilde can admire.

2B. Choose the line that best supports your choice for question 2A.
   A. "…the pretty bright-eyed lady who charmed us all last June…"
   B. "…the American invasion has done English society a great deal of good."
   C. "…acting is no longer considered absolutely essential for success…"
   D. "…make a big boom and paint the town red."
   E. "We sincerely hope she will…"

3. Wilde's overall assessment of American cities on the East Coast is best summarized as
   A. thrilling.
   B. controlling.
   C. classy.
   D. savage.
   E. boring.

4A. In England, a *vestry* was a committee that managed the property or business attached to a church or public area. The *vestry* mentioned in line 11 would probably resemble a
   A. trade union.
   B. town council.
   C. university lecture.
   D. Congressional hearing.
   E. tailor shop.

4B. The author's comparison of suburbia to Washington, D.C., implies which one of the following statements?
   A. Every region has its own political atmosphere.
   B. Life is easier in the city.
   C. Politics create the culture in a place.
   D. Politics are the same everywhere.
   E. A capital city is always political.

5. Which choice best identifies the implication in the first sentence of paragraph 2?
   A. Mrs. Brown-Potter will be a hit.
   B. Most actors are conceited.
   C. Mrs. Brown-Potter is not an impressive actress.
   D. Mrs. Brown-Potter is charming, but she will not succeed.
   E. British actresses are not as good as Mrs. Brown-Potter.

6A. In lines 21-51, Wilde describes his perception of American women. What is ironic about Wilde's list of American girls' faults, which includes "agitating," "reckless," and "strident"?
   A. Wilde describes English girls in exactly the same terms.
   B. American girls are shy when they are in foreign lands.
   C. The girls do not acknowledge history in any way.
   D. To Wilde, the negative elements are what make American girls charming.
   E. The girls are boring in England, but interesting in America.

6B. According to paragraph 2, the single greatest flaw of American girls is
   A. their poor communication.
   B. their mothers.
   C. the way they imitate class.
   D. too much conceit.
   E. their heavy accent.

7A. In line 54, "they" probably refers to
   A. young Americans.
   B. university professors.
   C. the upper class.
   D. American mothers.
   E. tourists arriving in London.

7B. According to Wilde, the American parents most resemble
   A. the Pilgrims who left England for America.
   B. children because they have no self-control.
   C. pioneers of the American Midwest.
   D. housekeepers, picking up after their children.
   E. schoolteachers who always criticize their students.

8A. The description of child-parent relationships in paragraph 3 is
   A. an extended pun because it plays on the word *parents*.
   B. unnecessary because it detracts from the passage.
   C. ironic because it exchanges the roles of parents and children.
   D. an example of exaggerated language.
   E. the primary point that the passage is trying to make.

8B. Choose the quotation that best supports your answer to question 8A.
   A. "...fair to the rising generation of America..."
   B. "...one who has had the opportunity of watching an American family..."
   C. "...this characteristic of their civilization."
   D. "...the young are always ready to give...the full benefits of their inexperience."
   E. "...they...bring up their parents properly..."

9A. The author of the passage probably feels that
   A. America produces good actors, but not good chefs.
   B. American culture is an abomination to self-respecting Londoners.
   C. too many people are attracted to American pastimes.
   D. American culture is ridiculous, but entertaining.
   E. America is a threat to the British way of life.

9B. When this passage was written, the intended audience was probably
   A. the American public.
   B. the British public.
   C. Wilde's fellow authors.
   D. people who traveled to America.
   E. a British emigrant to the United States.

10A. If Wilde were to eliminate the first paragraph of the essay, the essay could easily be re-titled:
   A. Seen But Not Heard.
   B. Wild Children of America.
   C. The Absent American Father.
   D. The Many Sides of Americans in England.
   E. The American Female.

10B. The essay is best described as
   A. humorous.
   B. historical.
   C. political.
   D. criticism.
   E. nonfiction.

Review Lessons 16-18

Exercise I

Inferences

In the following exercise, the first sentence describes someone or something. Infer information from the first sentence, and then choose the word from the Word Bank that best completes the second sentence.

auspicious	**miscreant**	**apotheosis**	**prurient**	**rebuke**
coalesce	**affinity**	**nonentity**		

1. The city health inspector condemned the house in which an old woman kept more than sixty cats in deplorable conditions.

   From this sentence, we can infer that the woman's __________ for cats has destroyed her home.

2. Permanent red spots on the stone countertop marked places in which fruit punch had been spilled and allowed to evaporate.

   From this sentence, we can infer that fruit punch will stain the countertop if it is allowed time to _________ with the stone.

3. News of the copper shortage drove prices up almost immediately, and suppliers reported record profits.

   From this sentence, we can infer that the copper shortage was __________ for the owners of copper mines.

4. The perfect example of a Greyhound won its division at the national dog show three years in a row.

   From this sentence, we can infer that the Greyhound was the __________ of its breed.

5. Nicole had worked in the office for eight weeks, and her managers still did not know her name or acknowledge her when they walked past her desk in the morning.

   From this sentence, we can infer that Nicole is treated as a[n] __________ at work.

Exercise II

Related Words

Some of the vocabulary words from Lessons 16 through 18 have related meanings. Complete the following sentences by choosing the word that best fits the context, based on information you infer from the use of the italicized word. Some word pairs will be antonyms, some will be synonyms, and some will simply be words often used in the same context.

1. When authorities attempted to arrest the crooked vice governor for criminal __________, the *recreant* hid behind his own children.
   A. affinity
   B. malfeasance
   C. nonentity
   D. apotheosis
   E. hiatus

2. Facing execution, Scheherazade __________ the king, her captor, with stories for 1,001 consecutive nights, and *beguiled* him in the process.
   A. palliated
   B. recanted
   C. coalesced
   D. rebuked
   E. regaled

3. Before Martin would be allowed to take __________ control of his family's fortune, he had to earn a college degree and learn how to manage *pecuniary* matters.
   A. platonic
   B. prurient
   C. tenacious
   D. vociferous
   E. fiscal

4. The __________ couple were always together, but their relationship was strictly *platonic.*
   A. fiscal
   B. impalpable
   C. jocular
   D. malleable
   E. miscreant

5. Quentin's __________ attempt to catch the *refractory* horse failed, so he sat down and created a more thorough plan.
   A. salacious
   B. fiscal
   C. pandemic
   D. desultory
   E. contiguous

6. Patricia __________ over her recent promotion to vice president of operations, knowing that it should make her happy, but the truth was that any sense of pride was *impalpable* to her because she no longer enjoyed her career.
   A. rebuked
   B. regaled
   C. flouted
   D. coalesced
   E. pontificated

7. After getting caught sneaking around the back of warehouse while carrying tire irons and wearing ski masks, the *miscreants* offered __________ explanations to the police as to what they had been doing.
   A. impalpable
   B. malleable
   C. vociferous
   D. specious
   E. refractory

8. Paul, who has a[n] __________ for insects that mimic plants, considers the orchid mantis to be the *apotheosis* of the game because it camouflages itself as a flower in order to capture its prey.
   A. nonentity
   B. affinity
   C. hiatus
   D. proletariat
   E. ennui

9. The __________ rumbling of an excavator *palliated* the trapped miners, who had thought they would never be rescued.
   A. auspicious
   B. refractory
   C. specious
   D. tenacious
   E. vociferous

10. The __________ account of the company's cover-up of hazardous products quickly became *pandemic* when the story reached the Internet.
    A. fiscal
    B. jocular
    C. malleable
    D. incendiary
    E. sentient

Exercise III

Deeper Meanings

Choose a word to replace the italicized word in each sentence. All of the possible choices for each sentence have similar definitions, but the correct answer will have a connotation that best suits the context. For example, the words "delete," "destroy," and "obliterate," all mean "to remove or wipe out," but no one would ever say, "I destroyed the name from the document." The correct choice will be the word with the best specific meaning and does not render the sentence awkward in tone or content. When choices seem close, look for a clue in the context that makes one choice better than the other. Note that the correct answer is not always the primary vocabulary word from the lesson.

flouted	**unyielding**	**tight**	**inimitable**	**told**
affinity	**difficult**	**neat**	**disobeyed**	**rebuked**
attraction				

1. Ever since childhood, Meagan, the owner of a bowling center and an expert bowler, has had a[n] *addiction* for the game.

   Better word: ____________________

2. Carl *ignored* the rules of the public pool by running while he was also waving at the lifeguard, only to slip and break his collarbone.

   Better word: ____________________

3. Maria *criticized* her son for having left the duck pen open all night, thus allowing foxes to eat all but one of the birds.

   Better word: ____________________

4. The seasoned jeweler had developed a[n] *unique* technique that not even the world's greatest artisans could understand, let alone emulate.

   Better word: ____________________

5. The *tenacious* lid on the pickle jar simply would not turn until Wayne ran hot water on it.

   Better word: ____________________

Exercise IV

Crossword Puzzle

Use the clues to complete the crossword puzzle. The answers consist of vocabulary words from Lessons 16 through 18.

Across

6. about to get hot
7. full of chuckles
8. all over the place
10. I take it back!
12. the best example
14. like clay or a young child
15. to scold
16. what draws you to it
17. an extra long work break

Down

1. just friends, nothing more
2. Don't get physical over these matters.
3. never heard of him
4. worse than boredom
5. all kinds of rude
8. what ice does for a broken toe
9. needs to turn the volume way down
11. very obvious
13. misleading

Exercise V

Subject Prompts

Here is a writing prompt similar to the one you will find on the writing portion of an assessment test. Follow the instructions below and write a brief, efficient essay.

Children of America live in a toy-laden culture. Action figures, dolls, vehicles, and board and video games hit the store shelves weeks before the films they are modeled upon, providing children with countless mental reruns of imagery, sounds, and contexts, eliminating the need for imagination—a world apart from the children of yesteryear, who fashioned their own toys or artwork for the things that interested them—usually the things they simply didn't have.

Knowingly, we endure the junky, short-lived plastic toys as standard materials for the entertainment of children, though adults are not much different: They carry smart phones, PDAs, and music players, most of which are primarily used for the same things the children's toys are used for—distraction and entertainment.

What fosters imagination and creativity in children and adults? Necessity may be the mother of invention, but imagination is no doubt the father. The ability to adapt, improvise, and simply improve upon civilization requires imagination, but is the human imagination endangered? Does "showing all" in detail make the imagination weak?

Imagine that you are a famous artist, author, or designer known for your original ideas and style and that you have the opportunity to address a million high school students on the topic of imagination. What would you say to them? How can the students hone and increase their imaginations? Can the imagination even be improved?

Take a stand on the importance of imagination, and use three subtopics to support your speech. Offer solutions or reasons that the issue should or should not be a concern.

Thesis: Write a *one-sentence* response to the above assignment. Make certain this single sentence offers a clear statement of your position.

Example: The best way to ensure that imagination will be available and usable is to limit the distractions that are detrimental to it.

____

____

Organizational Plan: List at least three subtopics you will use to support your main idea. This list is your outline.

1. ______________________________

2. ______________________________

3. ______________________________

Draft: Following your outline, write a good first draft of your essay. Remember to support all your points with examples, facts, references to reading, etc.

Review and Revise: Exchange essays with a classmate. Using the scoring guide for Word Choice on page 267, score your partner's essay (while he or she scores yours). Focus on word choice and the use of language conventions. If necessary, rewrite your essay to improve your word choice and/or your use of language.

Lesson Nineteen

1. **acrid** (a´ krəd) *adj.* marked by a sharp taste or smell; bitter
The burning plastic produced *acrid* fumes.

2. **fulminate** (ful´ mə nāt) *v.* to voice disapproval or protest
The crowd *fulminated* about destroying a historical landmark to make room for a shopping mall.
syn: denounce

3. **dross** (dros) *n.* refuse or waste
Landfills are filling rapidly, so communities must find a new way to dispose of *dross*.
syn: trash

4. **abnegation** (ab ni gā´ shən) *n.* unwillingness to admit reality or truth; denial
Maria was in a state of *abnegation* when she found out her husband had died in a car accident.
syn: rejection *ant: acceptance; admission*

5. **apex** (ā´ peks) *n.* the highest point of something
The *apex* of Mt. Everest is the highest point in the world.
syn: acme; pinnacle; summit *ant: bottom*

6. **insuperable** (in sōō´ pər ə bəl) *adj.* not able to be overcome
The *insuperable* tide dragged the swimmer away from the shore.
syn: indomitable; invulnerable

7. **verisimilitude** (ver ə sə mi´ lə tüd) *n.* the appearance of truth
The *verisimilitude* of the forged documents almost fooled the experts.
syn: authenticity; realism

8. **psychosomatic** (sī kō sə ma´ tik) *adj.* of or relating to symptoms caused by mental or emotional problems
The doctor refused to prescribe medication for Jane's *psychosomatic* headaches.

9. **gravitas** (gra´ və täs) *n.* seriousness
The judge's *gravitas* helped to increase the severity of the case.
syn: weightiness

10. **jejune** (ji jōōn´) *adj.* without interest; dull
Allen abandoned his *jejune* life on the farm to become a racecar driver.
syn: insipid; routine *ant: interesting; dramatic*

11. **hegemony** (hi je´ mə nē) *n.* influence or domination over
The Spanish explorers claimed *hegemony* over the native peoples of Latin America.
syn: dominion; reign

12. **truculent** (trək´ yə lənt) *adj.* marked by ferocity
Only one brave warrior volunteered to battle the *truculent* dragon.
syn: ravenous; savage *ant: tame; gentle*

13. **credulity** (kri dōō´ lə tē) *n.* willingness to believe too readily
Kim expressed *credulity* for claims of alien abductions despite the absence of any real evidence.
syn: faith; credence *ant: skepticism*

14. **viscous** (vis´ kəs) *adj.* having a thick or sticky consistency like glue
Mixing water and flour creates a *viscous* substance that is similar to paste.
syn: glutinous; adhesive

15. **polyglot** (pä´ lē glät) *n.* someone with knowledge of two or more languages
The Latin professor was a *polyglot* who spoke six different languages.

Exercise I

Words in Context

From the list below, supply the words needed to complete the paragraph. Some words will not be used.

truculent	**apex**	**hegemony**	**viscous**
abnegation	**fulminate**	**credulity**	**dross**

1. Jim's parents __________ at his naive __________ in conspiracy theories. "Why do you fill your head with such __________?" his mother asked.

   "You and dad are just slaves to the government's __________," said Jim. When the __________ aliens arrive and turn you into slaves, you'll reconsider my so-called __________."

From the list below, supply the words needed to complete the paragraph. Some words will not be used.

acrid	**abnegation**	**gravitas**	**verisimilitude**
viscous	**insuperable**	**apex**	

2. The black, __________ tar on the roof caught fire when lightning struck the __________ of the metal weathervane. The flames spread throughout the shed, finally igniting a pile of tires and filling the air with __________ smoke. The fire became __________ by the time the flames reached the office; the fire department did not have the equipment to control it. No one realized the __________ of the situation until the gas line beneath the office exploded, sending a fireball high into the air.

From the list below, supply the words needed to complete the paragraph. Some words will not be used.

psychosomatic	**apex**	**polyglot**
acrid	**jejune**	**verisimilitude**

3. Dr. Kerry, a[n] __________ who speaks four ancient languages, was enjoying the __________ day raking leaves when his cell phone rang. It was Dr. Orris, another archaeologist, and he wanted Dr. Kerry to look at an artifact that had the __________ of an ancient Mayan relic. Dr. Kerry reluctantly agreed, but first he went to the dermatologist to determine whether his newest skin abrasion was __________ or the consequence of touching poison oak leaves.

Exercise II

Sentence Completion

Complete the sentence in a way that shows you understand the meaning of the italicized vocabulary word.

1. Victoria reached the *apex* of her career early in life, and now she feels as though her career is…
2. The *polyglot* is an excellent spy because she…
3. Sean's *psychosomatic* headaches occurred whenever he remembered…
4. The autographed photo had the *verisimilitude* of a genuine item, but it…
5. Sophia did not realize the *gravitas* of Joe's condition until she saw that he had…
6. If the fishermen do not properly dispose of the *dross* after cleaning their catch, then…
7. Unless you want the *acrid* taste of powdered cement in your mouth, you should wear a mask when we begin to…
8. The president of the corporation sought economic *hegemony* over…
9. The speaker tried to enhance his usually *jejune* lectures by…
10. Most of the people thought that the prisoner was innocent, so they *fulminated* when the judge…
11. It surprised everyone when, in the third round, the *insuperable* boxer…
12. Kevin briefly experienced *abnegation* when he realized that his lottery ticket had…
13. The wounded dog was so *truculent* that the veterinarian was forced to…
14. Rebecca used the *viscous* epoxy to…
15. The child's excuse lacked *credulity*, so…

Exercise III

Roots, Prefixes, and Suffixes

Study the entries and answer the questions that follow.

The roots *apt* and *ept* mean "fit."
The roots *aster* and *astr* mean "star."
The root *capit* or *cap* means "head."
The prefix *dis–* means "apart" or "not."
The suffix *–al* means "pertaining to."

1. Using *literal* translations as guidance, define the following words without using a dictionary.

   A. adaptable
   B. adept
   C. astral
   D. asterisk
   E. captain
   F. decapitate

2. A *disaster* is a misfortune or a calamity. Write a possible explanation as to why the word *disaster* contains a root that means "star."

3. A[n] __________ pupil might have personal interests that fit a particular subject. An *inept* worker might not be __________ for a particular job.

4. In a *capitalist* economy, citizens are the __________ of their own *capital*, or wealth.

5. List as many words as you can think of that contain the roots *apt* or *ept*.

6. List as many words as you can think of that contain the roots *aster* or *astr*.

Exercise IV

Inference

Complete the sentence by inferring information about the italicized word from its context.

1. The noisy mob *fulminated* outside the courthouse because it did not agree with…

2. The *credulity* that you give to supermarket tabloids is absurd because they are…

3. Becky had difficulty getting the *viscous* pancake syrup from the container because it…

Exercise V

Writing

Here is a writing prompt similar to the one you will find on the writing portion of an assessment test.

Plan and write an essay based on the following statement:

> Caring is the greatest thing, caring matters most.
>
> –last words of Friedrich Von Hugel (1852-1925)

Assignment: Do you agree or disagree with Von Hugel's opinion about caring? Write an essay in which you support or refute Von Hugel's statement. Support your point with evidence from your own reading, classroom studies, and personal observation and experience. Consider the many forms of the quotation that you might have seen or heard in the past.

Thesis: Write a *one-sentence* response to the above assignment. Make certain this single sentence offers a clear statement of your position.

Example: Friedrich Von Hugel's last words form a pleasant idea, but it is doing—not caring—that truly matters most.

____

____

Organizational Plan: List at least three subtopics you will use to support your main idea. This list is your outline.

1. ____
2. ____
3. ____

Draft: Following your outline, write a good first draft of your essay. Remember to support all your points with examples, facts, references to reading, etc.

Review and Revise: Exchange essays with a classmate. Using the Holistic scoring guide on page 268, score your partner's essay (while he or she scores yours). If necessary, rewrite your essay to correct the problems indicated by the essay's score.

Exercise VI

English Practice

Improving Paragraphs

Read the following passage and then answer the multiple-choice questions that follow. The questions will require you to make decisions regarding the revision of the reading selection.

[1] Long workdays can be depressing, especially when it means arriving at work before daylight and leaving after dark. People in the northernmost parts of the United States endure this endless nightlife all winter long and now, doctors have found that a consistent lack of sunlight has negative psychological effects on people; however, life without daylight does indeed cause depression. The most vulnerable people in the United States are, of course, those who live in Alaska, where residents experience only several hours of dim sunlight during the winter months.

[2] Anchorage natives have adapted to short days and long nights, but adapting is a real problem for people who are new to the state. Winters are difficult enough in the pipeline city; subfreezing temperatures and snow merely enhance the entrapping effect of the unending winter darkness. During the winter in Anchorage, the sun does not rise until 10:15 a.m., well after people have arrived at work. The sun goes down at 3:45 p.m., and most people still have another hour or two of work before they can leave.

[3] The Trans-Alaskan Pipeline, an 800-mile artery of Alaska, employs nearly one thousand workers, many of whom work around-the-clock shifts. The occupational stress from working swing shifts, combined with the lack of vacation opportunities during the long winters, increases the probability of depression for the Alaskan workers. Winter is a tough time for animals, too, because they frequently get run over on unlighted roadways.

[4] Like animals in hibernation, people suffering from Seasonal Affective Disorder (SAD), overeat and sleep most of the day. They have trouble concentrating and functioning at work and in personal relationships. Victims of SAD often suffer disastrous economic consequences when depression prevails over the desire to properly maintain finances. Many sufferers declare bankruptcy or lose their jobs.

[5] An estimated one in four people suffer from SAD in Alaska. The depression is so prevalent that therapists report not having the resources to help all the people who seek treatment.

1. Which of the following changes would correct an error in paragraph 1?
   A. Replace *people* with *citizens*.
   B. Capitalize *northernmost*.
   C. Delete *of course*.
   D. Change *psychological* to *mental*.
   E. Delete *however*.

2. Which of the following changes would best clarify the topic of the passage?
   A. Expound on the problems that animals have during Alaskan winters, and explain that animals can also develop SAD.
   B. Introduce SAD in the first paragraph, and use the supporting paragraphs to explain the effects of the condition on people in Alaska.
   C. Include a paragraph about North Pacific weather patterns, and explain how precipitation can amplify the symptoms of SAD.
   D. Eliminate any information about workdays.
   E. Include information on how to treat Seasonal Affective Disorder.

3. Which of the following should be deleted from paragraph 3?
   A. sentence 1
   B. sentence 2
   C. sentence 3
   D. the word *unlighted*
   E. the word *opportunities*

4. Which of the following paragraph arrangements would improve the logical order of the passage?
   A. 2, 1, 3, 4, 5
   B. 1, 2, 4, 3, 5
   C. 1, 3, 2, 4, 5
   D. 2, 3, 4, 5, 1
   E. 1, 5, 3, 4, 2

5. Which of the following would be the most appropriate concluding sentence for the passage?
   A. Therefore, people should make it a point to get out into the sun more often.
   B. It is likely that Seasonal Affective Disorder will be a challenge people must face for years to come.
   C. Therapists should appeal to the government for additional funding and employees.
   D. Therapists will probably notify the Alaskan Pipeline officials of their discoveries.
   E. Perhaps, in the distant future, Alaska will build another pipeline—a pipeline that brings sunshine from California.

Lesson Twenty

1. **disseminate** (di se´ mə nāt) *v.* to disperse or scatter
   Health officials *disseminated* flyers to warn people about deer ticks.
   syn: distribute

2. **extemporaneous** (ek stem pə rā´ nē əs) *adj.* done without planning; spur of the moment; unexpected; makeshift
   William made *extemporaneous* repairs to the roof to stop the leak.
   syn: impromptu; spontaneous

3. **intractable** (in trak´ tə bəl) *adj.* difficult to manipulate or govern
   It took the blacksmith several days to hammer the *intractable* iron rods into elaborate railings.
   syn: unmanageable; rigid

4. **acerbic** (ə ser´ bik) *adj.* sarcastic in mood, tone, or temper; harsh
   The *acerbic* shopkeeper offended the customers and caused a drop in sales.

5. **diaspora** (dī as´ pə rə) *n.* a dispersion of people from their homeland
   Native American groups experienced a *diaspora*, and few ever recovered their lands.
   syn: displacement

6. **androgynous** (an drä´ jə nəs) *adj.* having features of both sexes; suitable for both male and female
   The *androgynous*-looking hats are designed to be worn by both men and women.

7. **discursive** (dis ker´ siv) *adj.* jumping from one topic to another without any order or reason
   The scientist had so many ideas that his lectures tended to be *discursive* and difficult to follow.
   syn: digressive; rambling

8. **augur** (o´ gər) *n.* someone who predicts future events according to omens
   The mysterious *augur* was watchful for ominous signs whenever he was faced with an important choice.
   syn: clairvoyant; oracle

9. **sinecure** (sī´ ni kyur) *n.* a job that provides income but requires little or no work
   The company employees were so motivated and productive that the manager's job was a *sinecure*.

10. **tendentious** (ten den´ chəs) *adj.* biased in perspective; preferring one view over another
The journalist's *tendentious* article about the incident angered many readers.
syn: jaundiced; partisan *ant: indifferent*

11. **politic** (pä´ lə tic) *adj.* prudent or shrewdly tactful
Ashley's *politic* manners made her an excellent lawyer and negotiator.
syn: sagacious; cunning

12. **requiem** (re´ kwē əm) *n.* a religious service or song for the deceased
The church held a *requiem* after the death of one of its parishioners.

13. **traduce** (trə dōōs´) *v.* to slander someone's reputation
Anthony's one time friend now *traduced* his name around campus because of his disgraceful behavior.
syn: smear; besmirch

14. **beatitude** (bē a´ tə tōōd) *n.* a state of happiness or joy
The parents lived in a type of *beatitude* in the hours following the birth of their first child.
syn: bliss; euphoria *ant: agony*

15. **maladroit** (ma lə droit´) *adj.* not resourceful or cunning; inept
After his original plan failed, the *maladroit* captain could not decide what to do next.
syn: incompetent

Exercise I

Words in Context

From the list below, supply the words needed to complete the paragraph. Some words will not be used.

maladroit	**augur**	**disseminate**	**sinecure**
extemporaneous	**beatitude**	**discursive**	

1. Brian experienced a[n] feeling of near-__________ when he was offered the job of night watchman. He hated hard work, and he assumed that the job would be a[n] __________ since he could recline in a chair during most of his shift.

   Brian's dream job lasted one day. During his first shift, the __________ security guard forgot to lock the door to the warehouse, and Brian was sleeping in his chair when workers arrived in the morning. The boss made a[n] __________ decision to fire Brian on the spot, and then he __________ a memo to the other security guards about taking their jobs seriously.

From the list below, supply the words needed to complete the paragraph. Some words will not be used.

acerbic	**discursive**	**politic**	**requiem**
intractable	**diaspora**	**androgynous**	

2. The FBI found it nearly impossible to track the Gatliones—a crime family whose __________ throughout the United States made it __________. Some of its __________ bosses had created businesses that concealed criminal operations, and phone taps were useless because the FBI could not decode the __________ conversations between gangsters and their henchmen. Agents occasionally arrested the family's hired thugs, but their __________ attitudes made it clear that they weren't going to release any information that would incriminate their bosses.

From the list below, supply the words needed to complete the paragraph. Some words will not be used.

acerbic	**requiem**	**augur**	**beatitude**
androgynous	**traduce**	**tendentious**	

3. The choir, dressed in white, __________ robes, sang movements of the __________ that the late composer had written for his own funeral. Superstitious people had the __________ idea that the death should be blamed on a[n] __________ who had convinced the composer that a visit from a raven meant certain death. They thought that the old seer had caused the composer to worry himself to death. Angry citizens __________ the old oracle and eventually ran him out of town.

Exercise II

Sentence Completion

Complete the sentence in a way that shows you understand the meaning of the italicized vocabulary word.

1. Many retired people find *sinecures* because they…
2. The Prussian general took the *intractable* men and…
3. Irish families experienced a *diaspora* during the potato famine, and now their family names are found in…
4. Both sides gave their *tendentious* accounts of what happened, and neither of them was…
5. Nelson was forced to give an *extemporaneous* speech when…
6. The *politic* investor knew that her stock would drop in value, so she…
7. Before the *requiem* began,…
8. Lanna appreciated the *beatitude* she felt during the church services until her little brother…
9. The *maladroit* waiter angered the customer by…
10. The community theater *disseminated* flyers that told people the…
11. The king's *augur* warned him not to…
12. The child's *discursive* explanation made it difficult for the detective to…
13. The restaurant owner claimed that the food critic *traduced* him by…
14. If you do not stop giving *acerbic* answers to your dad's questions, you will not be allowed to…
15. The *androgynous* hospital gowns were designed to…

Exercise III

Roots, Prefixes, and Suffixes

Study the entries and answer the questions that follow.

The prefixes *neo–* and *nova–* mean "new."
The root *tort* means "twist" or "bend."
The roots *reg*, *rig*, and *rect* mean "rule" or "govern."
The roots *cide* and *cis* mean "to kill."
The root *nat* means "to be born."
The root *phy* means "to grow."
The prefix *ex–* means "out."
The prefix *de–* means "off."

1. Using *literal* translations as guidance, define the following words without using a dictionary.

A.	direct	D.	retort
B.	incorrigible	E.	decide
C.	extort	F.	excise

2. The rebels killed the dictator-king in an act of __________ because the king's __________ had brutally ruled the country.

   If you want to get into good physical shape, you must allow yourself to be ruled by a good exercise __________.

3. You will find newborn babies in the __________ ward of the hospital.

   A *neophyte* at a sport might lose to experienced players because he or she is __________ to the game.

4. A *novice* who lacks carpentry experience might have difficulty __________ a home, or "making it new again."

5. Some would say that it is lying to __________ the truth by bending facts.

   A[n] __________ can bend his own body beyond the usual limits of normal human flexibility. Medieval __________ devices were sometimes used to stretch or twist people for punishment.

Exercise IV

Inference

Complete the sentence by inferring information about the italicized word from its context.

1. The automobile dealership fired the *maladroit* salesman because he could not…

2. If you want a large turnout at the bake sale, you should *disseminate* information about the event so that…

3. Eugene's poorly-prepared, *discursive* presentation confused everyone because it did not…

Exercise V

Critical Reading

Below is a pair of reading passages followed by several multiple-choice questions. Carefully read the passages and choose the best answer to each of the questions.

The following two speeches were given at the dedication of the National Cemetery at Gettysburg on November 19, 1863. Massachusetts Governor Edward Everett gave a speech of over 13,500 words that lasted more than two hours and is barely remembered by history. It was followed by President Abraham Lincoln's famous Gettysburg address, which is only 171 words long and took less than two minutes to deliver. A few days later, Everett wrote to Lincoln saying, "I should be glad, if I could flatter myself that I came as near to the central idea of the occasion, in two hours, as you did in two minutes." Everett's speech has been heavily abridged here.

Passage 1

We have assembled, friends, fellow citizens, at the invitation of the Executive of the great central State of Pennsylvania, seconded by the Governors of seventeen other loyal States of the Union, to pay the last tribute of respect to the brave men, who, in the hard fought battles of the first, second and third days of July last, laid down their lives for the country on these hillsides and the plains before us, and whose remains have been gathered into the Cemetery which we consecrate this day. As my eye ranges over the fields whose sods were so lately moistened by the blood of gallant and loyal men, I feel, as never before, how truly it was said of old, that it is sweet and becoming to die for one's country. I feel as never before, how justly, from the dawn of history to the present time, men have paid the homage of their gratitude and admiration to the memory of those who nobly sacrificed their lives, that their fellow men may live in safety and in honor. And if this tribute were ever due, when, to whom, could it be more justly paid than to those whose last resting place we this day commend to the blessing of Heaven and of men?

For consider, my friends, what would have been the consequences to the country, to yourselves, and to all you hold dear, if those who sleep beneath our feet, and their gallant comrades who survive to serve their country on other fields of danger, had failed in their duty on those memorable days….

And now, friends, fellow citizens, as we stand among these honored graves, the momentous question presents itself: Which of the two parties to the war is responsible for all this suffering, for this dreadful sacrifice of life, the lawful and constitutional government of the United States, or the ambitious men who have rebelled against it? I say "rebelled" against it, although Earl Russell, the British Secretary of State for Foreign Affairs, in his recent temperate and conciliatory speech in Scotland, seems to intimate that no prejudice ought to attach to that word, inasmuch as our English forefathers rebelled against Charles I. and James II., and our American fathers rebelled against George III....

I call the war which the Confederates are waging against the Union a "rebellion," because it is one, and in grave matters it is best to call things by their right names. I speak of it as a crime, because the Constitution of the United States so regards it, and puts "rebellion" on a par with "invasion." The Constitution and law not only of England, but of every civilized country, regard them in the same light; or rather they consider the rebel in arms as far worse than the alien enemy. To levy war against the United States is the constitutional definition of treason, and that crime is by every civilized government regarded as the highest which citizen or subject can commit....

The people of loyal America will never ask you, sir, to take to your confidence or admit again to a share in the government the hard-hearted men whose cruel lust of power has brought this desolating war upon the land, but there is no personal bitterness felt, even against them. They may live, if they can bear to live after wantonly causing the death of so many thousands of their fellow-men; they may live in safe obscurity beneath the shelter of the government they have sought to overthrow, or they may fly to the protection of the governments of Europe—some of them are already there, seeking, happily in vain, to obtain the aid of foreign powers in furtherance of their own treason. There let them stay. The humblest dead soldier, that lies cold and stiff in his grave before us, is an object of envy beneath the clods that cover him, in comparison with the living man, I care not with what trumpery credentials he may be furnished, who is willing to grovel at the foot of a foreign throne for assistance in compassing the ruin of his country.

But the hour is coming and now is, when the power of the leaders of the Rebellion to delude and inflame must cease. There is no bitterness on the part of the masses. The people of the South are not going to wage an eternal war, for the wretched pretext by which this Rebellion is sought to be justified....

And now, friends, fellow citizens of Gettysburg and Pennsylvania, and you from remoter States, let me again, as we part, invoke your benediction on these honored graves. You feel, though the occasion is mournful, that it is good to be here....God bless the Union; it is dearer to us for the blood of brave men which has been shed in its defense. The spots on which they stood and fell; these pleasant heights; the fertile plain beneath them; the thriving village whose streets so lately rang with the strange din of war; the fields beyond the ridge, where the noble Reynolds held the advancing foe at bay, and, while he gave up his own life, assured by his forethought and self-sacrifice the triumph of the two succeeding days; the little streams which wind through the hills, on whose banks in aftertimes the wondering ploughman will turn up, with the rude weapons of savage warfare, the fearful missiles of modern artillery; Seminary Ridge, the Peach Orchard, Cemetery, Culp, and Wolf Hill, Round Top, Little Round Top, humble names, henceforward dear and famous—no lapse of time, no distance of space, shall cause you to be forgotten. "The whole earth," said Pericles, as he stood over the remains of his fellow citizens, who had fallen in the first year of the Peloponnesian war, "the whole earth is the sepulcher of illustrious men." All time, he might have added, is the millennium of their glory. Surely I would do no injustice to the other noble achievements of the war, which have reflected such honor on both arms of the service, and have entitled the armies and the navy of the United States, their officers and men, to the warmest thanks and the richest rewards which a grateful people can pay. But they, I am sure, will join us in saying, as we bid farewell to the dust of these martyr-heroes, that wheresoever throughout the civilized world the accounts of this great warfare are read, and down to the latest period of recorded time, in the glorious annals of our common country, there will be no brighter page than that which relates The Battles of Gettysburg.

Passage 2

Four score and seven years ago our fathers brought forth on this continent, a new nation, conceived in Liberty, and dedicated to the proposition that all men are created equal. Now we are engaged in a great civil war, testing whether that nation, or any nation so conceived and so dedicated, can long endure. We are met on a great battle-field of that war. We have come to dedicate a portion of that field, as a final resting place for those who here gave their lives that that nation might live. It is altogether fitting and proper that we should do this.

But, in a larger sense, we can not dedicate—we can not consecrate—we can not hallow—this ground. The brave men, living and dead, who struggled here, have consecrated it, far above our poor power to add or detract. The world will little note, nor long remember what we say here, but it is for us the living, rather, to be dedicated here to the unfinished work which they who fought here have thus far so nobly advanced. It is rather for us to be here dedicated to the great task remaining before us—that from these honored dead we take increased devotion to that cause for which they gave the last full measure of devotion—that we here highly resolve that these dead shall not have died in vain—that this nation, under God, shall have a new birth of freedom—and that government of the people, by the people, for the people, shall not perish from the earth.

1A. The best substitute for the word *rebel* as Everett used it in passage 1 is
   A. southerner.
   B. traitor.
   C. slave-owner.
   D. soldier.
   E. confederate.

1B. Choose the statement that best supports your answer to question 1A.
   A. "…our English forefathers rebelled against Charles I."
   B. "…the wretched pretext by which this Rebellion is sought to be justified."
   C. "…they consider the rebel in arms as far worse than the alien enemy."
   D. "…the ambitious men who have rebelled against it[.]"
   E. "…it is sweet and becoming to die for one's country."

2A. According to passage 1, paragraph 2, which choice best describes the "sods [that] were so lately moistened"?
   A. all the men who died at Gettysburg
   B. only Union soldiers who died at Gettysburg
   C. wartime cemeteries throughout history
   D. the fields of Gettysburg
   E. battles to save a country from ruin

2B. Choose the quotation from passage 1 that best supports your answer to question 2A.
   A. "…laid down their lives for the country on these hillsides and the plains before us…"
   B. "…to pay the last tribute of respect to the brave men…"
   C. "…those whose last resting place we this day commend to the blessing of Heaven…"
   D. "…their fellow men may live in safety and in honor."
   E. "…it is sweet and becoming to die for one's country."

3A. As used in line 34, "no personal bitterness" most nearly expresses
A. a true feeling of forgiveness.
B. a personal attack on Confederate dead.
C. a personal recognition of the sacrifice of the dead.
D. knowledge that the rebellion was doomed.
E. personal hatred for the actions of the South.

3B. Which statement supports your answer to question 3A?
A. "…this desolating war upon the land…"
B. "…the hard-hearted men whose cruel lust of power…"
C. "…obtain the aid of foreign powers…"
D. "…an object of envy beneath the clods that cover him…"
E. "…willing to grovel at the foot of a foreign throne…"

4A. According to Everett, what will a future farmer find at Gettysburg?
A. the ruins of war
B. remains of dead soldiers
C. nothing worth the deaths
D. peace at last
E. military hardware

4B. In passage 1, why does Everett quote Pericles?
A. Pericles was a survivor of the Peloponnesian war.
B. Pericles understood what was worth fighting for.
C. Pericles knew that time could never diminish glory.
D. Pericles felt that the world would become a tomb because of wars.
E. Pericles understood the honor of death for the right cause.

5A. The clearest explanation of how Lincoln's speech begins is
A. with a dedication to the fallen soldiers.
B. with a historical reference his audience would know.
C. by quoting the previous speaker's remarks.
D. with a reference to the founding of the United States.
E. by revealing his sadness over the futility of the war.

6A. According to passage 2, why is Lincoln at Gettysburg?
A. to honor the end of the war
B. to praise the men who died
C. to dedicate a cemetery
D. to get over the horrors of war
E. to show the South who was victorious

6B. What does Lincoln say that contradicts your answer to 6A?
A. He says that there is no way to fully end the war.
B. He says that the soldiers never really knew what they fought for.
C. He says that the Union was worth preserving at all costs.
D. He says that nothing that is done can equate to the men's sacrifices.
E. He says that no one will remember what was said by him.

7A. Which statement below expresses a similarity between the speeches?
   A. They both attempt to put blame on the South.
   B. They both try to heal the wounds the war caused.
   C. They both want to honor the fallen at Gettysburg.
   D. They both state that the war will end soon.
   E. They both predict that equality will come to all men.

8A. Choose the statement that best explains Lincoln's phrase, "the last full measure of devotion."
   A. Soldiers gave their lives during the war.
   B. Soldiers were called on to sacrifice.
   C. Soldiers devoted themselves to the cause of war.
   D. Soldiers could not estimate what will happen.
   E. Soldiers will always be called on to fight.

8B. Which phrase from Everett's speech best exemplifies Lincoln's quotation in question 8A?
   A. "…causing the death of so many thousands of their fellow-men…"
   B. "Which of the two parties to the war is responsible…?"
   C. "…let me again, as we part, invoke your benediction on these honored graves."
   D. "…memory of those who nobly sacrificed their lives…"
   E. "There is no bitterness on the part of the masses."

9A. According to Lincoln's final paragraph, what is most important thing the people gathered at Gettysburg that day should do?
   A. make the battlefield sacred and holy
   B. continue to uphold the honor of the country
   C. give the soldiers the recognition they deserve
   D. remember the sacrifices that the dead made
   E. make sure the United States continues to exist

9B. Choose another sentence from passage 2 that states essentially the same sentiment as your answer to question 9A.
   A. "Now we are engaged in a great civil war…"
   B. "…gave their lives that that nation might live."
   C. "…any nation so conceived and so dedicated, can long endure."
   D. "…altogether fitting and proper that we should do this."
   E. "The world will little note, nor long remember what we say here…"

10A. Select the answer that best describes the main tone of *both* passages.
   A. somber and hopeful
   B. uplifting and spiritual
   C. angry and resentful
   D. respectful, yet ominous
   E. sad, yet relieved

10B. Which statement below does *not* support your answer to question 10A?

A. Both speakers refer to the dead soldiers and to the living who must continue their work.

B. Everett condemns soldiers from the South, but Lincoln does not mention them.

C. Lincoln realizes the inadequacy of his words to heal, but Everett warns of retribution.

D. Everett understands the common goals of the warring parties, and Lincoln wants the war over at all costs.

E. Both speakers use historical references to make the audience understand the cause of the Civil War.

Lesson Twenty-One

1. **peon** (pē´ än) *n.* various laborers who are generally landless
The farmer hired *peons* to work his fields during the summer months.
syn: serf; servant

2. **digress** (dī gres´) *v.* to deviate from the original subject or course
The professor usually *digressed* from his original topic during his class lectures.
syn: stray

3. **stolid** (stä´ ləd) *adj.* showing or having little or no emotion; unemotional
The *stolid* gambler revealed no clue that he was holding a winning hand.
syn: impassive; stoic *ant: expressive; agitated*

4. **bon mot** (bōn mō´) *n.* a witty remark or saying
Jerry ended every meeting with a *bon mot* about work productivity.
syn: quip

5. **plenary** (plē´ nə rē) *adj.* complete in every way; full
With the arrival of the bride, the wedding was *plenary* and could finally begin.
syn: thorough; entire *ant: incomplete; lacking*

6. **misogyny** (mə sä´ jə nē) *n.* a hatred toward females
People attribute Cody's *misogyny* to his jealousy of his sister's success.

7. **travesty** (tra´ və stē) *n.* a poor representation or imitation; distortion
The Broadway musical was a *travesty* of the original show of the same title.
syn: perversion; sham

8. **potboiler** (pät´ boi lər) *n.* a poorly done artistic work, often for quick profit
Critics described the novels as a series of *potboilers* with little literary value.

9. **furlough** (fər´ lō) *n.* a leave of absence
The soldier was granted a *furlough* after his heroic deeds.
syn: vacation; liberty

10. **plutocrat** (plōō´ tə krat) *n.* a member of the controlling upper-class
Thomas Jefferson was a *plutocrat,* who helped to shape America's government.
ant: plebian

11. **succor** (sə´ kər) *n.* something that gives relief or aid
The medicine will be *succor* for the ailing people.
syn: comfort; ease *ant: aggravation; annoyance*

12. **xeric** (zir´ ik) *adj.* characterized by or adapted to a dry habitat
Do not add too much water to *xeric* plants such as cacti; they require very little.

13. **clandestine** (klan des´ tən) *adj.* marked by secrecy
Only trusted agents could attend the *clandestine* meeting of the rebels.
syn: undercover; hidden

14. **redoubtable** (ri dau´ tə bəl) *adj.* arousing fear
The drill sergeant was known for his *redoubtable* demeanor with new recruits.
syn: dreadful; dire *ant: wonderful; fortunate*

15. **vignette** (vin yet´) *n.* a short, descriptive literary sketch
Harold's autobiography is a collection of *vignettes* about events in his life.

Exercise I

Words in Context

From the list below, supply the words needed to complete the paragraph. Some words will not be used.

vignette	**redoubtable**	**succor**	**plenary**
digress	**clandestine**	**xeric**	**furlough**

1. Even the __________ creatures and people of the desert were unaware of the __________ testing facility deep beneath the sand and soil. Constructed as a countermeasure to the __________ threat of biological weapons, the hidden facility featured a[n] __________ laboratory in which scientists could identify and exploit organisms without the risk of contaminating the public. Some of the researchers were leading professors who had taken __________ from their teaching duties. Program managers ensured that research did not __________ from the mission of the laboratory—to minimize the threat of biological agents in the United States.

From the list below, supply the words needed to complete the paragraph. Some words will not be used.

peon	**xeric**	**bon mot**	**potboiler**
plutocrat	**stolid**	**succor**	**travesty**
vignette	**misogyny**	**plenary**	

2. A six-dollar tub of popcorn was Meredith's only __________ while she watched the lousy __________ at the movie theater. The film made a[n] __________ of the book on which it was based, mostly because it omitted the best __________ from the original story. In the book, the central character is a[n] __________ who suffers under the __________ of a wealthy heiress who wants to rid her estate of any women other than herself. The servant becomes __________ after years of emotional abuse, and she dies alone and penniless. In the movie, the peasant woman becomes a wealthy __________ after discovering that her real father left her an enormous inheritance. The script is loaded with modern clichés and __________ that do not belong in the movie's seventeenth-century setting.

Exercise II

Sentence Completion

Complete the sentence in a way that shows you understand the meaning of the italicized vocabulary word.

1. The remake of the classic film was a *travesty* of the original because…
2. The *stolid* judge showed no reaction to the witness, even when she…
3. The king ordered the *peons* to…
4. No one noticed the *clandestine* camera because it looked like…
5. The wrongfully imprisoned woman received a *plenary* pardon that…
6. The *xeric* vegetation required…
7. At this time, I'd like to *digress* from the topic of art to…
8. The movie sequel was a *potboiler* that used the popularity of the first film to…
9. Dr. Hafner, the creative writing professor, took a *furlough* from his duties in order to…
10. The knight had a *redoubtable* reputation on the battlefield because he…
11. The detective on the police drama series recited a tacky *bon mot* every time he…
12. The trailer for the new movie featured a *vignette* in which the lead character…
13. The air-dropped rations were *succor* for the…
14. Grandpa's *misogyny* was apparent by…
15. Some believe that *plutocrats* create laws that…

Exercise III

Roots, Prefixes, and Suffixes

Study the entries and answer the questions that follow.

The root *plic* means "to fold."
The root *domin* means "lord" or "master."
The prefixes *com–* and *con–* mean "together" or "very."
The prefix *im–* means "in."
The roots *vince* and *vict* mean "to conquer" or "to defeat."
The prefix *e–* means "from" or "out."
The prefix *in–* means "against" or "not."
The prefix *pre–* means "in front of" or "before."

1. Using *literal* translations as guidance, define the following words without using a dictionary.

   A. evict
   B. convict
   C. convince
   D. invincible
   E. predominate
   F. province

2. The animal that controls the other animals in a group is often called the __________ animal.

   If no one can take control of a person, then that person is said to be __________.

   If you become the master of a group, then you __________ it.

3. The word *implicate* means "to connect incriminatingly," or "to connect to a crime." Originally, *implicate* meant "to entangle," or "to interweave." Explain why a word that once meant "to entangle" has come to mean "to connect to a crime."

4. If someone increases the number of folds in a situation, then he or she is said to __________ matters.

   When someone gives *explicit* instructions, he or she __________ the information to make it understandable.

   If you are into the folds of a subject, then you have a[n] __________ understanding of it.

5. List as many words as you can think of that contain the roots *vince* or *vict*.

Exercise IV

Inference

Complete the sentence by inferring information about the italicized word from its context.

1. No one knew the cause of Steve's *misogyny*, but it was apparent when he worked around women because he...

2. The *stolid* cowboy did not even flinch when...

3. The company phone list contained the numbers to a few key personnel, but the president wanted a *plenary* list that...

Exercise V

Writing

Here is a writing prompt similar to the one you will find on the writing portion of an assessment test.

Plan and write an essay based on the following statement:

> Passing judgment on nontraditional families seems to be customary for what Barbara Kingsolver calls "the Family of Dolls," the traditional Barbie and Ken household that has never been disassembled by divorce. The ever-ambiguous "family values" suggests that traditional families offer the most stability for children, nurturing them in a community of successful relationships from which they can model their own lives. Divorced people, gay families, Brady Bunch families, and single parents put their children at risk and are failures.
>
> –adapted from "Stone Soup" by Barbara Kingsolver

Assignment: Write an essay in which you support or refute Barbara Kingsolver's position. Be certain to support your own position with examples from literature, current events, or your own personal experience or observation.

Thesis: Write a *one-sentence* response to the above assignment. Make certain this single sentence offers a clear statement of your position.

Example: In a nation where non-traditional families outnumber traditional families, reorganized families are as successful as traditional families in raising capable, thriving children who are at no more risk for failure than children from any other family.

____

____

Organizational Plan: List at least three subtopics you will use to support your main idea. This list is your outline.

1. ________________________________

2. ________________________________

3. ________________________________

Draft: Following your outline, write a good first draft of your essay. Remember to support all your points with examples, facts, references to reading, etc.

Review and Revise: Exchange essays with a classmate. Using the Holistic scoring guide on page 268, score your partner's essay (while he or she scores yours). If necessary, rewrite your essay to correct the problems indicated by the essay's score.

Exercise VI

English Practice

Identifying Sentence Errors

Identify the grammatical error in each of the following sentences. If the sentence contains no error, select answer choice E.

1. Even (A) if I was (B) invited, I wouldn't have (C) gone to the picnic (D). No error (E)

2. If I had saved (A) enough money, (B) I would of (C) traveled to San Francisco last year (D). No error (E)

3. Jane (A) has a favorite pastime: (B) to play (C) the piano (D). No error (E)

4. They're (A) running away is (B) not going to get (C) them out of trouble with the law (D). No error (E)

5. The doctor (A) she advised (B) me to cut (C) down on (D) salt. No error (E)

Improving Sentences

The underlined portion of each sentence below contains some flaw. Select the answer choice that best corrects the flaw.

6. <u>The woman Shakespeare wrote about in sonnet 130 must have been real special.</u>
   A. The woman that Shakespeare wrote about in sonnet 130 must have been real special.
   B. The woman Shakespeare wrote about in "Sonnet 130" must have been very special.
   C. The woman whom Shakespeare wrote about in Sonnet 130 must have been real special.
   D. The woman Shakespeare wrote about in "Sonnet 130" must have been real special.
   E. The woman Shakespeare wrote about in sonnet 130 must have been very special.

7. <u>One student which is in our class asked What does this poem mean?</u>
   A. One student who is in our class asked What does this poem mean?
   B. One student which is in our class, asked What does this poem mean?
   C. One student who is in our class, asked "What does this poem mean?"
   D. One student which is in our class, asked "What does this poem mean"?
   E. One student who is in our class asked, "What does this poem mean?"

8. <u>How come all these poems was about love death and time.</u>
   A. How come all these poems were about love death and time?
   B. Why was all these poems about love, death, and time?
   C. How come all these poems were about love, death and time?
   D. Why were all these poems about love death, and time?
   E. Why were all these poems about love, death, and time?

9. <u>Racing faster than all the drivers, Karl finished first, lapping the second-place finisher.</u>
   A. Karl finished first, racing faster than all the drivers, and lapping the second-place finisher.
   B. Racing faster than all the other drivers, Karl finished first, lapping the second-place finisher.
   C. Racing faster than all the drivers, Karl finished first, and he lapped the second-place finisher.
   D. Lapping the second-place finisher, Karl finished first, racing faster than all the drivers.
   E. Racing faster than all the drivers, Karl finished first, beating the second-place finisher by a lap.

10. When did the teacher <u>ask On what page did we stop reading yesterday?</u>
   A. When did the teacher ask "On what page did we stop reading yesterday?"
   B. "When did the teacher ask, 'On what page did we stop reading yesterday'?"
   C. When did the teacher ask, "On what page did we stop reading yesterday?"?
   D. When did the teacher ask, "On what page did we stop reading yesterday"?
   E. When did the teacher ask, "On what page did we stop reading yesterday?"

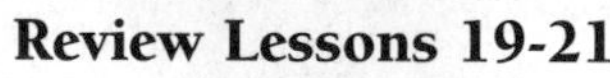

Review Lessons 19-21

Exercise I

Inferences

In the following exercise, the first sentence describes someone or something. Infer information from the first sentence, and then choose the word from the Word Bank that best completes the second sentence.

sinecure	**diasporas**	**acerbic**	**politic**	**gravitas**
vignettes	**potboilers**	**verisimilitude**		

1. Unsupervised, seven-year-old Tanner made dozens of purchases and bids on the Internet auction site, racking up thousands of dollars on his parents' credit card.

   From this sentence, we can infer that Tanner did not understand the __________ of his actions.

2. The publisher rejected the author's novel because the setting locations are described weakly, as though the author had never actually visited or seen them before.

   From this sentence, we can infer that the author's writing lacks __________.

3. When asked how he was feeling after waiting to be seen for two hours, the pale, obviously sick man in the doctor's office replied, "Oh, I feel wonderful; I just enjoy your company!"

   From this sentence, we can infer that the ill patient's long wait caused him to be __________ with his reply to the doctor's question.

4. Every year, around the holidays, television networks air movies and shows that are cheaply produced, have very simple, predictable storylines, and would be considered terrible if they didn't happen to be relevant to the season.

   From this sentence, we can infer that some holiday television productions are __________ created to fill network airtime around the holidays.

5. After the governor was elected, his brother-in-law was hired to be an advisor, a vaguely defined position which required only that he show up for occasional banquets and ribbon cuttings.

   From this sentence, we can infer that the governor's brother-in-law received a[n] __________ after the governor was elected.

Exercise II

Related Words

Some of the vocabulary words from Lessons 19 through 21 have related meanings. Complete the following sentences by choosing the word that best fits the context, based on information you infer from the use of the italicized word. Some word pairs will be antonyms, some will be synonyms, and some will simply be words often used in the same context.

1. The *politic* fur trader warned his __________ sidekick that saying the wrong thing to the hostile tribal leader would get the both of them killed.
   A. acrid
   B. insuperable
   C. clandestine
   D. extemporaneous
   E. maladroit

2. Only wealthy *plutocrats* could afford to pay for successful election campaigns, so it was they who maintained __________ over the small nation.
   A. hegemony
   B. misogyny
   C. travesty
   D. requiem
   E. apex

3. Budget cuts forced Dee to take a *furlough* from her job only two years before retirement, but she was lucky enough to find a[n] __________ in which she could earn money with little effort to fill the gap until her pension would begin.
   A. abnegation
   B. sinecure
   C. apex
   D. requiem
   E. peon

4. The conqueror enjoyed a *redoubtable* reputation during his campaign, owing chiefly to the __________ horsemen and battle-hardened warriors in the ranks of his army.
   A. clandestine
   B. extemporaneous
   C. truculent
   D. acrid
   E. tendentious

5. The troubled daycare worker didn't try to hide her __________ treatment of the children she liked; she was patient with her favorites, and spoke in an *acerbic* tone with those whom she disliked.
   A. insuperable
   B. truculent
   C. redoubtable
   D. tendentious
   E. acrid

6. The herbal drug company preys on the __________ of people who develop *psychosomatic* disease symptoms simply by hearing someone tell them they are sick.
   A. apex
   B. abnegation
   C. plutocrat
   D. credulity
   E. requiem

7. Having already said their goodbyes, the __________ sailors manned their stations and performed valiantly against the *insuperable* forces of the tropical super-typhoon.
   A. acrid
   B. stolid
   C. acerbic
   D. clandestine
   E. tendentious

8. Opie's *vignettes* about growing up in a circus family had a[n] __________ that only a genuine circus performer could convey from first-hand experience.
   A. abnegation
   B. apex
   C. gravitas
   D. misogyny
   E. verisimilitude

9. Suffering *abnegation* because of his habitual __________, Ben refused to accept that his new supervisor was, in fact, a woman.
   A. beatitude
   B. travesty
   C. misogyny
   D. requiem
   E. polyglot

10. The spy easily changed her *clandestine* identities when traveling among her three assigned countries because she was a[n] __________ who was fluent in all the regional languages.
   A. polyglot
   B. requiem
   C. peon
   D. apex
   E. credulity

Exercise III

Deeper Meanings

Choose a word to replace the italicized word in each sentence. All of the possible choices for each sentence have similar definitions, but the correct answer will have a connotation that best suits the context. For example, the words "delete," "destroy," and "obliterate," all mean "to remove or wipe out," but no one would ever say, "I destroyed the name from the document." The correct choice will be the word with the best specific meaning and does not render the sentence awkward in tone or content. When choices seem close, look for a clue in the context that makes one choice better than the other. Note that the correct answer is not always the primary vocabulary word from the lesson.

misunderstanding	**apex**	**unknowing**	**maximum**
abnegation	**go**	**intractable**	**horrifying**
redoubtable	**tip**	**redirect**	**immovable**
change	**busy**		

1. Gino's *blindness* about his lack of skills on the basketball court led him to a few embarrassing losses, but at least he got some practice.

   Better word: ____________________

2. No matter how much training he received, the *wild* Labrador rocketed across the street and all over the neighborhood as soon as his leash was removed.

   Better word: ____________________

3. At a price of $20,000 at the height of the Great Depression, when most cars sold for $500, the Duesenberg Model J sat at the *roof* of the decadent, luxury automobile market.

   Better word: ____________________

4. The couple needed to *divert* both their salaries into paying the mortgage and away from their expensive vacation.

   Better word: ____________________

5. Just the *hard* name of the class, "Statistical Thermodynamics," dissuaded many students from signing up for it.

   Better word: ____________________

Exercise IV

Crossword Puzzle

Use the clues to complete the crossword puzzle. The answers consist of vocabulary words from Lessons 19 through 21.

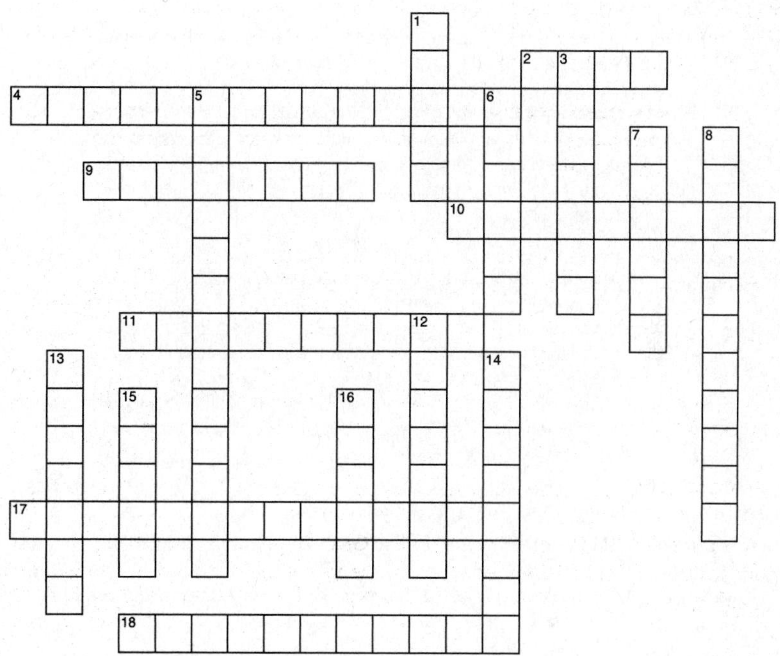

Across

2. the tippy-top
4. made up on the spot, just happens
9. speaks Latin, Greek, Spanish, and Klingon
10. boss with big bucks
11. can't stick to the subject
17. just like the real thing
18. does what it wants

Down

1. refuse, garbage
3. cool and clever
5. pain in the brain
6. always a cool operator
7. a comfort
8. secret-agent stuff
12. like pancake syrup
13. stray from the main topic
14. a short tale
15. Bleh, that tastes nasty.
16. like the Sahara and burnt cookies

Exercise V

Subject Prompts

Here is a writing prompt similar to the one you will find on the writing portion of an assessment test. Follow the instructions below and write a brief, efficient essay.

How much do you value your right to be anonymous? Do you even have a right to be anonymous? The laws vary from state to state as to the extent to which you must comply with police officers when you are detained, whether or not you have committed a crime or are even suspected of having committed a crime. In most states, you must at least provide your name, if not an actual photo identification, when asked for it by an officer. If you fail to provide the identification, the police can arrest or detain you. Detractors of identification laws often mock them with the phrase, "Papers, please!"—an allusion to nations occupied by Nazis during World War II, wherein identification papers were required for any type of travel.

Do you have a right to be anonymous if you are not breaking any laws? Take a position and assume the role of defender or prosecutor in a trial for someone who was walking down the street and subsequently arrested for not providing identification to officers. Write your opening speech to the jury and explain your reasons whether the defendant is an innocent victim or a guilty criminal. Provide at least three reasons based on your experience, observation, or opinion as to why your stance on the issue is correct.

Thesis: Write a *one-sentence* response to the above assignment. Make certain this single sentence offers a clear statement of your position.

Example: Detaining innocent people for the sake of knowing their identity is an abuse of police authority.

____

____

Organizational Plan: List at least three subtopics you will use to support your main idea. This list is your outline.

1. ______________________________

2. ______________________________

3. ______________________________

Draft: Following your outline, write a good first draft of your essay. Remember to support all your points with examples, facts, references to reading, etc.

Review and Revise: Exchange essays with a classmate. Using the Holistic scoring guide on page 268, score your partner's essay (while he or she scores yours). If necessary, rewrite your essay to correct the problems indicated by the essay's score.

Scoring Guide for Writing

Organization

6 = **Clearly Competent**
The paper is clearly organized around the central point or main idea. The organization may grow from the writer's argument or a slightly predictable structure. Ideas follow a logical order.
The work is **free of surface errors** (grammar, spelling, punctuation, etc.).

5 = **Reasonably Competent**
The organization of the paper is clear, but not fully implemented. The structure might be predictable. Ideas follow a logical order, but transitions might be simple or obvious.
Minor surface errors are present, but they **do not interfere** with the reader's understanding of the work.

4 = **Adequately Competent**
The organization of the paper is apparent, but not consistently implemented. The structure is predictable. Some ideas follow a logical order, but transitions are simple and obvious.
Surface errors are present, but they **do not severely interfere** with the reader's understanding.

3 = **Nearly Competent**
There is evidence of a simple organizational plan. Ideas are grouped logically in parts of the paper, but do not flow logically throughout. Transitions are needed.
Surface errors are **apparent** and **begin to interfere** with the reader's understanding of the work.

2 = **Marginally Incompetent**
The organizational plan of the paper is obscured by too few details and/or irrelevant details. Some of the ideas are grouped logically in parts of the paper. Transitions are needed or are incorrect.
Surface errors are **frequent and severe enough** to **interfere** with the reader's understanding of the work.

1 = **Incompetent**
There is no clear organizational plan and/or insufficient material. Ideas are not grouped logically. Transitions are absent.
Surface errors are **frequent** and **extreme**, and **severely interfere** with the reader's understanding of the work.

Scoring Guide for Writing

Development

6 = **Clearly Competent**
The **paper takes a position** on the issue and **offers sufficient material** (details, examples, anecdotes, supporting facts, etc.) to create a **complete discussion**. **Every word and sentence is relevant**. Ideas are **fully supported**.
The paper visits **different perspectives** of the argument or addresses **counterarguments** to the writer's position. The paper **focuses** on the argument evoked by the prompt. There is a **clear**, **purposed**, well-developed **introduction** and **conclusion**.
The work is **free of surface errors** (grammar, spelling, punctuation, etc.).

5 = **Reasonably Competent**
The essay **takes a position** on the issue and **offers sufficient material** for a complete discussion, but the reader is left **with a few unanswered questions**. Ideas are **supported**. The paper **partially visits different perspectives** of the argument or addresses **counterarguments**. **Most** of the paper **focuses** on the argument evoked by the prompt. There is **no irrelevant material**. There is a clear **introduction** and **conclusion**.
Minor surface errors are present, but they **do not interfere** with the reader's understanding of the work.

4 = **Adequately Competent**
The paper **takes a position** on the issue but **does not provide** enough details, examples, or supporting facts for a complete discussion, leaving a **few unanswered questions**. The paper includes **some attention** to **counterarguments** and differing perspectives. **Irrelevant material** is present. **Most** of the paper **focuses** on the topic and the specific argument.
Surface errors are present, but they **do not severely interfere** with the reader's understanding.

3 = **Nearly Competent**
The essay **takes a position** on the issue but **does not include** sufficient details, examples, or supporting facts for a discussion. The paper **may include incomplete or unclear counterarguments**. The paper **might repeat** details or rhetoric. The paper focuses on the topic, but **does not maintain** the specific argument.
Surface errors are **apparent** and **begin to interfere** with the reader's understanding of the work.

2 = **Marginally Incompetent**
The paper **may not take a position** on the issue, or the paper may take a position but **fail to support** it with sufficient details. Examples and ideas are **vague** and **irrelevant**. The paper might **repeat ideas extensively**. The paper **might maintain focus** on the general topic.
Surface errors are **frequent and severe enough** to **interfere** with the reader's understanding of the work.

1 = **Incompetent**
The paper **might attempt to take a position**, but it **fails to provide** examples, fact, or rhetoric to support the position. The paper may be **repetitious** with **little** or **no focus** on the general topic.
Surface errors are **frequent** and **extreme**, and **severely interfere** with the reader's understanding of the work.

Scoring Guide for Writing

Sentence Formation And Variety

6 = **Clearly Competent**
Sentences are **varied**, **complete**, and **assist the reader** in the flow of the discussion.
The work is **free of surface errors** (grammar, spelling, punctuation, etc.).

5 = **Reasonably Competent**
Sentences are **somewhat varied**, **generally correct**, and **do not distract** the reader from the flow of the discussion.
Minor surface errors are present, but they **do not interfere** with the reader's understanding of the work.

4 = **Adequately Competent**
Some sentences show **variety**, and **most** are **complete** and **generally correct**.
Surface errors are present, but they **do not interfere** with the reader's understanding.

3 = **Nearly Competent**
Sentences show a **little variety**, but the structure may be **dull**. Sentences are **generally complete** and grammatically correct, but **some errors** distract the reader.
Surface errors are **apparent** and **begin to interfere** with the reader's understanding of the work.

2 = **Marginally Incompetent**
Sentence Structure is usually simple. Problems in sentence structure and grammar distract the reader and provide little or no variety.
Surface errors are **frequent and severe enough** to **interfere** with the reader's understanding of the work.

1 = **Incompetent**
Sentence structure is **simple, generally erroneous** and **lacks variety**.
Surface errors are **frequent** and **extreme**, and **severely interfere** with the reader's understanding of the work.

Scoring Guide for Writing

Word Choice

6 = **Clearly Competent**
The essay shows a **good command** of language. Word choice is **specific**, **clear**, and **vivid**, favoring **powerful nouns** and **verbs** to weaker adjective and adverb phrases. **Clear, specific words** are used, instead of vague, general terms.
The work is **free of surface errors** (grammar, spelling, punctuation, etc.).

5 = **Reasonably Competent**
Language is **competent**. Word choice is **clear** and **accurate**. Words and phrases are **mostly** vivid, specific, and powerful.
Minor surface errors are present, but they **do not interfere** with the reader's understanding of the work.

4 = **Adequately Competent**
Language is **adequate**, with **appropriate** word choice. **Most** words and phrases are vivid, specific, and powerful.
Serious surface errors are present, but they **do not interfere** with the reader's understanding.

3 = **Nearly Competent**
Language shows a **basic control** and word choice is **usually appropriate** but **inconsistent**.
Surface errors are **apparent** and **begin to interfere** with the reader's understanding of the work.

2 = **Marginally Incompetent**
Word choice is usually **vague**.
Surface errors are **frequent** and **severe enough** to **interfere** with the reader's understanding of the work.

1 = **Incompetent**
Word choice is **simple**, **vague**, and **inexact**. The writer makes **no attempt** to choose the best words for the topic, audience, and purpose.
Surface errors are **frequent** and **extreme,** and **severely interfere** with the reader's understanding of the work.

Scoring Guide for Writing

Holistic

6 = Clearly Competent

The paper is **clearly organized** around the central idea. Ideas follow a **logical order**.

The paper **takes a position** on the issue and **offers sufficient material** (details, examples, anecdotes, supporting facts, etc.) to create a complete discussion. There is a **clear**, **purposed**, **well developed** introduction and conclusion.

The paper visits **different perspectives** of the argument or addresses **counterarguments** to the writer's position.

Sentences are **varied**, **complete**, and **assist the reader** in the flow of the discussion.

The paper shows a **good command** of language. Word choice is **specific**, **clear**, and **vivid**, favoring **powerful nouns** and **verbs** to weaker adjective and adverb phrases.

The work is **free of surface errors** (grammar, spelling, punctuation, etc.).

5 = Reasonably Competent

The organization of the paper is **clear**, but **not fully implemented**. Ideas follow a **logical order**, but transitions **might be simple** or obvious. The structure **might be predictable**.

The paper **takes a position** on the issue and **offers sufficient material** for a complete discussion, but the reader is left with **a few unanswered questions**. There is a clear **introduction** and **conclusion**.

The paper visits **some different perspectives** of the argument or addresses **counterarguments**.

Sentences are **somewhat varied**, **generally correct**, and **do not distract** the reader from the flow of the discussion.

Language is **competent**. Words and phrases are **mostly vivid**, **specific**, and **powerful**.

Minor surface errors are present, but they **do not interfere** with the reader's understanding of the work.

4 = Adequately Competent

The organization of the paper is **apparent**, but **not consistently** implemented. The structure is **predictable. Some** ideas follow a **logical order**, but transitions are **simple** and **obvious. Most** of the paper **focuses** on the topic and the specific argument.

The paper **takes a position** on the issue, but **does not provide** the details, examples, or supporting facts for a complete discussion, leaving **a few unanswered questions**.

The paper includes **little attention** to counterarguments and differing perspectives.

Irrelevant material is present.

Language is **adequate**, with appropriate word choice. **Most** words and phrases are vivid, specific, and powerful.

Some sentences show **variety**, and **most** are **complete** and **generally correct**.

Surface errors are present, but they **do not interfere** with the reader's understanding.

3 = Nearly Competent

There is **evidence of a simple organizational plan**. The essay **takes a position** on the issue but **does not include** sufficient details, examples, or supporting facts for a discussion. Ideas are **grouped logically** in parts of the paper, **but do not flow** logically throughout. The paper **focuses** on the topic, but **does not maintain** the specific argument.

The paper **may include incomplete** or **unclear** counterarguments.

Language shows a **basic control,** and word choice is **usually appropriate** but **inconsistent**. Sentences show a **little variety**, but the structure may be **dull**.

Sentences are **generally complete** and **grammatically correct**, but some errors **distract** the reader.

The paper might **repeat** details or rhetoric.

Surface errors are **apparent** and **begin to interfere** with the reader's understanding of the work.

2 = Marginally Incompetent

The organizational plan of the paper is **obscured by too few details** and/or **irrelevant details**. The paper **may not take a position** on the issue, or the paper may take a position but **fail to support** it with sufficient details. **Some** of the ideas are **grouped logically** in parts of the paper. The paper **generally maintains focus** on the general topic.

Examples and ideas are **vague** and **irrelevant**.

Sentence structure is **usually simple**. **Problems** in sentence structure and grammar **distract** the reader and provide **little** or **no variety**. **Word choice** is usually **vague**.

The paper might **repeat** ideas **extensively**.

Surface errors are **frequent and severe enough** to **interfere** with the reader's understanding of the work.

1 = Incompetent

There is **no clear organizational plan** and/or **insufficient material**. The paper **might attempt** to **take a position**, but it **fails** to provide examples, fact, or rhetoric to support the position. Ideas are **not grouped logically**.

The paper may be **repetitious** with little or **no focus** on the general topic.

Sentence structure is **simple** and **generally erroneous** and **lacking variety**. Word choice is **simple**, **vague**, and **inexact**. The writer makes **no attempt** to choose the best words for the topic, audience, and purpose.

Surface errors are **frequent** and **extreme,** and **severely interfere** with the reader's understanding of the work.

Relevant State Standards

High School - Grades 9-10

These are only the minimum standards that the product line meets; if these standards seem out of order, they typically go in "keyword" order; from the Language Usage category of standards, to Comprehension, Analysis, Writing, Research/Applied, and Technology/ Media categories. Therefore, these standards may be in a different order than the order given by your local Department of Education. Also, if one state standard meets multiple categories, that particular standard is listed the first time it appears, to reduce redundancy. Again, please refer to your local Department of Education for details on the particular standards.

Bias/Validity standards are included, as are Voice/Style standards, as both categories include use of words for different effects on the audience (connotation, denotation, distortion, formality, etc.) and thus are logical inclusions.

Depending on state, standards pertaining to use of dialect and idiomatic expressions might be met by this product. Please refer to your local Department of Education for details.

Notation is as close as possible to the notation given by the Department of Education of the respective state.

States:

Alaska:
R4.1.1-4; R4.4.1-2; R4.5.1; R4.5.2-3; W4 (all); R4.1.5; R4.2.1-2; R4.3.1-4; R4.3.5-6; R4.7.1; R4.9.2; R4.9.1; R4.6.1-4; R4.9.1

Indiana:
10.1.1-4; 10.2.3; 10.3.1; 10.2.1; 10.3.7-8; 10.4 (all); 10.6 (all); 10.5 (all); 10.3.11; 10.7.12; 10.3.12; 10.3.6; 10.3.2; 10.4.10-12

Nebraska (standards set at grade 12):
12.1.1; 12.1.5; 12.1.6

Texas (TEKS section 110.43):
b6 (all); b7 (all); b8B; b11D; b12A; b2 (all); b3 (all); b12B-C; B8D; B9A; B11A, F; B5 (entire)

Virginia:
10.4; 10.3; 10.7; 10.8; 10.3D; 10.9

Common Core State Standards for English Language Arts

Standards		Exercises
Reading Standards for Informational Text		
Key Ideas and Details		
RI.9-10.1	Cite strong and thorough textual evidence to support analysis of what the text says explicitly as well as inferences drawn from the text.	**Critical Reading: Level One** Lessons: 2, 4, 6, 8, 10, 12, 14, 16, 18, 20
RI.9-10.2	Determine a central idea of a text and analyze its development over the course of the text, including how it emerges and is shaped and refined by specific details; provide an objective summary of the text.	**Critical Reading: Level One** Lessons: 2, 4, 6, 8, 10, 12, 14, 16, 18, 20
Craft and Structure		
RI.9-10.4	Determine the meaning of words and phrases as they are used in a text, including figurative, connotative, and technical meanings; analyze the cumulative impact of specific word choices on meaning and tone (e.g., how the language of a court opinion differs from that of a newspaper).	**Critical Reading: Level One** Lessons: 2, 4, 6, 8, 10, 12, 14, 16, 18, 20 **Inference: Level One** Lessons: 1-21
RI.9-10.6	Determine an author's point of view or purpose in a text and analyze how an author uses rhetoric to advance that point of view or purpose.	**Critical Reading: Level One** Lessons: 2, 4, 6, 8, 10, 12, 14, 16, 18, 20
Writing Standards		
Text Types and Purposes		
W.9-10.1	Write arguments to support claims in an analysis of substantive topics or texts, using valid reasoning and relevant and sufficient evidence.	**Writing: Level One** Lessons: 1, 3, 5, 7, 9 11, 13, 15, 17, 19, 21
W.9-10.1a	Introduce precise claim(s), distinguish the claim(s) from alternate or opposing claims, and create an organization that establishes clear relationships among claim(s), counterclaims, reasons, and evidence.	**Writing: Level One** Lessons: 1, 3, 5, 7, 9 11, 13, 15, 17, 19, 21
W.9-10.1b	Develop claim(s) and counterclaims fairly, supplying evidence for each while pointing out the strengths and limitations of both in a manner that anticipates the audience's knowledge level and concerns.	**Writing: Level One** Lessons: 1, 3, 5, 7, 9 11, 13, 15, 17, 19, 21
W.9-10.1c	Use words, phrases, and clauses to link the major sections of the text, create cohesion, and clarify the relationships between claim(s) and reasons, between reasons and evidence, and between claim(s) and counterclaims.	**Writing: Level One** Lessons: 1, 3, 5, 7, 9 11, 13, 15, 17, 19, 21

W.9-10.1d	Establish and maintain a formal style and objective tone while attending to the norms and conventions of the discipline in which they are writing.	**Writing: Level One** Lessons: 1, 3, 5, 7, 9 11, 13, 15, 17, 19, 21
W.9-10.1e	Provide a concluding statement or section that follows from and supports the argument presented.	**Writing: Level One** Lessons: 1, 3, 5, 7, 9 11, 13, 15, 17, 19, 21
W.9-10.2	Write informative/explanatory texts to examine and convey complex ideas, concepts, and information clearly and accurately through the effective selection, organization, and analysis of content.	**Writing: Level One** Lessons: 1, 3, 5, 7, 9 11, 13, 15, 17, 19, 21
W.9-10.2a	Introduce a topic; organize complex ideas, concepts, and information to make important connections and distinctions; include formatting (e.g., headings), graphics (e.g., figures, tables), and multimedia when useful to aiding comprehension.	**Writing: Level One** Lessons: 1, 3, 5, 7, 9 11, 13, 15, 17, 19, 21
W.9-10.2b	Develop the topic with well-chosen, relevant, and sufficient facts, extended definitions, concrete details, quotations, or other information and examples appropriate to the audience's knowledge of the topic.	**Writing: Level One** Lessons: 1, 3, 5, 7, 9 11, 13, 15, 17, 19, 21
W.9-10.2c	Use appropriate and varied transitions to link the major sections of the text, create cohesion, and clarify the relationships among complex ideas and concepts.	**Writing: Level One** Lessons: 1, 3, 5, 7, 9 11, 13, 15, 17, 19, 21
W.9-10.2d	Use precise language and domain-specific vocabulary to manage the complexity of the topic.	**Writing: Level One** Lessons: 1, 3, 5, 7, 9 11, 13, 15, 17, 19, 21
W.9-10.2e	Establish and maintain a formal style and objective tone while attending to the norms and conventions of the discipline in which they are writing.	**Writing: Level One** Lessons: 1, 3, 5, 7, 9 11, 13, 15, 17, 19, 21
W.9-10.2f	Provide a concluding statement or section that follows from and supports the information or explanation presented (e.g., articulating implications or the significance of the topic).	**Writing: Level One** Lessons: 1, 3, 5, 7, 9 11, 13, 15, 17, 19, 21

Range of Writing		
W.9-10.10	Write routinely over extended time frames (time for re-search, reflection, and revision) and shorter time frames (a single sitting or a day or two) for a range of tasks, purposes, and audiences.	**Writing: Level One** Lessons: 1, 3, 5, 7, 9 11, 13, 15, 17, 19, 21
Language Standards		
Conventions of Standard English		
L.9-10.1a	Demonstrate command of the conventions of standard English grammar and usage when writing or speaking.	**Identifying Sentence Errors: Level One** Lessons: 1, 5, 9, 13, 17, 21 **Improving Sentences: Level One** Lesson: 1, 5, 9, 13, 17, 21 **Improving Paragraphs: Level One** Lesson: 3,7,11, 15, 19 **Writing: Level One** Lessons: 1, 3, 5, 7, 9 11, 13, 15, 17, 19, 21
L.9-10.2	Demonstrate command of the conventions of standard English capitalization, punctuation, and spelling when writing.	**Identifying Sentence Errors: Level One** Lessons: 1, 5, 9, 13, 17, 21 **Improving Sentences: Level One** Lessons: 1, 5, 9, 13, 17, 21 **Improving Paragraphs: Level One** Lessons: 3,7,11, 15, 19 **Writing: Level One** Lessons: 1, 3, 5, 7, 9 11, 13, 15, 17, 19, 21

Vocabulary Acquisition and Use		
L.9-10.4	Determine or clarify the meaning of unknown and multiple-meaning words and phrases based on grades 9–10 reading and content, choosing flexibly from a range of strategies.	**Critical Reading: Level One** Lessons: 1-21
L.9-10.4a	Use context (e.g., the overall meaning of a sentence, paragraph, or text; a word's position or function in a sentence) as a clue to the meaning of a word or phrase.	**Word in Context: Level One** Lessons: 1-21 **Inference: Level One** Lessons: 1-21 **Critical Reading: Level One** Lessons: 1-21
L.9-10.4b	Identify and correctly use patterns of word changes that indicate different meanings or parts of speech (e.g., analyze, analysis, analytical; advocate, advocacy).	**Roots, Prefixes, and Suffixes: Level One** Lessons: 1-21
L.9-10.4d	Verify the preliminary determination of the meaning of a word or phrase (e.g., by checking the inferred meaning in context or in a dictionary).	**Inference: Level One** Lessons: 1-21
L.9-10.5	Demonstrate understanding of figurative language, word relationships, and nuances in word meanings.	**Related Words, Deeper Meaning: Level One** Lessons: 1-3, 4-6, 7-9, 10-12, 13-15, 16-18, 19-21
L.9-10.5b	Analyze nuances in the meaning of words with similar denotations.	**Critical Reading: Level One** Lessons: 2, 4, 6, 8, 10, 12, 14, 16, 18, 20
L.9-10.6	Acquire and use accurately general academic and domain-specific words and phrases, sufficient for reading, writing, speaking, and listening at the college and career readiness level; demonstrate independence in gathering vocabulary knowledge when considering a word or phrase important to comprehension or expression.	**Level One:** Lessons: 1-21

History/Social Studies		
Key Ideas and Details		
RH.9-10.1.	Cite specific textual evidence to support analysis of primary and secondary sources, attending to such features as the date and origin of the information.	**Critical Reading: Level One** Lessons: 2, 4, 6, 8, 10, 12, 14, 16, 18, 20
Craft and Structure		
RH.9-10.4	Determine the meaning of words and phrases as they are used in a text, including vocabulary describing political, social, or economic aspects of history/social science.	**Critical Reading: Level One** Lessons: 2, 4, 6, 8, 10, 12, 14, 16, 18, 20
RH.9-10.6	Compare the point of view of two or more authors for how they treat the same or similar topics, including which details they include and emphasize in their respective accounts.	**Critical Reading: Level One** Lessons: 4, 8, 12, 16, 20
Integration of Knowledge and Ideas		
RH.9-10.9	Compare and contrast treatments of the same topic in several primary and secondary sources.	**Critical Reading: Level One** Lessons: 4, 8, 12, 16, 20